Perceiving Behaving Becoming

A NEW FOCUS FOR EDUCATION

Yearbook 1962

Prepared by the ASCD 1962 Yearbook Committee
Arthur W. Combs, Chairman

Association for Supervision and Curriculum Development
A department of the National Education Association
1201 Sixteenth Street, N.W., Washington 6, D.C.

A department of the
National Education Association
1201 Sixteenth Street, Northwest
Washington 6, D.C.

Price $4.50

Library of Congress Catalogue Card Number: 44-6213

FROM THE ASSOCIATION

IT MAY SEEM paradoxical to say that *Perceiving, Behaving, Becoming: A New Focus for Education* is timely. How can it be timely in a period in which attention in education is riveted on the technological revolution, alternative proposals for organizational structures, and updating knowledge in government-favored academic areas? *Perceiving, Behaving, Becoming* is timely precisely because continuous consideration of the basic foundations of the educational program is inescapable. Regardless of what technological devices are adopted, what organizational patterns prevail, what curricular content emerges, the three basic foundations of education—social, psychological and philosophical—are central in the making of the educational program.

Essentially the 1962 Yearbook of the Association for Supervision and Curriculum Development provides bold new insights on one of the three foundations, the psychological, with related implications affecting social and philosophical aspects. *Perceiving, Behaving, Becoming* deals with the truly adequate person, adequate in the sense of Webster's synonym *sufficient* and in the sense of the authors' equivalent phrases, *fully functioning* and *self-actualizing*, rather than adequate in the corrupted usage, "good enough to get by." The yearbook describes how schools may help develop such persons.

Here is no trivial contribution by scholars avoiding reality; here the authors deal with the heart of the educational process as they propose a new focus for education. If they prove to be correct in their espousal of a "third force" in psychology, neither behavioristic nor Freudian, a hopeful vista as to man's potentiality stretche ahead. The theories and applications of *Perceiving, Behaving, Be coming* merit intent and open-minded study by the reader.

Many people were responsible for this well-integrated yearbook Arthur W. Combs, chairman, deserves the warmest appreciatio from members of the Association for Supervision and Curriculun Development and from all readers. The debt of ASCD to the fou busy scholarly authors who contributed basic papers for use an analysis is incalculable; we thank Earl C. Kelley, Carl R. Rogers A. H. Maslow and Arthur W. Combs deeply. The members of th

Yearbook Committee, listed on a page which follows, have earned our warm congratulations. All members of the Executive Committee read and commented upon the original manuscript, but we owe a special thanks to Lavone Hanna who served as Executive Committee official reader.

Margaret Gill, executive secretary of the Association, read and commented upon the original manuscript. Robert R. Leeper, editor and associate secretary, ASCD, worked with the manuscript in its several stages, did final editing on the volume and directed its production. Janet A. Leban, of the NEA Publications Division, assisted in editing, paging, proofreading and other aspects of production. Ruth P. Ely, editorial associate, secured permissions to quote. Dolores J. Minor, ASCD staff assistant, helped with copy and the checking of corrections. Design of cover, title page and chapter headings is by the NEA Publications Division, Charles E. Ford, artist.

November 1961

WILLIAM VAN TIL, *President*
The Association for Supervision and Curriculum Development

CONTENTS

THE 1962 YEARBOOK COMMITTEE

ARTHUR W. COMBS, *Chairman and Editor*
Professor of Education, University of Florida, Gainesville, Florida

NORA M. BARRON
Principal, Highcroft Country Day School, Wayzata, Minnesota

JOHN P. CAUSEY
Assistant Director of Elementary Education, Board of Education of Montgomery County, Rockville, Maryland

MILTON J. GOLD
Associate Professor, Hunter College, New York, New York

JOHN D. GREENE
Director of Instruction, Box 2950, Baton Rouge, Louisiana

LAVONE HANNA, *Executive Committee Member*
San Francisco State College, 1600 Holloway Avenue, San Francisco 17, California

CARL W. HASSEL
Superintendent, Public Schools, Moorestown, New Jersey

AGNES ANN KANTZ
Teacher, Midland, Texas

LEONARD KORNBERG
Department of Education, Queens College, Flushing 67, New York

EDNA T. LAYTON
Classroom Teacher and Assistant Director of Curriculum, Hempstead Public Schools, Hempstead, New York

GERTRUDE M. LEWIS
Specialist for Upper Grades, Elementary School Section, U.S. Office of Education, Washington 25, D.C.

MARY JANE LOOMIS
Professor of Education, Coordinator of Elementary Studies, Center for School Experimentation, College of Education, Ohio State University, Columbus, Ohio

CAMERON W. MEREDITH
Head, Education Division, Southwestern Illinois Campus, Southern Illinois University, East St. Louis, Illinois

George L. Miller, Jr.
William Stewart School, University of Utah, Salt Lake City 21 Utah

Gennette Nygard
Coordinator of Elementary Education, Arlington County Public Schools, Arlington, Virginia

Charles S. Partin, Jr.
Assistant Superintendent, Board of Public Instruction, Escambia County, 215 West Garden Street, Pensacola, Florida

Manette Swett
Teacher, P. K. Yonge Laboratory School, Gainesville, Florida

Doris A. Young
Associate Professor of Education, Purdue University, Lafayette, Indiana

Paul E. Zintgraff
Assistant Superintendent, Curricular Services, Department of Education, San Diego County, 6401 Linda Vista Road, San Diego 11, California

CHAPTER 1

WHAT CAN MAN BECOME?

WHATEVER WE DO in teaching depends upon what we think people are like. The goals we seek, the things we do, the judgments we make, even the experiments we are willing to try, are determined by our beliefs about the nature of man and his capacities. It has always been so. Teachers who believe children *can,* will try to teach them. Teachers who believe children are *unable,* give up trying or spend their days on a treadmill, hopelessly making motions they never expect will matter. The beliefs we hold about people can serve as prison walls limiting us at every turn. They can also set us free from our shackles to confront great new possibilities never dreamed of before. No beliefs will be more important to education than those we hold about the nature of man and the limits of his potentials. Whenever our ideas about human capacities change, the goals of teaching must change, too. Whatever we decide is the best that man can become must necessarily set the goal of education.

We have grown accustomed to the great shifts in thinking brought to us almost daily by the physical sciences. We expect them. But breakthroughs occur in the social sciences as well. When they do, what is more, they may be as momentous and far reaching as those in the physical sciences. Indeed, it is even possible that new understandings about man and his behavior may prove to be far more significant for man's destiny in the years to come. Whenever we change our basic ideas about man and his behavior, great changes are called for in every aspect of our relationships with other people. This is just what has happened to our understandings about the nature of human capacity and adjustment. Man, it now appears, can become much more than we have dreamed.

For a half-century or more we have been preoccupied with a conception of human adjustment or mental health stated as a function of the norm. Our standards of human adjustment have been primarily statistical, defined in terms of the famous bell-shaped curve. The well adjusted were those who clustered about the norm. Those who departed from average were deviates from the mean—abnormal. Good adjustment thus became synonymous with average. The ideas we hold about what people are like have inevitable effects on the things we do in dealing with them, and this statistical concept of the healthy personality is no exception. It has had widespread effects upon our way of life. But nowhere has its effect been more marked than in our thinking about the goals of education. Such a view of human health seems to require on the one hand the discouragement of difference, individuality and creativity, and on the other hand encouragement of "the organization man," conformity and the most banal forms of togetherness. On such a basis we should have to classify some of the greatest figures in human history as badly maladjusted. Many teachers have long felt there was something wrong with this conception. Adjustment and health are presumed to be something worth seeking, but who, after all, wants to be average?

It is apparent that we need a definition of the supremely healthy personality—not in terms of averages, but in terms of ultimates—that gives us something to shoot for. To set our goals we need to see beyond what man is. We need to know what man can become. This is just what some social scientists are finding out. A number of them have asked, "What does it mean to be a supremely healthy, fully functioning person? What is a self-actualizing person and how do you produce such an individual?" The answers they are producing to these questions, furthermore, pose great challenges to education. The world we live in needs such people as never before, and it is the task of education to produce them.

NEW CONCEPTS OF HUMAN POTENTIALITY

Instead of looking at human adjustment as a matter of averages, some social scientists are seeking to define the crowning achievement in human growth and development. They have asked, "What kind of person would it be who has truly achieved the ultimate in self-realization? What sort of man shall we strive for?" They are seeking to discover what people would be like who have achieved high degrees of self-actualization, of psychological freedom—the maximum fulfillment of their potentialities. Others are searching for ways such people are produced. "How do they come about? What factors went into making them this kind of person?" they ask. Out of these investigations have come fascinating new insights about the nature of human potentialities. Little by little we are beginning to understand what truly self-actualizing, truly adequate personalities are like, how they grow and develop.

These new understandings lead to quite different conceptions of how we need to deal with people from those growing out of a statistical approach to the problem. They are particularly significant for education. The fullest possible flowering of human potentiality is the business of education. It is our reason for being. Whatever we decide is the nature of the fully functioning, self-actualizing individual must become at once the goal of education. Accordingly, we need the very best definitions science can provide us. If better definitions are devised, moreover, we need to inject these into the stream of educational thought with the least possible delay. This is the purpose of the ASCD 1962 Yearbook: to explore some of the implications of what these new ideas about the truly adequate person mean for teaching and learning.

THE YEARBOOK TASK

A Bridge to Practice

One of the great handicaps to progress in human institutions is the lag which often exists between the production of new ideas in the learned disciplines and their expression in our social institutions. It sometimes happens that many years may pass before a new idea discovered in the laboratory or formulated in theory finds its way into the daily operations of human practice. In medicine, for example, thousands of people may die before a new understanding about the nature of a disease can find its way into the practices of the physician. In industry, established firms have been driven to bankruptcy through failure to remain awake to new conceptions as they appeared on the scene. The same lag exists between the social sciences and the schools. There is often a wide gap between our understanding of the nature of human behavior on the one hand and the utilization of such understandings in the classroom on the other.

There was a time when this kind of lag could be met in a leisurely fashion. The tempo of events in the world today, however, no longer permits us the luxury of so relaxed an approach to the dissemination of knowledge. Survival itself is at stake. It is essential that the best we know be converted into practice as quickly as possible. Accordingly, the ASCD Executive Committee conceived this yearbook as a kind of bridge between the learned disciplines of the social sciences on the one hand and the applied field of endeavor of the public schools on the other. The 1962 Yearbook Committee was charged with the task of examining current theory about the adequate personality with an eye to its implications for educational thought and practice.

THE INVITED PAPERS

We began our project with a brief sketch of new ideas about the nature of the self-actualizing, fully functioning personality provided by four experts. We invited each of four persons outstanding in this field to prepare a description of self-actualizing persons as he saw them.

The authors we chose to do this were busy people. However, they readily grasped the significance of our yearbook effort, and graciously acceded to our request. One wrote us, "This yearbook about which you wrote me sounds significant. I have steadfastly refused every speaking engagement, every writing engagement, for the coming year because I am trying to get some research under way which seems to me important. However, I guess I will have to make an exception in my current attitude and accept the responsibility for the paper you described." Another said, "Yes, I will do what you asked. I must tell you frankly that I sort of heaved a sigh of regret when I got your letter—I had hoped to be free for this sabbatical year to reject requests that didn't come from within my own self—but this is so clearly a matter of duty and of the clearest obligation that I feel I must help if I can. I agree with you absolutely about the importance of the projected yearbook."

We are deeply grateful to the four authors who provided us with these fine papers and for their enthusiastic cooperation in this project.

THE AUTHORS OF THE INVITED PAPERS

Earl C. Kelley

Earl C. Kelley is no stranger to education. He has spent most of his life in education, serving at various times as teacher, administrator, supervisor and college professor. Currently he is a professor of education at Wayne State University in Detroit, where he has been since 1940. He is widely known as a consultant to school systems from coast to coast and has often appeared on programs at ASCD conferences. He is even more widely known for his writing. His penetrating analyses of educational problems and his deep understanding of teachers and pupils are evident in everything he does. He has an ability to cut directly and unequivocally to the heart of a matter in a fashion that is sometimes disconcerting to the faint-hearted, but always helpful and rewarding. He is a truly courageous and creative thinker, with a deep appreciation of his fellows and of his profession.

In 1946, Dr. Kelley visited the Dartmouth Eye Institute at Hanover, New Hampshire, as a research consultant. There he became intrigued with the experiments on perception carried on by Adelbert Ames and his co-workers. Dr. Kelley saw at once the vast implications of these concepts for education and brought them to the attention of the profession in his book, *Education for What Is Real,* published in 1947. He has continued his interest in perceptual approaches to the understanding of human behavior and has developed these ideas more fully in a number of articles over the past 10 years. In his paper for this yearbook, Dr. Kelley has applied the perceptual approach to a discussion of "The Fully Functioning Self." Of our invited authors, Dr. Kelley is probably best known to educators. Accordingly, we have chosen his paper to open our yearbook.

Carl R. Rogers

Carl R. Rogers is presently a professor in the departments of Pyschology and Psychiatry at the University of Wisconsin. He is probably best known for his development of the "client-centered" approach to counseling and psychotherapy which he introduced about 1939. While this concept for helping people was sharply criticized in the early days of its presentation, it has now become one of the most widely accepted approaches to counseling theory and practice.

Dr. Rogers' interest in human personality, however, extends far beyond the problems of maladjustment and therapy. Out of his rich experience in counseling and psychotherapy, he has added immeasurably to our understanding of human behavior in a far broader frame of reference. In recent years he has contributed fascinating new conceptions of man's becoming and of the helping relationship. These concepts point the way to a philosophy and practice of working with people in all phases of human interaction, including teaching.

Before going to Wisconsin, Dr. Rogers was a professor at the University of Chicago. There he established and, for 12 years, directed the Counseling Center. He has been president of the American Psychological Association and of its division of clinical psychology. He has published outstanding research on personality theory and counseling. He is also a most prolific and talented author of a long list of scholarly books and articles. Dr. Rogers' training and research are primarily in the field of psychology, but his work is well known and admired far outside his own field. Many educators are already familiar with his work. We are honored indeed to include his paper, "Toward Becoming a Fully Functioning Person," as the second of our invited contributions.

Abraham H. Maslow

Abraham H. Maslow is currently chairman of the Department of Psychology at Brandeis University. He is a graduate of the University of Wisconsin and taught psychology at Columbia University and Brooklyn College before moving to his present post at Brandeis. He has been president of several divisions of the American Psychological Association. Dr. Maslow is one of a group of modern psychologists who are deeply interested in human values as keys to understanding personality.

Like our other authors, Dr. Maslow has written extensively in his field and is probably one of the most provocative thinkers in modern psychology. As an exponent of what has been called the "new look" or "third force" in psychology, his work has been the subject of much comment and discussion. This year will see the publication of *Toward a Psychology of Being*. Dr. Maslow is a brilliant psychologist and a challenging and exciting personality. It would be hard to find a more creative and courageous thinker. His studies on the self-actualizing personality, creativity and the nature of the "peak experience" are among the most stimulating in modern psychological thought. It is a pleasure to include his article, "Some Basic Propositions of Growth and Self-Actualization Psychology," among our invited papers.

Arthur W. Combs

Arthur W. Combs is presently professor of education in two departments, Educational Foundations and Personnel Services, at the University of Florida. He has contributed extensively to the fields of personality theory and counseling and psychotherapy and is perhaps best known as co-author, with Donald Snygg, of *Individual Behavior; A Perceptual Approach to Behavior*. This book provides a broad framework for modern perceptual approaches to understanding behavior.

Dr. Combs began his professional career as a public school teacher in 1935. Later, he became a school psychologist, then returned to Ohio State University for his doctorate in 1945. Before going to Florida he served for 12 years at Syracuse University, where he taught clinical psychology and was head of the University Personal Counseling Service. He is a past president of the New York State Psychological Association and a diplomate of the American Board of Examiners in Professional Psychology. He is widely known as a consultant on educational and human relations problems. He is editor of this yearbook. We are pleased to present his article, "A Perceptual Approach to the Truly Adequate Personality," as the last of the four invited papers.

THE YEARBOOK COMMITTEE

To explore the implications of the ideas presented by our four invited authors, a Yearbook Committee was selected by the Executive Committee of ASCD. In consultation with the editor, committee members were carefully chosen according to the following criteria:

1. Highly recommended by their peers

2. From all sections of the country

3. Representative of all aspects of education, including elementary, secondary, supervision, administration, governmental agencies and teacher training institutions.

Over the three years of its operation, the committee regretted losing several of its original members who found themselves unable to continue their association with the project. The list of members still on our roster as this yearbook goes to press is presented in the opening pages of the yearbook.

HOW THE YEARBOOK WAS WRITTEN

The four invited papers provided the Yearbook Committee with its working base. With these papers in hand, the committee proceeded by four steps with its task: (a) During the first year the committee studied these four papers and extracted from them the most pertinent and promising ideas for teaching. (b) During the second year the committee formed itself into a series of subcommittees to explore much further the implications of these ideas for every aspect of educational thought and practice. (c) In the third year these subcommittee reports were turned over to writing teams assigned to write the various chapters. (d) Finally, the manuscript for each chapter was reviewed and edited by a small editorial committee responsible for final preparation of the manuscript.

At first glance the task of writing a book with a committee of 19 people would seem to present insurmountable obstacles—especially one written by a committee deliberately chosen, as this was, for diversity of background and the widest possible geographic representation. Indeed, the obstacles *would* have been insurmountable had we not had a committee of high professional caliber, able to work together with almost unlimited patience and forbearance. The committee, to be sure, had its problems. Members did not always agree either with our invited authors or with other members of the committee. The remarkable thing, however, is not the disagreement, but the high proportion of agreement finally reached among the 19 distinct individuals who made up our group.

Not all matters discussed in this volume can fairly be said to represent the unanimous opinion of the committee members. We do agree, however, that the experience of working together on this volume has been interesting and challenging to all of us. At times it has been frustrating, to be sure, but never dull! The experience of kicking ideas around with a group of respected colleagues has been exciting and stimulating and has contributed important qualities to our own growth and development.

We do not expect readers of this yearbook to agree with all of our interpretations any more than all members of our committee agree. The concepts we present here are the reactions of the committee to the challenging concepts developed in the four invited papers. We are under no illusions that we have any final answers. Like teachers everywhere, we are seeking for better understanding and better practices. We present these concepts to our colleagues in the profession, therefore, as we have presented them to each other—as hypotheses, proposals, questions and opinions that:

1. Corroborate our present practices
2. Raise questions about what we are doing
3. Point the way to new possibilities.

If our readers find these discussions as stimulating and challenging as we have, or just plain fun, we shall be content.

THE ASCD 1962 YEARBOOK COMMITTEE

CHAPTER 2

THE FULLY FUNCTIONING SELF

EARL C. KELLEY • WAYNE STATE UNIVERSITY

IN A DISCUSSION of the self, it will perhaps be helpful to attempt to say as well as we can what it is we are trying to discuss. This is done at the risk of using the conversation stopper, "Let's define it." Many a fine discussion has ended at this point.

The self consists, in part at least, of the accumulated experiential background, or backlog, of the individual. It is what has been built, since his life began, through unique experience and unique purpose, on the individual's unique biological structure. The self is therefore unique to the individual.

This self is built almost entirely, if not entirely, in relationship to others. While the newborn babe has the equipment for the development of the self, there is ample evidence to show that nothing resembling a self can be built in the absence of others. Having a cortex is not enough; there must be continuous interchange between the individual and others. Language, for example, would not be possible without social relationships. Thus, it is seen that man is necessarily a social being.

The self has to be achieved; it is not given. All that is given is the equipment and at least the minimal (mother and child) social environment. Since the self is achieved through social contact, it has to be understood in terms of others. "Self and other" is not a duality, because they go so together that separation is quite impossible.

The self consists of an organization of accumulated experience over a whole lifetime. It is easy to see, therefore, that a great deal of the self has been relegated to the unconscious, or has been "forgotten." This does not mean that these early experiences have been lost. It merely means that they cannot readily be brought into consciousness. We must recognize the fact that the unconscious part of the self functions, for weal or woe, depending on the quality of the experiences.

It is intended here, however, to deal with the conscious self. The unconscious self (not a separation but a continuum) is difficult to deal with for the very reason that it is below the level of consciousness. We want here to look especially at how the individual sees himself. This is indeed the critical point, because it is what the person *sees* that is enabling or disabling. The crucial matter is not so much what you are, but what you think you are. And all of this is always in relationship to others.

The fully functioning personality (self) needs to have certain characteristics. Here, perhaps, is as good a place as any to discuss word trouble. We live in a moving, changing, becoming-but-never-arriving world, yet our language was built by people who believed this to be a static world. I have often spoken of the adequate self, but "adequate" will not do, because it is static. In fact, "inadequate" is a more useful word than "adequate." If there were a word that combines "aspiring-becoming," it would come close to our needs. I have chosen "fully functioning," which I think I learned from Carl Rogers, as the best I can do. This expression at least implies movement.

In order for a person to be fully functioning, when he looks at his self, as he must, he must see that it is enough—enough to perform the task at hand. He must see in his experiential background some history of success. He needs to see process, the building and becoming nature of himself. This being so, he will see that today has no meaning in the absence of yesterdays and tomorrows. In fact, there could be no today except for both yesterday and tomorrow. He must like what he sees, at least well enough for it to be operational.

MANY PEOPLE DO NOT LIKE THEIR SELVES

Unfortunately, many people in the world today suffer from inadequate concepts of self, which naturally lead to mistaken notions of others. Perhaps everybody is afflicted thus to some degree. There may be some rare spirits who are not, but they are few indeed.

We see evidence of this all around us. We see people ridden by unreasonable fears. The fearful person looks at his self and sees that it is not sufficient to meet what he fears. Middle-aged graduate students are afraid to stick their necks out. They are afraid to write; they suffer from stage fright. The question uppermost in their minds is, "What will people think?" Their selves are veritable skeletons in their closets, and if one has a skeleton in his closet, it is best not to do anything except to keep quiet. Any move may reveal it. So they try to sit tight so that they may not be revealed to others. This is a great loss to others—to mankind—for new paths are forbidding and exploration is fraught with terrors.

This Is Crippling

An inadequate concept of self, so common in our culture, is crippling to the individual. Our psychological selves may become crippled in much the same way as our physical selves may be crippled by disease or by an accident. They are the same, in effect, because each limits what we can do. When we see ourselves as inadequate, we lose our "can-ness." There becomes less and less that we can do.

Perhaps it is unfortunate that we cannot see the psychological self in the same way that we see the physical self. Our hearts go out to the physical cripple—we do not enter him in a foot race—but we expect the psychological cripple to step lively and meet all of the vicissitudes of life as though he were whole. Both kinds of cripples need therapy, though of different sorts. Many benefit by therapy, though all do not.

How Do We Get That Way?

Now we come to the question, "How do we get that way?" We get that way in the same way that a physical cripple does—by the lives we lead. Of course there are some cases of congenital defect, but if these were the only cripples we had, we would be fortunate indeed.

The newborn babe has enormous potential for health, but this health has to be built out of his experience with others. It has to be achieved, and it has to be achieved in relationship to others. The health potential then lies strictly in the quality of the people around him, since the infant, for many years to come, has, himself, no control over whom he will associate with.

Damage to the self, so disabling to so many of us, comes from the fact that we grow up in an authoritarian culture. While it is true that this is a democracy in governmental form, we have not achieved democracy in the home, the school or the church. The fact that we have a democratically chosen president or governor has no effect upon the developing child. He is built by the people close to him, and he does not elect them. The people close to him, having themselves been crippled, know no better than to continue the process.

The evils of authoritarianism are more extensive than is ordinarily understood. It is easy to see on a grand scale, as when a Hitler gains power. We all abhor a Hitler, but we seem to think that tyranny in small doses or on a small scale is somehow good. All in all, it appears that small tyrants do more harm than grand ones. The small tyrant operates on the growing edge of the personality of the young.

The trouble with the tyrant is basically that he does not have any faith in anyone except himself. He gets that way by living with people who never had any faith in him. Of course he does not really have any faith in himself either, but he has longed for and striven for a position of power over others weaker than himself. Getting his concept of others from his concept of himself, he believes that nothing worthwhile will happen unless he forces it to happen.

Lack of faith in others—the feeling that one has to see to it that others, who are perverse by nature, do what they should—starts a chain reaction of evils, one piled upon another. The burden one bears when he feels that he must watch others and coerce them must be unbearable. And so it turns out to be, for the tyrant deprives himself of others, and grows in the direction of more loneliness and hostility.

From this we can see what happens to the newborn babe as he faces the tyrant. Of course, the tyrant loves his baby in such manner as he is able to love. But he still regards the infant as a "thing," naturally in need of correction. One might think that the very young would not know the difference. But there are ample data to show that even in the first few days after birth, the child knows the difference between being loved and being viewed as in need of coercion. He knows whether the parent is doing things *with* him or *to* him. And the personality at that stage must be tender.

After five or six years of the authoritarian home, the child goes to school. The school is a place inhabited by adults, and too often these adults hold adult concepts of what a child ought to be. These concepts are unverified by the study of children. Here he meets preconceived standards, grade levels, and all of the other paraphernalia of the adult-centered school. If he does not measure up to these standards, then obviously he is perverse and in need of coercion. The fact that these standards are not derived from the child, that there is nothing about them in the Bible, that they arise and reside only in the minds of adults, bothers the adults not at all. Thus, coercion and criticism become the daily fare, while the deviations in behavior brought about by the uniqueness of the personality are stopped. Conformity is the way to the good life, and the best way to conform is to withdraw. One cannot be unique and extend himself and still conform. His uniqueness will show. Shells look a great deal alike, and so if one crawls into his shell, his differences will not be so apparent.

In our authoritarian culture, many forces converge upon the young individual which have the effect of making him think less of himself. The church is one of these forces. The concept of guilt, with its imaginary burden of sin, cannot help one to think well of himself. Of course one can acquire these damaging concepts without getting them at church. But those who have salvation to dispense hold a powerful weapon. When one is made to feel unworthy, he is crippled in some degree, because he cannot do what he otherwise might.

There is a distinction here between the effects of religion and the effects of the church as often administered. It is not religion per se which makes one think ill of himself. It is the representatives of religion who use authoritarian methods to gain their ends. Likewise schooling or education can be expanding in their nature. It is that the representatives of the school—teachers and administrators—often have their own ends to be served, not those of their learners. They act from their own fears, which cause them to dampen and delimit the expanding personalities of their young, thus defeating the very purpose for their being.

Nor is it intended here to deny the need for standards. A fully functioning personality cannot operate without standards. Such standards are the basis for aspiration, the basis for the hope for tomorrow. But it is doubtful that extrinsic, materialistic standards can be successfully applied. Standards have to be the product of values held, and of the life that has been led. The better the quality of the life that has been experienced, the better the values held and the standards which result from these values. Standards will be unique—not the same for everyone—even as the experience from which they are derived has been unique. They will be in terms of other human beings.

BASIS FOR HEALTHY GROWTH

The dynamic which changes a speck of protoplasm into a fully functioning human being is growth. The questions, then, are: What does he grow on? What are the environmental conditions which feed him?

We need to consider that in growing up one is developing both his physical structure and his psychological structure. We are most familiar with the physical structure and are apt to think of that as growth. We know what the body needs to develop and that lack of development will result in physical crippling. We can identify the diseases of malnutrition and know that a man will not become truly a man in the best sense without an adequate supply of the required stuff of physical growth.

All of the time that the physical body is being developed, so also is the psychological self. The physical body fortunately stops growing after about 20 years. The psychological self, however, continues to grow throughout life. As the physical body has its own unique food requirements, so does the psychological self. This is a different kind of stuff, however, with a different point of intake. We feed the psychological self through the perceptive process. This is what comes into consciousness when stimuli from the environment impinge on the organism. It is the stuff of growth for the personality, and it builds attitudes, habits and knowledge. The perceptive stuff of growth provides the experiential background from which we operate. This controls what we do with the body. The quality of the perceptive stuff of growth therefore determines the quality of the behavior of the individual.

It is necessary here to make clear the fact that the physical body and the psychological self do not constitute a duality, even though it is necessary to speak of them one at a time. The organism is unitary in its operation. There is no body apart from personality, no psychological self without a body to inhabit. What affects one affects all. But that does not prevent speaking of a part. Although we know that hand and foot, attitude, emotion and habit are all one, we still can talk of the hand as having certain characteristics while the foot has others. Speaking of parts does not deny the unitary nature of the individual.

WE SELECT WHAT WE WILL PERCEIVE

Since in this paper we are primarily concerned with the development of the fully functioning self, we will discuss what feeds the self and how it is fed. As we have noted, perception is the stuff of growth for the psychological self. The perceptive process is the only avenue by which the self can be fed. Recent understandings as to the nature of this process have enabled us to see more clearly than before how the self is built.

One of the most revealing facts about perception is that it is *selective* We do not see everything in our surroundings. There are thousands of coincidences in the situation in which we find ourselves at any point of time. To perceive them all would cause pandemonium. We therefore *choose* that which the self feeds upon. The direction of the growth of the self depends upon those choices.

The choices seem to be on the basis of experience and unique purpose. We all have a background of experience upon which perception is in part based. We cannot see that which we have no experience to see. But experience is not enough to account for what happens, for there are many objects in our surroundings with which we have had experience, but which we do not perceive.

The additional element which appears to determine perceptive intake is purpose. There is ample evidence now to show that all living tissue is purposive, and, of course, in man this purpose is partly, but only partly, on the conscious level. In perception, purpose operates automatically most of the time. And so, just as we do not eat everything, our psychological selves are particular as to what they feed on. What they take in has to suit their purposes, and has to fit onto their past experiences.

ENHANCEMENT AND DEFENSE

The self "looks out" upon the surrounding scene largely in terms of its own enhancement or defense. It tends to extend in the direction of that which promises to make it better off. It withdraws from that which seems likely to endanger it. This is largely true throughout life and entirely true in the early stages when the self is being established—when "self" and "other" first come into being. Altruism is a highly sophisticated concept, and, if it is achieved at all, it comes late. It is the result of great understanding of the self-other interdependency.

THE SELF NEEDS BOUNDARIES

If the self is going to reach out toward facilitating factors and withdraw from endangering ones, it has to have something to reach out from, something to hide behind. It helps to understand this if we assume that the self has to have boundaries in much the same sense that the physical self has to have a skin. The self has certain things that it will let in, others that it will keep out. The boundaries are not, of course, physical—to be seen—but neither is the self. A physical concept, however, helps us to comprehend it. So if we can imagine a physical shell, or armor, necessary for the confinement of the self, we then can imagine how it functions.

Some kind of boundary—a selective screen—is therefore essential to the maintenance of the self. We could not manage the affairs of living without something of this kind. It follows that the nature of the environment, whether it is seen to be facilitating or endangering, will determine the permeability of this screen. That is, the more facilitating the environment, the less need for protection. The more endangering the environment, the greater need for protection. Thus, under adverse conditions, the screen develops into a shell, so that very little is admitted. When this process is continued over a long period of time, that which enabled us to be selective in our perception becomes almost impermeable.

Boundaries then become barriers. Protection becomes isolation. The self becomes a prisoner in its own fort. We have all seen persons off whom words or ideas seemed to bounce. They have built their barriers against other people so strong that they have become inaccessible. Since fear feeds on itself, especially when a person is in isolation, it has a tendency to extend itself beyond the people who are endangering, to include all people.

When the fearful person withdraws within his psychological shell, communication is shut off. It is just as difficult for such a person to give as it is for him to receive. The self then is denied that which it feeds on. The psychological self feeds on ideas, which come from other people. Without the stuff of growth, the self becomes less adequate, and the whole person loses its ability to do, to venture, to create. The individual comes to see himself as impoverished, but he is not able to do much about it by himself.

THE LIFE GOOD TO LIVE

Such a person, however, by having enhancing relationships with others, can break down some of the barriers which separate him from others. By good experiences, he can become less fearful and more open. This process, too, feeds on itself, and confidence can be built by the quality of his experience with others. Confidence opens the barriers so that the perceptive stuff of growth can again be received. He has to learn not to see others as threats, but as assets. Of course, this will not happen unless others cease to act toward him as threats. The parent or teacher who depends upon threats or other techniques of fear will not be able to open the self of one who is in his power.

Fortunate indeed, and not too common in this authoritarian culture, is the person who has had the opportunity to grow up with people whom he can see as facilitating. Most of us have to build our shell against others, and if we are to have fully functioning selves, we have to have experiences which will open these shells.

For the development of a fully functioning self, a person needs to have opportunity to live the life good to live. This life, or his world, needs to be populated by people whom he can view as facilitating. It is almost entirely a matter of people, not things. Facilitating people can be poor in material things. In fact, some of the happiest and most open people are found in poor material circumstances. The most closed and fearful people, the most authoritarian people, may be surfeited by the material goods of the earth. While this is no plea for poverty and privation, it seems that the very possession of great quantities of material goods is apt by its very nature to make the holder fearful that he will lose his goods to others. Vague fear always causes the personality to close up and to become less accessible.

The life good to live does not depend upon the material status of the person. It depends upon the quality of the people around him. He needs people who are open, so that he can feel their quality. He needs people who respect him as a person from the very beginning. It is paradoxical that many parents love their young, but do not respect them. Parents and teachers often say that the child is, of course, too young to be able to make any decisions for himself. It is true that the newborn infant cannot make decisions. But the babe can feel the difference between being held in respect and being regarded as though he had no personality. Respect for the budding self brings it out. Disrespect starts the process of closing up, which in some of our older children and adults is often so complete.

The life good to live is a cooperative one. No child is too young to sense whether or not he lives in a cooperative relation with the people around him. The reason that cooperation is so important is that the cooperative atmosphere is one of involvement. The growing self must feel that it is involved, that it is really part of what is going on, that in some degree it is helping shape its own destiny, together with the destiny of all. Perhaps there is no one quality more important for the developing self than this feeling of involvement in what is taking place. This is what gives a person a "reason to be." The lack of consultation and involvement is the cause of the continuing war between parents and their children, between teachers and learners, between teachers and administrators, employers and employees, ad infinitum. When the person is a part of something, then he becomes responsible.

Whenever the cooperative life is proposed, the authoritarians say, "Oh yes, you want children (or workers or teachers) to do just as they please!" This is a gross misunderstanding of the cooperative way of life, and the shell on such people is so thick that we are baffled in our efforts to reach them. The fact is that in the cooperative life there is much less freedom "to do just as they please" than there is under the surveillance of the autocrat. For the obligation is owed, and the responsibility is felt, to ourselves and to those who facilitate us. The obligation is with us 24 hours a day, rather than just when the autocrat is looking. We do not neglect or sabotage our own projects. This happens to the other's project, particularly if he has met us with threat or fear.

The cooperative life, where everyone from his beginning receives the respect due to a person, and, as he is able, becomes involved in and responsible for what goes on, is not an easy life. The obligation is continuous and pressing. But the difficulties of such a life are inherent in the living, and they cause the self to extend and stretch and grow. These difficulties have quite the opposite effect from those thought up by and inflicted on us by someone else. The latter, not having meaning to the person, cause him to withdraw and begin to calculate how he can protect himself.

THE FULLY FUNCTIONING PERSON

What is a person with a fully functioning self like? This can be answered only in terms of his behavior. Conclusions can be drawn from this behavior. The temptation here is to vest this person, like Rose Aylmer, with "every virtue, every grace." Rather than simply listing virtues, there are some characteristics not necessarily cherished in our culture, which such a person would logically have. From what has been stated here, it might be inferred that nobody has escaped with a fully functioning self. And it seems to be likely that very few survive home, church and school without damage to the self.

Yet there are a good many people who, through contact with facilitating persons, have been reopened and whose selves function well. To argue otherwise would be to deny the potential for change and improvement on which life itself depends. In fact, it can be considered that no one can experience elation who has never known despair; no one can be courageous without having known fear. So the human personality is not doomed to endure its present state, but can be brought into flower by enhancing experiences. As Karen Horney has said, "My own belief is that man has the capacity as well as the desire to develop his potentialities and become a decent human being, and that these deteriorate if his relationship to others and hence to himself is, and continues to be, disturbed. I believe that man can change and keep on changing as long as he lives."[1]

The fully functioning personality thinks well of himself. He looks at himself and likes what he sees well enough so that he can accept it. This is essential to doing, to "can-ness." He does not see himself as able to do anything and everything, but he sees himself as able in terms of his experience. He feels he can do what is reasonable to expect on the basis of his experience.

Those who do not like what they see when they look at themselves are the fearful ones—not just afraid of present danger, but taking a fearful view of everything in general. Fear renders them helpless, and this leads to alienation from others and hostility toward others, thus shutting themselves off from the stuff they feed upon. The harmful ramifications of not accepting self are endless, because one attitude leads to another.

He thinks well of others. This comes about automatically because of the one-ness of the self-other relationship. It is doubtful that there can be a self except in relation to others, and to accept one implies the acceptance of the other. The acceptance of others opens a whole world with which to relate. It is the opposite of the hostility which results from non-acceptance of self.

He therefore sees his stake in others. He sees that other people are the stuff out of which he is built. He has a selfish interest then in the quality of those around him and has responsibility in some degree for that quality. The whole matter of selfishness and altruism disappears when he realizes that self and other are interdependent—that we are indeed our brother's keeper, and he is ours. Coming into the awareness of mutual need modifies human behavior. He comes to see other people as opportunities, not for exploitation, but for the building of self. He becomes a loving person, so that he can get closer to the real source of his power.

[1] Karen Horney. *Our Inner Conflicts.* New York: W. W. Norton & Co., 1945. p. 19.

He sees himself as a part of a world in movement—in process of becoming. This follows from the whole notion of self and others and the acceptance that they can feed off each other and hence can improve. When one looks outward rather than inward, the idea of change—in self, in others, in things—becomes apparent. The acceptance of change as a universal phenomenon brings about modifications of personality. The person who accepts change and expects it behaves differently from the person who seeks to get everything organized so that it will be fixed from now on. He will not search for the firm foundation on which he can stand for the rest of his life. He will realize that the only thing he knows for sure about the future is that tomorrow will be different from today and that he can anticipate this difference with hopeful expectation.

Optimism is the natural outcome of an accepting view of self and hence of others. Such a person is a doer, a mobile person, one who relates himself in an active way with others. Such activity would be meaningless unless the person had hopes for improvement. As has been stated, today has no meaning except in relation to an expected tomorrow. This is the basis for hope, without which no one can thrive. Improvement is that which enhances and enriches self and others. Neither can be enhanced by itself.

The fully functioning personality, having accepted the ongoing nature of life and the dynamic of change, *sees the value of mistakes.* He knows he will be treading new paths at all times, and that, therefore, he cannot always be right. Rigid personalities suffer much from their need to be always right. The fully functioning personality will not only see that mistakes are inevitable in constantly breaking new ground, but will come to realize that these unprofitable paths show the way to better ones. Thus, a mistake, which no one would make if he could foresee it, can be profitable. In fact, much of what we know that is workable comes from trying that which is not. In our culture, it seems that most of our moral code is based on the values of rigid people who cannot bear to be wrong, and so, making a mistake is almost sinful. The effective person cannot afford to have his spirit of adventure thus hampered. He knows that the only way to find out is to go forward and to profit from experience—to make experience an asset.

The fully functioning self, seeing the importance of people, *develops and holds human values.* There is no one, of course, who does not come to hold values. Values come about through the life one lives, which determines what one comes to care about. The better the life, the better the values accumulated. The one who sees human beings as essential to his own enhancement develops values related to the welfare of people. Holding these values in a world which most people consider to be static, he encounters problems in meeting static mores. He is, therefore, on the creative edge of the generally accepted mores or morals. Values in terms of what is good for all people are continuously in conflict with materialistic values held by the majority.

He knows no other way to live except in keeping with his values. He has no need continuously to shift behavior, depending upon the kind of people nearest him. He has no need for subterfuge or deceit, because he is motivated by the value of facilitating self and others. While treading new paths is fraught with risk, he does not have to engage in a continuous guessing game to make his behavior match new people and also be consistent with what he has done before. A fully functioning person, holding human values, does not have to ask himself constantly what it was he said last week.

We are tempted to call this courage and integrity. This is another way of saying that one has what it takes to live as life really exists and to do it all in one piece. Can we call it courage when there is no alternative?

Since life is ever-moving and ever-becoming, *the fully functioning person is cast in a creative role.* But more than simply accepting this role, he sees creation going on all around him. He sees that creation is not something which occurred long ago and is finished, but that it is now going on and that he is part of it. He sees the evil of the static personality because it seeks to stop the process of creation to which we owe our world and our being. He exults in being a part of this great process and in having an opportunity to facilitate it. Life to him means discovery and adventure, flourishing because it is in tune with the universe.

Other Publications by the Author

Earl C. Kelley. *Education for What Is Real.* New York: Harper & Brothers, 1947. 114 p.

Earl C. Kelley. *The Workshop Way of Learning.* New York: Harper & Brothers, 1951. 169 p.

Earl C. Kelley and Marie I. Rasey. *Education and the Nature of Man.* New York: Harper & Brothers, 1952. 209 p.

CHAPTER 3

TOWARD BECOMING A FULLY FUNCTIONING PERSON

CARL R. ROGERS • UNIVERSITY OF WISCONSIN

I AM SURE that each of us has puzzled from time to time as to his own goals, and the goals which he believes would be desirable for others. "What is my purpose in life?" "What am I striving for?" "What do I want to be?" These are questions which every individual asks himself at one time or another, sometimes calmly and meditatively, sometimes in agonizing uncertainty or despair. They are old, old questions which have been asked and answered in every century of history. Yet they are also questions which every individual must ask and answer for himself, in his own way. They are questions which I, as a therapist, hear expressed in many differing ways as men and women in personal distress try to learn, or understand, or choose the directions which their lives are taking.

THE PROBLEM

As I have worked for many years with troubled individuals, I believe that I can discern a pattern, a trend, a direction, an orderliness, a commonality, in the tentative answers to these questions which these people have found for themselves. And so I would like to share with the reader the picture of the optimum human person, as I have formed this picture from my experience with my clients. It is my perception of what human beings appear to be striving for, when they feel free to choose their own direction. It is also my picture of what constitutes personal or psychological health.

The Background from Which the Problem Is Approached

I shall have to make it clear at the outset that my observations are made from a background of client-centered therapy. Quite possibly all successful psychotherapy has a similar personality outcome, but I am less sure of that than formerly, and hence wish it to be clear that I speak from a particular perspective. The trends I have observed have occurred in a relationship which, when it is at its best, partakes of these characteristics. The therapist has been willing to *be* his real feelings, has been willing to be genuine, in the relationship with the client. He has been able to enter into an intensely personal and subjective relationship with the client—relating not as a scientist to an object of study, not as a physician expecting to diagnose and cure, but as a person to a person.

The therapist feels this client to be a person of unconditional self-worth; of value no matter what his condition, his behavior, or his feelings. The therapist is able to let himself go in understanding this person; no inner barriers keep him from sensing what it feels like to be the client at each moment of the relationship, and he has been able to convey to the client something of this empathic understanding. It means that the therapist has been comfortable in entering this relationship fully, without knowing cognitively where it will lead, satisfied with providing a climate which will free the client to become himself.

For the client, this optimal therapy has meant an exploration of increasingly strange and unknown and dangerous feelings in himself; the exploration proving possible only because he is gradually realizing that he is accepted unconditionally. Thus, he becomes acquainted with elements of his experience which have in the past been denied to awareness as too threatening, too damaging to the structure of the self. He finds himself experiencing these feelings fully, completely, in the relationship, so that for the moment he *is* his fear, or his anger, or his tenderness, or his strength. And as he lives and accepts these widely varied feelings, in all their degrees of intensity, he discovers that he has experienced *himself*, that he *is* all these feelings. He finds his behavior changing in constructive fashion in accordance with his newly experienced and newly accepted self. He approaches the realization that he no longer needs to fear what experience may hold, but can welcome it freely as a part of his changing and developing self.

This is a thumbnail sketch of what client-centered therapy (5) might be at its optimum. I give it here to suggest the kind of situation in which I have observed certain trends occurring in clients who have participated in such therapy. I would like now to proceed to my main concern: what are these directions, and what personality characteristics appear to develop in the client as a result of this kind of experience?

CHARACTERISTIC DIRECTIONS

What follows is based both upon clinical observation and upon research. It tries to present the trends I have seen in our clients, but it also pushes these trends to the limit, as it were, in order better to see the kind of person who would emerge if therapy were optimal, the kind of person who might be said to be the goal which individuals discover they are aiming toward.

An Increasing Openness to Experience

A major observation is that the individual moves toward being open to his experience. This is a phrase which has come to have increasingly definite meaning for me. It is the polar opposite of defensiveness. Defensiveness I have described in the past as being the organism's response to experiences which are perceived or anticipated as incongruent with the structure of the self. In order to maintain the self-structure, such experiences are given a distorted symbolization in awareness, which reduces the incongruity. Thus, the individual defends himself against any threat of alteration in the concept of self by not perceiving those meanings in his experience which contradict his present self-picture.

In the person who is open to his experience, however, every stimulus, whether originating within the organism or in the environment, would be freely relayed through the nervous system without being distorted by a defensive mechanism. There would be no need of the mechanism of "subception" (4) whereby the organism is forewarned of any experience threatening to the self. On the contrary, whether the stimulus was the impact of a configuration of form, color or sound in the environment on the sensory nerves, or a memory trace from the past, or a visceral sensation of fear or pleasure or disgust, the person would be "living it," would have it completely available to awareness.

Perhaps I can give this concept a more vivid meaning if I illustrate it from a recorded interview. A young professional man reports in the forty-eighth interview the way in which he has become more open to some of his bodily sensations, as well as other feelings.

Client: It doesn't seem to me that it would be possible for anybody to relate all the changes that you feel. But I certainly have felt recently that I have more respect for, more objectivity toward, my physical make-up. I mean I don't expect too much of myself. This is how it works out: It feels to me that in the past I used to fight a certain tiredness that I felt after supper. Well now I feel pretty sure that I really am *tired*—that I am not making myself tired—that I am just physiologically lower. It seemed that I was just constantly criticizing my tiredness.

Therapist: So you can let yourself *be* tired, instead of feeling along with it a kind of criticism of it.

Client: Yes, that I shouldn't be tired or something. And it seems in a way to be pretty profound that I can just not fight this tiredness, and along with it goes a real feeling of *I've* got to slow down, too, so that being tired isn't such an awful thing. I think I can also kind of pick up a thread here of why I should be that way in the way my father is and the way he looks at some of these things. For instance, say that I was sick, and I would report this, and it would seem that overtly he would want to do something about it, but he would also communicate, "Oh, my gosh, more trouble." You know, something like that.

Therapist: As though there were something quite annoying really about being physically ill.

Client: Yeah, I am sure that my father has the same disrespect for his own physiology that I have had. Now last summer I twisted my back; I wrenched it; I heard it snap and everything. There was real pain there all the time at first, real sharp. And I had the doctor look at it and he said it wasn't serious; it should heal by itself as long as I didn't bend too much. Well this was months ago—and I have been noticing recently that—hell, this is a real pain and it's still there—and it's not my fault, I mean it's—

Therapist: It doesn't prove something bad about you—

Client: No—and one of the reasons I seem to get more tired than I should maybe is because of this constant strain and so on. I have already made an appointment with one of the doctors at the hospital that he would look at it and take an X-ray or something. In a way I guess you could say that I am just more accurately sensitive—or objectively sensitive to this kind of thing. I can say with certainty that this has also spread to what I eat and how much I eat. And this is really a profound change, as I say, and of course my relationship with my wife and the two children is—well you just wouldn't recognize it if you could see me inside—as you have—I mean—there just doesn't seem to be anything more wonderful than really and genuinely—really *feeling* love for your own children and at the same time *receiving* it. I don't know how to put this. We have such an increased respect—both of us—for Judy, and we've noticed just—as we participated in this—we have noticed such a tremendous change in her—it seems to be a pretty deep kind of thing.

Therapist: It seems to me you are saying that you can listen more accurately to yourself. If your body says it's tired, you listen to it and believe it, instead of criticizing it, if it's in pain you can listen to that, if the feeling is really loving your wife or children, you can *feel* that, and it seems to show up in the differences in them, too.

Here, in a relatively minor but symbolically important excerpt, can be seen much of what I have been trying to say about openness to experience. Formerly he could not freely feel pain or illness, because being ill meant being unacceptable. Neither could he feel tenderness and love for his child, because such feelings meant being weak, and he had to maintain his façade of being strong. But now he can be genuinely open to the experience of his organism—he can be tired when he is tired, he can feel pain when his organism is in pain, he can freely experience the love he feels for his daughter, and he can also feel and express annoyance toward her, as he goes on to say in the next portion of the interview. He can fully live the experiences of his total organism, rather than shutting them out of awareness.

I have used this concept of availability to awareness to try to make clear what I mean by openness to experience. This might be misunderstood. I do not mean that this individual would be self-consciously aware of all that was going on within himself, like the centipede who became aware of all his legs. On the contrary, he would be free to live a feeling subjectively, as well as be aware of it. He might experience love, or pain, or fear, living in this attitude subjectively. Or he might abstract himself from this subjectivity and realize in awareness, "I am in pain"; "I am afraid"; "I do love." The crucial point is that there would be no barriers, no inhibitions, which would prevent the full experiencing of whatever was organismically present, and availability to awareness is a good measure of this absence of barriers.

Openness to experience is not a construct which is easy to measure with our present instruments, but such research as exists tends to support the notion that it is characteristic of those who are coping effectively with life. Chodorkoff (1), for example, found in a very careful study that the better adjusted subjects perceived themselves more accurately. They were, that is, more open to the facts of their experience and thus perceived themselves in much the same way as they were seen by a group of competent and unbiased observers. Even more interestingly, they tended accurately to recognize threatening experiences (in this case tachistoscopically presented threatening words) more quickly than they recognized neutral experiences. They thus seemed very open even to stimuli which were threatening. The poorly adjusted group showed the reverse trend, and seemed to have a set toward keeping threatening experiences inadequately differentiated and inadequately symbolized.

Toward Becoming a Process

A second major trend which I have observed is that the individual moves toward more acceptantly being a process, a fluidity, a changing. He lives in a more existential fashion, living fully in each moment. Let me see if I can explain what I mean.

I believe it would be evident that for the person who was fully open to his experience, completely without defensiveness, each moment would be new. The complex configuration of inner and outer stimuli which exists in this moment has never existed before in just this fashion. Consequently, such a hypothetical person would realize that, "What I will be in the next moment, and what I will do, grow out of that moment, and cannot be predicted in advance either by me or by others." Not infrequently we find clients expressing this sort of feeling. Thus one, at the end of therapy, says in rather puzzled fashion, "I haven't finished the job of integrating and reorganizing myself, but that's only confusing, not discouraging, now that I realize this is a continuing process. . . .It is exciting, sometimes upsetting, but deeply encouraging to feel yourself in action and apparently knowing where you are going even though you don't always consciously know where that is."

One way of expressing the fluidity which is present in such existential living is to say that the self and personality emerge *from* experience, rather than experience being translated or twisted to fit a preconceived self-structure. It means that one becomes a participant in and an observer of the ongoing process of organismic experience, rather than being in control of it. As one client put it: "I have a feeling that what I have to do is to take more the position of passenger, rather than driver. See how things go when they're left alone. It's awful kind of scary—feeling that nobody's at the wheel. Of course it's a tremendously challenging feeling, too. Perhaps *this* is the key to freedom."

Or again, the same client, a bit later: "I'm not changing from *me* into something else, I'm changing from *me* to *me*. More like being an amoeba than a caterpillar-butterfly. The amoeba changes shape, but it's still an amoeba. In a way that's sort of a relief. I can keep the parts of me I really like. I don't have to chuck the whole thing, and start all over again."

Such living in the moment, then, means an absence of rigidity, of tight organization, of the imposition of structure on experience. It means instead a maximum of adaptability, a discovery of structure *in* experience, a flowing, changing organization of self and personality.

It is this tendency toward existential living which appears to me very evident in people who are involved in the process of psychological health. It means discovering the structure of experience in the process of living the experience. Most of us, on the other hand, bring a preformed structure and evaluation to our experience and never relinquish it, but cram and twist the experience to fit our preconceptions, annoyed at the fluid qualities which make it so unruly in fitting our carefully constructed pigeonholes. To open one's self to what is going on *now*, and to discover in that present process whatever structure it appears to have—this to me is one of the qualities of the healthy life, the mature life, as I see clients approach it.

An Increasing Trust in His Organism

Still another characteristic of the person who is living the process of health appears to be an increasing trust in his organism as a means of arriving at the most satisfying behavior in each existential situation. Again let me try to explain what I mean.

In choosing what course of action to take in any situation, many people rely upon guiding principles, upon a code of action laid down by some group or institution, upon the judgment of others (from wife and friends to Emily Post), or upon the way they behaved in some similar past situation. Yet as I observe the clients whose experiences in living have taught me so much, I find that increasingly such individuals are able to trust their total organismic reaction to a new situation because they discover to an ever-increasing degree that if they are open to their experience, doing what "feels right" proves to be a competent and trustworthy guide to behavior which is truly satisfying.

As I try to understand the reason for this, I find myself following this line of thought. The hypothetical person who is fully open to his experience would have access to all of the available data in the situation, on which to base his behavior; the social demands; his own complex and possibly conflicting needs; his memories of similar situations; his perception of the uniqueness of this situation. The data would be very complex indeed. But he could permit his total organism, his consciousness participating, to consider each stimulus, need and demand, its relative intensity and importance, and out of this complex weighing and balancing, discover that course of action which would come closest to satisfying all his needs in the situation.

An analogy which might come close to a description would be to compare this person to a giant electronic computing machine. Since he is open to his experience, all of the data from his sense impressions, from his memory, from previous learning, from his visceral and internal states, are fed into the machine. The machine takes all of these multitudinous pulls and forces which are fed in as data, and quickly computes the course of action which would be the most economical vector of need satisfaction in this existential situation. This is the behavior of our hypothetical person.

The defects which in most of us make this process untrustworthy are the inclusion of information which does *not* belong to this present situation, or the exclusion of information which *does*. It is when memories and previous learnings are fed into the computations as if they were *this* reality, and not memories and learnings, that erroneous behavioral answers arise. Or when certain threatening experiences are inhibited from awareness, and hence are withheld from the computation or fed into it in distorted form, this too produces error. But our hypothetical person would find his organism thoroughly trustworthy, because all of the available data would be used, and it would be present in accurate rather than distorted form. Hence his behavior would come as close as possible to satisfying all his needs—for enhancement, for affiliation with others, and the like.

In this weighing, balancing and computation, his organism would not by any means be infallible. It would always give the best possible answer for the available data, but sometimes data would be missing. Because of the element of openness to experience, however, any errors, any following of behavior which was not satisfying, would be quickly corrected. The computations, as it were, would always be in process of being corrected, because they would be continually checked against their consequences.

Perhaps the reader will not like my analogy of an electronic computing machine. Let me put it in more human terms. The client I previously quoted found himself expressing annoyance to his daughter, as well as affection, when he "felt like it." Yet he found himself doing it in a way which not only released the tension in himself, but which freed this small girl to voice her annoyances. He describes the differences between communicating his annoyance and directing his feeling of anger at, or imposing it on, her: " 'Cause it just doesn't feel like I'm imposing my feelings on her, and it seems to me I must show it on my face. Maybe she sees it as 'Yes, daddy is angry, but I don't have to cower.' Because she never *does* cower. This in itself is a topic for a novel, it just feels that good." In this instance, being open to his experience, he selects, with astonishing intuitive skill, a subtly guided course of behavior which meets his need for release of angry tension, but also satisfies his need to be a good father and his need to find satisfaction in his daughter's healthy development. Yet he achieves all this by simply doing the thing that feels right to him.

Another way of saying this is that the individual guides his behavior by the meanings which he discovers in the immediate feeling process which is going on within him. Gendlin (3) terms this immediately present feeling process "experiencing," and shows how the individual can turn again and again to his experiencing to discover further meanings in it. The experiencing is thus a referent by which the individual may guide his behavior.

Observation has shown that clients who appear to have gained the most from therapy come to trust their experiencing. They accept the realization that the meanings implicit in their experiencing of a situation constitute the wisest and most satisfying indication of appropriate behavior. I think of one client who, toward the close of therapy, when puzzled about an issue, would put his head in his hands and say, "Now what *is* it I'm feeling? I want to get next to it. I want to learn what it is." Then he would wait, quietly and patiently, until he could discern the exact flavor of the feelings occurring in him. Often I sense that the client is trying to listen to himself, is trying to hear the messages and meanings which are being communicated by his own physiological reactions. No longer is he so fearful of what he may find. He comes to realize that his own inner reactions and experiences, the messages of his senses and his viscera, are friendly. He comes to want to be close to his inner sources of information rather than closing them off.

Again there is a bit of research evidence to indicate that this trust of one's own experiencing is associated with the healthy personality. Crutchfield (2), in a most interesting study, presented potential military leaders with a situation in which the individual's clear perception and experience of a given situation appeared to be at variance with the judgment of all the other members of the group. Should he now rely on the evidence of his own senses or defer to the judgment of the group? The evidence shows that those who trusted their own experiencing were better adjusted individuals, more mature, with greater leadership ability. Those who distrusted their own sensing of the situation and adopted the group judgment were the less mature, less well adjusted persons.

It seems to be this trust of his own experiencing which guided the scientific behavior of Einstein, holding him toward a given direction, long before he could give any completely conscious and rational basis for it. During this initial period he simply trusted his total organismic reaction. He says, "During all those years there was a feeling of direction, of going straight toward something concrete. It is, of course, very hard to express that feeling in words, but it was decidedly the case, and clearly to be distinguished from later considerations about the rational form of the solution" (6, 183-84). This is the type of behavior which is also, I believe, characteristic of the person who has gained greatly from therapy.

SOME IMPLICATIONS

The three trends I have tried to describe—toward openness to experience, living as a process, and trust of one's own experiencing—add up to the fact that the person in whom they are observed is becoming a more fully functioning person. This picture of a more fully functioning individual has many implications, but I will restrict myself to pointing out three which I believe have special importance.

Integration Is Implied

The trends I have presented describe an individual who is becoming integrated. He is unified within himself from the surface level to the level of depth. He is becoming "all of one piece." The distinctions between "role self" and "real self," between defensive façade and real feelings, between conscious and unconscious, are all growing less the further these trends continue. All that the individual experiences and is, within the envelope of his organism, is increasingly available to his conscious self, to himself as a person. There is a continuing growth of good communication between all the different aspects and facets of himself.

Creativity Is Implied

Watching my clients, I have come to a much better understanding of creative people. El Greco, for example, must have realized, as he looked at some of his early work, that "good artists do not paint like that." But somehow he trusted sufficiently his own experiencing of life, the process of himself, so that he could go on expressing his own unique perceptions. It was as though he could say, "Good artists do not paint like this, but *I* paint like this." Or, to move to another field, Ernest Hemingway was surely aware that "good writers do not write like this." But fortunately he moved toward being Hemingway, being himself, rather than toward someone else's conception of a good writer.

Einstein seems to have been unusually oblivious to the fact that good physicists did not think his kind of thoughts. Rather than drawing back because of his inadequate academic preparation in physics, he simply moved toward being Einstein, toward thinking his own thoughts, toward being as truly and deeply himself as he could. This is not a phenomenon which occurs only in the artist or the genius. Time and again in my clients, I have seen simple people become significant and creative in their own spheres, as they have developed more trust of the processes going on within thmselves, and have dared to feel their own feelings, live by values which they discover within, and express themselves in their own unique ways.

Such a person would, I believe, be recognized by the student of evolution as the type most likely to adapt and survive under changing environmental conditions. He would be able creatively to make sound adjustments to new as well as old conditions. He would be a fit vanguard of human evolution.

Trustworthiness of Human Nature Is Implied

It will have been evident that one implication of the view presented here is that the basic nature of the human being, when functioning freely, is constructive and trustworthy. For me this is an inescapable conclusion from a quarter century of experience in psychotherapy. When we are able to free the individual from defensiveness, so that he is open to the wide range of his own needs, as well as to the wide range of environmental and social demands, his reactions may be trusted to be positive, forward-moving, constructive. We do not need to ask who will socialize him, for one of his own deepest needs is for affiliation and communication with others. When he is fully himself, he cannot help but be realistically socialized. We do not need to ask who will control his aggressive impulses, for when he is open to all of his impulses, his need to be liked by others and his tendency to give affection are as strong as his impulses to strike out or to seize for himself. He will be aggressive in situations in which aggression is realistically appropriate, but there will be no runaway need for aggression. His total behavior, in these and other areas, when he is open to all his experience, is balanced and realistic—behavior which is appropriate to the survival and enhancement of a highly social animal.

I have little sympathy with the rather prevalent concept that man is basically irrational, and that his impulses, if not controlled, would lead to destruction of others and self. Man's behavior is exquisitely rational, moving with subtle and ordered complexity toward the goals his organism is endeavoring to achieve. The tragedy for most of us is that our defenses keep us from being aware of this rationality, so that consciously we are moving in one direction, while organismically we are moving in another. But in our hypothetical person there would be no such barriers, and he would be a participant in the rationality of his organism. The only control of impulses which would exist or which would prove necessary is the natural and internal balancing of one need against another and the discovery of behaviors which follow the vector most closely approximating the satisfaction of all needs. The experience of extreme satisfaction of one need (for aggression, sex, etc.) in such a way as to do violence to the satisfaction of other needs (for companionship, tender relationship, etc.) —an experience very common in the defensively organized person—would simply be unknown in our hypothetical individual. He would participate in the vastly complex self-regulatory activities of his organism—the psychological as well as physiological thermostatic controls—in such a fashion as to live harmoniously, with himself and with others.

BECOMING A FULLY FUNCTIONING PERSON

Let me conclude by drawing together these observational threads into a more unified strand. As I have observed individuals who appear to have made important strides toward psychological health, I believe they may be thought of as moving toward an implicit goal—that of becoming a fully functioning person.

I find such a person to be a human being in flow, in process, rather than having achieved some state. Fluid change is central in the picture.

I find such a person to be sensitively open to all of his experience—sensitive to what is going on in his environment, sensitive to other individuals with whom he is in relationship, and sensitive perhaps most of all to the feelings, reactions, and emergent meanings which he discovers in himself. The fear of some aspects of his own experience continues to diminish, so that more and more of his life is available to him.

Such a person experiences in the present, with immediacy. He is able to live in his feelings and reactions of the moment. He is not bound by the structure of his past learnings, but these are a present resource for him, insofar as they relate to the experience of the moment. He lives freely, subjectively, in an existential confrontation of this moment of life.

Such a person is trustingly able to permit his total organism to function freely in all its complexity in selecting, from the multitude of possibilities, that behavior which in this moment of time will be most generally and genuinely satisfying. He thus is making use of all of the data his nervous system can supply, using this data in awareness, but recognizing that his total organism may be, and often is, wiser than his awareness.

Such a person is a creative person. With his sensitive openness to his world, and his trust of his own ability to form new relationships with his environment, he is the type of person from whom creative products and creative living emerge.

Finally, such a person lives a life which involves a wider range, a greater richness, than the constricted living in which most of us find ourselves. It seems to me that clients who have moved significantly in therapy live more intimately with their feelings of pain, but also more vividly with their feelings of ecstasy; that anger is more clearly felt, but so also is love; that fear is an experience they know more deeply, but so is courage; and the reason they can thus live fully in a wider range is that they have this underlying confidence in themselves as trustworthy instruments for encountering life.

I believe it will have become evident why, for me, adjectives such as happy, contented, enjoyable, do not seem quite appropriate to any general description of this process I have called psychological health, even though the person in this process would experience each one of these feelings at appropriate times. But the adjectives which seem more generally fitting are adjectives such as enriching, exciting, rewarding, challenging, meaningful. This process of healthy living is not, I am convinced, a life for the fainthearted. It involves the stretching and growing of becoming more and more of one's potentialities. It involves the courage to be. It means launching oneself fully into the stream of life. Yet the deeply exciting thing about human beings is that when the individual is inwardly free, he chooses this process of becoming.

SELECTED REFERENCES

1. Bernard Chodorkoff. "Self-Perception, Perceptual Defense, and Adjustment." *Journal of Abnormal and Social Psychology* 49: 508-12; 1954.

2. R. S. Crutchfield. "Conformity and Character." *American Psychologist* 10: 191-98; 1955.

3. Eugene Gendlin. "Experiencing: A Variable in the Process of Therapeutic Change." *American Journal of Psychotherapy* 15: 233-45; 1961.

4. R. S. Lazarus and R. A. McCleary. "Autonomic Discrimination Without Awareness: A Study of Subception." *Psychological Review* 58: 113-22; 1951.

5. Carl R. Rogers. *Client-Centered Therapy: Its Current Practice, Implications and Theory.* Boston: Houghton Mifflin Co., 1951. 506 p.

6. Max Wertheimer. *Productive Thinking.* New York: Harper & Brothers, 1945. 224 p.

Other Publications by the Author

Carl R. Rogers. *Client-Centered Therapy: Its Current Practice, Implications and Theory.* Boston: Houghton Mifflin Co., 1951. 506 p.

Carl R. Rogers. *On Becoming a Person.* Boston: Houghton Mifflin Co., 1961. 420 p.

CHAPTER 4

SOME BASIC PROPOSITIONS OF A GROWTH AND SELF-ACTUALIZATION PSYCHOLOGY

A. H. MASLOW • BRANDEIS UNIVERSITY

When the philosophy of man (his nature, his goals, his potentialities, his fulfillment) changes, then everything changes. Not only the philosophy of politics, of economics, of ethics and values, of interpersonal relations and of history itself change, but also the philosophy of education, the theory of how to help men become what they can and deeply need to become.

We are now in the middle of such a change in the conception of man's capacities, potentialities and goals. A new vision is emerging of the possibilities of man and of his destiny, and its implications are many, not only for our conceptions of education, but also for science, politics, literature, economics, religion, and even our conceptions of the non-human world.

I think it is finally possible to begin to delineate this view of human nature as a total, single, comprehensive system of psychology even though much of it has arisen as a reaction *against* the limitations (as philosophies of human nature) of the two most comprehensive psychologies now available, behaviorism, or associationism, and classical, Freudian psychoanalysis. Finding a single label for it is still a difficult task, perhaps a premature one. I have called it the "holistic-dynamic" psychology to express my conviction about its major roots. Some have called it "organismic," following Goldstein. Sutich and others are calling it the "self-psychology." We shall see. My own guess is that, in a few decades, if it remains suitably eclectic and comprehensive, it will be called simply "psychology."

I think I can be of most service by writing primarily for myself and out of my own work rather than from that of other thinkers, even though I am sure that the areas of agreement among them are very large. A selection of works of this "third force" is listed in the references. Because of space limitation, I will present only some of the major propositions of this point of view, especially those of importance to the educator. In general, I should warn the reader that at many points I am out ahead of the data, sometimes *way* out.

BASIC PROPOSITIONS

1. We have, each one of us, an essential inner nature which is intrinsic, given, "natural" and, usually, very resistant to change.

It makes sense to speak here of the hereditary, constitutional and very early acquired roots of the *individual* self, even though this biological determination of self is only partial, and far too complex to describe simply. In any case, this is "raw material" rather than finished product, to be reacted to by the person, by his significant others, by his environment, etc.

I include in this essential inner nature instinctoid needs, capacities, talents, anatomical equipment, physiological balances, prenatal and natal injuries, and traumata to the neonatus. Whether defense and coping mechanisms, "style of life," and other characterological traits, all shaped in the first few years of life, should be included, is still a matter for discussion. I would say "yes" and proceed on the assumption that this raw material very quickly starts growing into a self as it meets the world outside and begins to have transactions with it.

2. Each person's inner nature has some characteristics which all other selves have (species-wide) and some which are unique to the person (idiosyncratic). The need for love characterizes every human being that is born (although it can disappear later under certain circumstances). Musical genius, however, is given to very few and these differ markedly from each other in style, e.g., Mozart and Debussy.

3. It is possible to study this inner nature scientifically and objectively (that is, with the right kind of "science") and to discover what it is like (*discover*—not invent or construct). It is also possible to do this subjectively, by inner search and by psychotherapy, and the two enterprises supplement and support each other.

4. Even though weak, this inner nature rarely disappears or dies, in the usual person, in the United States (such disappearance or dying is possible, however). It persists underground, unconsciously, even though denied and repressed. Like the voice of the intellect, it speaks softly, but it *will* be heard, even if in a distorted form. That is, it has a dynamic force of its own, pressing always for open, uninhibited expression. Effort must be used in its suppression or repression, from which fatigue can result. This force is one main aspect of the "will to health," the urge to grow, the pressure to self-actualization, the quest for one's identity. It is

this that makes psychotherapy, education and self-improvement possible in principle.

5. However, this inner core, or self, grows into adulthood only partly by (objective or subjective) discovery, uncovering and acceptance of what is "there" beforehand. Partly it is also a creation of the person himself. Life is a continual series of choices for the individual in which a main determinant of choice is the person as he already is (including his goals for himself, his courage or fear, his feeling of responsibility, his ego-strength or "will power," etc.). We can no longer think of the person as "fully determined" where this phrase implies "determined only by forces external to the person." The person, insofar as he *is* a real person, is his own main determinant. Every person is, in part, "his own project," and makes **himself.**

6. No psychological health is possible unless this essential core of the person is fundamentally accepted, loved and respected by others and by himself (the converse is not necessarily true, i.e., that if the core is respected, etc., then psychological health must result, since other pre-requisite conditions must also be satisfied).

The psychological health of the chronologically immature is called healthy growth. The psychological health of the adult is called, variously, self-fulfillment, emotional maturity, individuation, productiveness, self-actualization, etc.

Healthy growth is conceptually subordinate, for it is usually defined now as "growth toward self-actualization," etc. Some psychologists speak simply in terms of one overarching goal or end, or tendency of human development, considering all immature growth phenomena to be only steps along the path to self-actualization (5, 11).

Self-actualization is defined in various ways, but a solid core of agreement is perceptible. All definitions accept or imply: (a) acceptance and expression of the inner core or self, i.e., actualization of these latent capacities and potentialities, "full functioning," availability of the human and personal essence; and (b) minimal presence of ill health, neurosis, psychosis, of loss or diminution of the basic human and personal capacities.

7. If this essential core (inner nature) of the person is frustrated, denied or suppressed, sickness results, sometimes in obvious forms, sometimes in subtle and devious forms, sometimes immediately, sometimes later. These psychological illnesses include many more than those listed by the American Psychiatric Association. For instance, the character disorders and disturbances are now seen as far more important for the fate of the world than the classical neuroses or even the psychoses. From this new point of view, new kinds of illness are most dangerous, e.g., "the diminished or stunted person," i.e., the loss of any of the defining characteristics of

humanness, or personhood, the failure to grow to one's potential; valuelessness (see proposition 19); etc.

That is, general illness of the personality is seen as any falling short of growth, or of self-actualization. And the main source of illness (although not the only one) is seen as frustation of the basic needs, of idiosyncratic potentials, of expression of the self, and of the tendency of the person to grow in his own style, especially in the early years of life.

8. This inner nature, as much as we know of it so far, is definitely not "evil," but is either what we adults in our culture call "good" or else it is neutral. The most accurate way to express this is to say it is "prior to good and evil." There is little question about this if we speak of the inner nature of the infant and child. The statement is much more complex if we speak of the "infant" as he still exists in the adult.

This conclusion is supported by all the truth-revealing and uncovering techniques that have anything to do with human nature: psychotherapy, objective science, subjective science, education and art. For instance, uncovering therapy lessens hostility, fear, greed, etc., and increases love, courage, creativeness, kindness, altruism, etc., leading us to the conclusion that the latter are "deeper," more natural, and more basic than the former, i.e., that what we call "bad" behavior is lessened or removed by uncovering, while what we call "good" behavior is strengthened and fostered by uncovering.

9. "Evil" behavior has mostly referred to unwarranted hostility, cruelty, destructiveness, "mean" aggressiveness. This we do not know enough about. To the degree that this quality of hostility is instinctoid, mankind has one kind of future. To the degree that it is reactive (a response to bad treatment), mankind has a very different kind of future. My opinion is that the weight of the evidence so far indicates that *destructive* hostility is reactive, because uncovering therapy reduces it and changes its quality into "healthy" self-affirmation, forcefulness, righteous indignation, etc. In any case, the *ability* to be aggressive and angry is found in all self-actualizing people, who are able to let it flow forth freely when the external situation "calls for" it.

The situation in children is far more complex. At the very least, we know that the healthy child is also able to be justifiably angry, self-protecting and self-affirming, i.e., reactive aggression. Presumably, then, a child should learn not only how to control his anger, but also how and when to express it.

10. This inner core, even though it is biologically based and instinctoid, is weak rather than strong. It is easily overcome, suppressed or repressed. It may even be killed off permanently. Humans no longer have instincts in the animal sense—powerful, unmistakable inner voices which

tell them unequivocally what to do, when, where, how and with whom. All that we have left are instinct-remnants. And furthermore, these are weak, subtle and delicate, very easily drowned out by learning, by cultural expectations, by fear, by disapproval, etc. They are *hard* to know, rather than easy. Authentic selfhood can be defined in part as being able to hear these impulse-voices within oneself, i.e., to know what one really wants or does not want, what one is fit for and what one is *not* fit for, etc.

11. For all these reasons, it is at this time best to bring out and encourage, or, at the very least, to recognize this inner nature, rather than to suppress or repress it. Pure spontaneity consists of free, uninhibited, uncontrolled, trusting, unpremeditated expression of the self, i.e., of the psychic forces, with minimal interference by consciousness. Control, will, caution, self-criticism, measure, deliberateness, are the brakes upon this expression made intrinsically necessary by the laws of the social and natural worlds outside this psychic world, and, secondarily, made necessary by fear of the psyche itself. Speaking in a very broad way, controls upon the psyche, which come from *fear of the psyche,* are largely neurotic or *psychotic,* or not intrinsically or theoretically necessary. (The healthy psyche is not terrible or horrible and therefore does not have to be feared, as it has been for thousands of years. Of course, the *unhealthy* psyche is another story.) This kind of control is usually lessened by psychological health, by deep psychotherapy, or by any *deeper* self-knowledge and self-acceptance. There are also, however, controls upon the psyche which do not come out of fear, but out of the necessities for keeping it integrated, organized and unified. And there are also "controls," probably in another sense, which are necessary as capacities are actualized and as higher forms of expression are sought for, e.g., acquisition of skills by the artist, the intellectual, the athlete. But these controls are eventually transcended and become aspects of spontaneity, as they become self.

The balance between spontaneity and control varies, then, as the health of the psyche and the health of the world vary. Pure spontaneity is not long possible because we live in a world which runs by its own nonpsychic laws. It *is* possible in dreams, fantasies, love, imagination, the first stages of creativity, artistic work, intellectual play, free association, etc. Pure control is not permanently possible, for then the psyche dies. Education must be directed then *both* toward cultivation of controls and cultivation of spontaneity and expression. In our culture and at this point in history, it is necessary to redress the balance in favor of spontaneity, the ability to be expressive, passive, unwilled, trusting in processes other than will and control, unpremeditated, creative, etc. But it must be recognized that there have been and will be other cultures and other eras in which the balance was or will be in the other direction.

12. Coordinate with this "acceptance" of the self, of fate, of one's call, is the conclusion that the main path to health and self-fulfillment is via basic need gratification rather than via frustration. This contrasts with the suppressive regime, the mistrust, the control, the policing that is necessarily implied by basic evil in the human depths. Intra-uterine life is completely gratifying and nonfrustrating and it is now generally accepted that the first year or so of life also had better be primarily gratifying and nonfrustrating. Asceticism, self-denial, deliberate rejection of the demands of the organism, at least in the West, tend to produce a diminished, stunted or crippled organism, and even in the East, bring self-actualization to very few exceptionally strong individuals.

13. In the normal development of the normal child, it is now known that *most* of the time, if he is given a really free choice, he will choose what is good for his growth. This he does because it tastes good, feels good, gives pleasure or *delight*. This implies that *he* "knows" better than anyone else what is good for him. A permissive regime means not that adults gratify his needs directly, but make it possible for *him* to gratify his needs and to make his own choices, i.e., let him *be*. It is necessary, in order for children to grow well, that adults have enough trust in them and in the natural processes of growth, i.e., not interfere too much, not *make* them grow, or force them into predetermined designs, but rather *let* them grow and *help* them grow in a Taoistic rather than an authoritarian way.

14. But we know also that the *complete absence* of frustration is dangerous. To be strong, a person must acquire frustration-tolerance, the ability to perceive physical reality as essentially indifferent to human wishes, the ability to love others and to enjoy their need-gratification as well as one's own (not to use other people only as means). The child with a good basis of safety, love and respect-need-gratification is able to profit from nicely graded frustrations and become stronger thereby. If they are more than he can bear, if they overwhelm him, we call them traumatic, and consider them dangerous rather than profitable.

It is via the frustrating unyieldingness of physical reality and of animals and of other people that we learn about *their* nature, and thereby learn to differentiate wishes from facts (which things wishing makes come true, and which things proceed in complete disregard of our wishes), and are thereby enabled to live in the world and adapt to it as necessary.

We learn also about our own strengths and limits by overcoming difficulties, by straining ourselves to the utmost, by meeting challenge, even by failing. There can be great enjoyment in a great struggle, and this can displace fear.

15. To make growth and self-actualization possible, it is necessary to understand that capacities, organs and organ systems press to function and express themselves and to be used and exercised, and that such use is satisfying and disuse irritating. The muscular person likes to use his muscles, indeed *has* to use them in order to "feel good" and to achieve the subjective feeling of harmonious, successful, uninhibited functioning (spontaneity) which is so important an aspect of good growth and psychological health. So also for intelligence, for the uterus, the eyes, the capacity to love. Capacities clamor to be used, and cease their clamor only when they *are* well used. That is, capacities are also needs. Not only is it fun to use our capacities, but it is also necessary. The unused capacity or organ can become a disease center or else atrophy, thus diminishing the person.

16. The psychologist proceeds on the assumption that for his purposes there are two kinds of worlds, two kinds of reality, the natural world and the psychic world, the world of unyielding facts and the world of wishes, hopes, fears, emotions, the world which runs by nonpsychic rules and the world which runs by psychic laws. This differentiation is not very clear except at its extremes, where there is no doubt that delusions, dreams and free associations are lawful and yet utterly different from the lawfulness of logic and from the lawfulness of the world which would remain if the human species died out. This assumption does not deny that these worlds are related and may even fuse.

I may say that this assumption is acted upon by *many* or *most* psychologists, even though they are perfectly willing to admit that it is an insoluble philosophical problem. Any therapist *must* assume it or give up his functioning. This is typical of the way in which psychologists bypass philosophical difficulties and act "as if" certain assumptions were true even though unprovable, e.g., the universal assumption of "responsibility," "will power," etc.

17. Immaturity can be contrasted with maturity from the motivational point of view, as the process of gratifying the deficiency-needs in their proper order. Maturity, or self-actualization, from this point of view, means to transcend the deficiency-needs. This state can be described then as meta-motivated, or unmotivated (if deficiencies are seen as the only motivations). It can also be described as self-actualizing, Being, expressing, rather than coping. This state of Being, rather than of striving, is suspected to be synonymous with selfhood, with being "authentic," with being a person, with being fully human. The process of growth is the process of *becoming* a person. *Being* a person is different.

18. Immaturity can also be differentiated from maturity in terms of the cognitive capacities (and also in terms of the emotional capacities).

Immature and mature cognition have been best described by Werner and Piaget. I wish to add another differentiation, that between D-cognition and B-cognition (D=Deficiency; B=Being). D-cognition can be defined as the cognitions which are organized from the point of view of basic needs or deficiency-needs and their gratification and frustration. That is, D-cognition could be called selfish cognition, in which the world is organized into gratifiers and frustrators of our own needs, with other characteristics being ignored or slurred. The cognition of the object, in its own right and its own Being, without reference to its need-gratifying or need-frustrating qualities, that is, without primary reference to its value for the observer or its effects upon him, can be called B-cognition (or self-transcending, or unselfish, or objective cognition). The parallel with maturity is by no means perfect (children can also cognize in a selfless way), but in general, it is mostly true that with increasing selfhood or firmness of personal identity (or acceptance of one's own inner nature) B-cognition becomes easier and more frequent. (This is true even though D-cognition remains for *all* human beings, including the mature ones, the main tool for living-in-the-world.)

To the extent that perception is desire-less and fear-less, to that extent is it more veridical, in the sense of perceiving the true or essential or intrinsic whole nature of the object (without splitting it up by abstraction). Thus the goal of objective and true description of any reality is fostered by psychological health. Neurosis, psychosis, stunting of growth, all are, from this point of view, cognitive diseases as well, contaminating perception, learning, remembering, attending and thinking.

19. A by-product of this aspect of cognition is a better understanding of the higher and lower levels of love. D-love can be differentiated from B-love on approximately the same basis as D-cognition and B-cognition, or D-motivation and B-motivation. No ideally good relation to another human being, especially a child, is possible without B-love. Especially is it necessary for teaching, along with the Taoistic, trusting attitude that it implies. This is also true for our relations with the natural world, i.e., we can treat it in its own right or we can treat it as if it were there only for our purposes.

20. Though, in principle, growth toward self-actualization is easy, in practice it rarely happens (by my criteria, certainly in less than one percent of the adult population). For this, there are many, many reasons at various levels of discourse, including all the determinants of psychopathology that we now know. We have already mentioned one main cultural reason, i.e., the conviction that man's intrinsic nature is evil or dangerous, and one biological determinant for the difficulty of achieving a mature self, namely that humans no longer have strong instincts.

There is a subtle but extremely important difference between regarding psychopathology as blocking or evasion or fear of growth toward self-actualization and thinking of it in a medical fashion, as akin to invasion from without by tumors, poisons or bacteria, which have no relationship to the personality being invaded.

21. Growth has not only rewards and pleasures but also many intrinsic pains, and always will have. Each step forward is a step into the unfamiliar and is possibly dangerous. It also means giving up something familiar and good and satisfying. It frequently means a parting and a separation, with consequent nostalgia, loneliness and mourning. It also often means giving up a simpler and easier and less effortful life, in exchange for a more demanding, more difficult life. Growth forward *is in spite of* these losses and therefore requires courage and strength in the individual, as well as protection, permission and encouragement from the environment, especially for the child.

22. It is therefore useful to think of growth or lack of it as the resultant of a dialectic between growth-fostering forces and growth-discouraging forces (regression, fear, pains of growth, ignorance, etc.). Growth has both advantages and disadvantages. Non-growing has not only disadvantages but also advantages. The future pulls, but so also does the past. There is not only courage but also fear. The total ideal way of growing healthily is, in principle, to enhance all the advantages of forward growth and all the disadvantages of not-growing, and to diminish all the disadvantages of growth forward and all the advantages of not-growing.

Homeostatic tendencies, "need-reduction" tendencies, and Freudian defense mechanisms are not growth-tendencies, but defensive, pain-reducing postures of the organism. But they are quite necessary and normal (not pathological, necessarily) and are generally prepotent over growth-tendencies.

23. All this implies a naturalistic system of values, a by-product of the empirical description of the deepest tendencies of the human species and of specific individuals(8). The study of the human being by science or by self-search can discover where he is heading, what his purpose is in life, what is good for him and what is bad for him, what will make him feel virtuous and what will make him feel guilty, why choosing the good is often difficult for him, what the attractions of evil are. (Observe that the word *ought* need not be used. Also such knowledge of man is relative to man only and does not purport to be "absolute.")

24. The state of being without a system of values is psychopathogenic, we are learning. The human being needs a framework of values, a philosophy of life, a religion or religion-surrogate to live by and understand by, in about the same sense that he needs sunlight, calcium or love.

This I have called the "cognitive need to understand." The value-illnesses which result from valuelessness are called variously anhedonia, anomie, apathy, amorality, hopelessness, cynicism, etc., and can become somatic illness as well. Historically, we are in a value interregnum in which all externally given value systems have proven to be failures (political, economic, religious, etc.), e.g., nothing is worth dying for. What man needs but does not have, he seeks for unceasingly, and he becomes dangerously ready to jump at *any* hope, good or bad. The cure for this disease is obvious. We need a validated, usable system of human values that we can believe in and devote ourselves to (be willing to die for), because they are true rather than because we are exhorted to "believe and have faith." Such an empirically based *Weltanschauung* seems now to be a real possibility, at least in theoretical outline.

Much disturbance in children and adolescents can be understood as a consequence of the uncertainty of adults about their values. As a consequence, many youngsters in the United States live not by adult values, but by adolescent values, which of course are immature, ignorant and heavily determined by confused adolescent needs. An excellent projection of these adolescent values is the cowboy, or "Western," movie.

25. At the level of self-actualizing, many dichotomies become resolved, opposites are seen to be unities and the whole dichotomous way of thinking is recognized to be immature. For self-actualizing people, there is a strong tendency for selfishness and unselfishness to fuse into a higher, superordinate unity. Work tends to be the same as play; vocation and avocation become the same thing. When duty is pleasant and pleasure is fulfillment of duty, then they lose their separateness and oppositeness. The highest maturity is discovered to include a childlike quality, and we discover healthy children to have some of the qualities of mature self-actualization. The inner-outer split, between self and all else, gets fuzzy and much less sharp, and they are seen to be permeable to each other at the highest levels of personality development.

26. One especially important finding in self-actualizing people is that they tend to integrate the Freudian dichotomies and trichotomies, i.e., the conscious, preconscious and the unconscious (as well as id, ego, superego). The Freudian "instincts" and the defenses are less sharply set off against each other. The impulses are more expressed and less controlled; the controls are less rigid, inflexible, anxiety-determined. The superego is less harsh and punishing and less set off against the ego. The primary and secondary cognitive processes are more equally available and more equally valued (instead of the primary processes being stigmatized as pathological). Indeed in the "peak experience" the walls between them tend to fall altogether.

This is in sharp contrast with the classical Freudian position in which these various forces were sharply dichotomized as (a) mutually exclusive, (b) with antagonistic interests, i.e., as antagonistic forces rather than as complementary or collaborating ones.

27. Healthy people are more integrated in another way. In them the conative, the cognitive, the affective and the motor are less separated from each other, and are more synergic, i.e., working collaboratively without conflict to the same ends. The conclusions of rational, careful thinking are apt to come to the same conclusions as those of the blind appetites. What such a person wants and enjoys is apt to be just what is good for him. His spontaneous reactions are as capable, efficient and right as if they had been thought out in advance. His sensory and motor reactions are more closely correlated. His sensory modalities are more connected with each other (physiognomical perception). Furthermore, we have learned the difficulties and dangers of those age-old rationalistic systems in which the capacities were thought to be arranged hierarchically, with rationality at the top.

28. This development toward the concept of a healthy unconscious, and of a healthy irrationality, sharpens our awareness of the limitations of purely abstract thinking, of verbal thinking and of analytic thinking. If our hope is to describe the world fully, a place is necessary for preverbal, ineffable, metaphorical, primary process, concrete-experience, intuitive and esthetic types of cognition, for there are certain aspects of reality which can be cognized in no other way. Even in science this is true, now that we know (a) that creativity has its roots in the nonrational, (b) that language is and must always be inadequate to describe total reality, (c) that any abstract concept leaves out much of reality, and (d) that what we call "knowledge" (which is usually highly abstract and verbal and sharply defined) often serves to blind us to those portions of reality not covered by the abstraction. That is, it makes us more able to see some things, but *less* able to see other things. Abstract knowledge has its dangers as well as its uses.

Science and education, being too exclusively abstract, verbal and bookish, do not have enough place for raw, concrete, esthetic experience, especially of the subjective happenings inside oneself. For instance, organismic psychologists would certainly agree on the desirability of more creative education in perceiving and creating art, in dancing, in (Greek style) athletics and in phenomenological observation.

The ultimate of abstract, analytical thinking is the greatest simplification possible, i.e., the formula, the diagram, the map, the blueprint, certain types of abstract paintings. Our mastery of the world is enhanced thereby, but its richness may be lost as a forfeit, *unless* we learn to value

B-cognition, perception-with-love-and-care, free floating attention—all of which enrich the experience instead of impoverishing it.

29. This ability of healthier people to dip into the unconscious and preconscious, to use and value their primary processes instead of fearing them, to accept their impulses instead of always controlling them, to be able to regress voluntarily without fear, turns out to be one of the main conditions of creativity. We can then understand why psychological health is so closely tied up with certain universal forms of creativeness (aside from special talent) as to lead some writers to make them almost synonymous.

This same tie between health and integration of rational and irrational forces (conscious and unconscious, primary and secondary processes) also permits us to understand why psychologically healthy people are more able to enjoy, to love, to laugh, to have fun, to be humorous, to be silly, to be whimsical and fantastic, to be pleasantly "crazy," and in general to permit and value and enjoy emotional experiences in general and peak experiences in particular and to have them more often. And it leads us to the strong suspicion that learning *ad hoc* to be able to do all these things may help the child move toward health.

30. Esthetic perceiving and creating and esthetic peak experiences are seen to be a central aspect of human life and of psychology and education rather than a peripheral one. This is true for several reasons: (a) All the peak experiences are (among other characteristics) integrative of the splits within the person, between persons, within the world, and between the person and the world. Since one aspect of health is integration, the peak experiences are moves toward health and are themselves momentary healths. (b) These experiences are life-validating, i.e., they make life worthwhile. These are certainly an important part of the answer to the question, "Why don't we all commit suicide?"

31. Self-actualization does not mean a transcendence of all human problems. Conflict, anxiety, frustration, sadness, hurt and guilt can all be found in healthy human beings. In general, the movement, with increasing maturity, is from neurotic pseudo problems to the real, unavoidable, existential problems inherent in the nature of man (even at his best) living in a particular kind of world. Even though he is not neurotic he may be troubled by real, desirable and necessary guilt rather than neurotic guilt (which is not desirable or necessary), by an intrinsic conscience (rather than the Freudian superego). Even though he has transcended the problems of Becoming, there remain the problems of Being. To be untroubled when one *should* be troubled can be a sign of sickness. Sometimes, smug people have to be scared "*into* their wits."

32. Self-actualization is not altogether general. It takes place via femaleness *or* maleness, which are prepotent to general-humanness. That is, one must first be a healthy, femaleness-fulfilled woman before general-human self-actualization becomes possible.

There is also a little evidence that different constitutional types actualize themselves in somewhat different ways (because they have different inner selves to actualize).

33. Another crucial aspect of healthy growth to selfhood is dropping away the techniques used by the child, in his weakness and smallness, for adapting himself to the strong, large, all-powerful, omniscient, god-like adults. He must replace these with the techniques of being strong and independent and of being a parent himself. This involves especially giving up the child's desperate wish for the exclusive, total love of his parents while learning to love others. He must learn to gratify his own needs and wishes, rather than the needs of his parents, and he must learn to gratify them himself, rather than depending upon the parents to do this for him. He must give up being good out of fear and in order to keep their love, and must be good because *he* wishes to be. He must discover his own conscience and give up his internalized parents as a sole ethical guide. All these techniques by which weakness adapts itself to strength are necessary for the child, but immature and stunting in the adult.

34. From this point of view, a society or a culture can be either growth-fostering or growth-inhibiting. The sources of growth and of humanness are essentially within the human person and are not created or invented by society, which can only help or hinder the development of humanness, just as a gardener can help or hinder the growth of a rosebush, but cannot determine that it shall be an oak tree. This is true even though we know that a culture is a *sine qua non* for the actualization of humanness itself, e.g., language, abstract thought, ability to love; but these exist as potentialities in human germ plasm prior to culture.

This makes theoretically possible a comparative sociology, transcending and including cultural relativity. The "better" culture gratifies all basic human needs and permits self-actualization. The "poorer" cultures do not. The same is true for education. To the extent that it fosters growth toward self-actualization, it is "good" education.

As soon as we speak of "good" or "bad" cultures, and take them as means rather than as ends, the concept of "adjustment" comes into question. We must ask, "What kind of culture or subculture is the 'well adjusted' person well adjusted *to*?" Adjustment is, very definitely, *not* necessarily synonymous with psychological health.

35. The achievement of self-actualization (in the sense of autonomy) paradoxically makes *more* possible the transcendence of self, and of self-consciousness and of selfishness. It makes it *easier* for the person to be homonomous, i.e., to merge himself as a part in a larger whole than himself. The condition of the fullest homonomy is full autonomy, and, to some extent, vice versa—one can attain to autonomy only via successful homonomous experiences (child dependence, B-love, care for others, etc.). It is necessary to speak of levels of homonomy (more and more mature), and to differentiate a "low homonomy" (of fear, weakness and regression) from a "high homonomy" (of courage and full, self-confident autonomy).

36. An important existential problem is posed by the fact that self-actualized persons (and *all* people in their peak experiences) occasionally live out-of-time and out-of-the-world (atemporal and aspatial), even though mostly they *must* live in the outer world. Living in the inner psychic world (which is ruled by psychic laws and not by the laws of outer-reality), i.e., the world of experience, of emotion, of wishes and fears and hopes, of love, of poetry, art and fantasy, is different from living in and adapting to the nonpsychic reality which runs by laws the person never made and which are not essential to his nature even though he has to live by them. The person who is not afraid of this inner, psychic world can enjoy it to such an extent that it may be called "heaven" by contrast with the more effortful, fatiguing, externally responsible world of "reality," of striving and coping, of right and wrong, of truth and falsehood. This is true even though the healthier person can adapt more easily and enjoyably to the "real" world, and has better "reality testing," i.e., does not confuse it with his inner, psychic world.

It seems quite clear now that confusing these inner and outer realities, or having either closed off from experience, is highly pathological. The healthy person is able to integrate them both into his life and therefore has to give up neither, being able to go back and forth voluntarily. The difference is the same as the one between the person who can *visit* the slums and the one who is forced to live there always. (*Either* world is a slum if one cannot leave it.) Then paradoxically that which was sick and pathological and the "lowest" becomes part of the healthiest and "highest" aspect of human nature. Slipping into "craziness" is frightening only for those who are not fully confident of their sanity. Education must help the person to live in both worlds.

37. The foregoing propositions generate a different understanding of the role of action in psychology. Goal-directed, motivated, coping, striving, purposeful action is an aspect or by-product of the necessary transactions between a psyche and a nonpsychic world.

a. The D-need gratifications come from the world outside the person, not from within. Therefore adaptation to this world is made necessary, e.g., reality-testing, knowing the nature of this world, learning to differentiate this world from the inner world, learning the nature of people and of society, learning to delay gratification, learning to conceal what would be dangerous, learning which portions of the world are gratifying and which dangerous or useless for need-gratification, learning and the approved and permitted cultural paths to gratification and techniques of gratification.

b. The world is in itself interesting, beautiful and fascinating. Exploring it, manipulating it, playing with it, contemplating it, enjoying it, are all motivated kinds of action (cognitive, motor and esthetic needs).

But there is also action which has little or nothing to do with the world, at any rate at first. Sheer expression of the nature or state or powers (*Funktionslust*) of the organism is an expression of Being rather than of striving. And the contemplation and enjoyment of the inner life not only is a kind of "action" in itself but is also antithetical to action in the world, i.e., it produces stillness and cessation of muscular activity. The ability to wait is a special case of being able to suspend action.

38. From Freud we learned that the past exists *now* in the person. Now we must learn, from growth theory and self-actualization theory, that the future also *now* exists in the person in the form of ideals, hopes, goals, unrealized potentials, mission, fate, destiny, etc. One for whom no future exists is reduced to the concrete, to hopelessness, to emptiness. For him, time must be endlessly "filled." Striving, the usual organizer of most activity, when lost, leaves the person unorganized and unintegrated.

Of course, being in a state of Being needs no future, because it is already *there*. Then Becoming ceases for the moment and its promissory notes are cashed in the form of the ultimate rewards, i.e., the peak experiences, in which time disappears.

SELECTED REFERENCES

1. Gordon W. Allport. *Becoming: Basic Considerations for a Psychology of Personality*. New Haven, Conn.: Yale University Press, 1955. 106 p.

2. Andras Angyal. *Foundations for a Science of Personality*. New York: Commonwealth Fund, 1941. 398 p.

3. C. Bühler. Forthcoming book.

4. Erich Fromm. *Man for Himself; An Inquiry into the Psychology of Ethics*. New York: Holt, Rinehart, and Winston, 1947. 254 p.

5. Kurt Goldstein. *Organism; A Holistic Approach to Biology Derived from Pathological Data in Man*. New York: American Book Co., 1939. 533 p.

6. Karen Horney. *Neurosis and Human Growth; The Struggle Toward Self-Realization.* New York: W. W. Norton & Co., 1950. 391 p.

7. Abraham H. Maslow. *Motivation and Personality.* New York: Harper & Brothers, 1954. 411 p.

8. Abraham H. Maslow, editor. *New Knowledge in Human Values.* New York: Harper & Brothers, 1959. 268 p.

9. Rollo May and others, editors. *Existence; A New Dimension in Psychiatry and Psychology.* New York: Basic Books, 1958. 445 p.

10. Clark Moustakas, editor. *The Self; Explorations in Personal Growth.* New York: Harper & Brothers, 1956. 284 p.

11. Carl R. Rogers and Rosalind F. Dymond, editors. *Psychotherapy and Personality Change; Co-ordinated Research Studies in the Client-Centered Approach.* Chicago: University of Chicago Press, 1954. 446 p.

Other Publications by the Author

Abraham H. Maslow. *Motivation and Personality.* New York: Harper & Brothers, 1954. 411 p.

Abraham H. Maslow, editor. *New Knowledge in Human Values.* New York: Harper & Brothers, 1959. 268 p.

Abraham H. Maslow. *Toward a Psychology of Being.* New York: D. Van Nostrand, in press.

CHAPTER 5

A PERCEPTUAL VIEW OF THE ADEQUATE PERSONALITY

ARTHUR W. COMBS • UNIVERSITY OF FLORIDA

THERE ARE two ways we may approach the question of what it means to be a truly healthy, adequate, self-actualizing person. We may attempt to describe what such people are like or we can seek to discover the dynamics of how such people get to be that way. Each of these approaches is, of course, important to our understanding of such people. To provide the professional worker in human relations fields with effective guides for action, however, we need to know particularly the nature of the processes producing adequate personalities. When we understand these "causes," we may be in a favorable position to establish the conditions by which an increasing number of persons can be helped to achieve richer, more satisfying lives.

There are a number of ways in which the problems of causation might be approached. My own favored frame of reference is to view these problems from a perceptual orientation. Perceptual psychologists have stated, as a basic axiom, that all behavior is a product of the perceptual field of the behaver at the moment of action. That is to say, how any person behaves will be a direct outgrowth of the way things seem to him at the moment of his behaving. To change behavior in this frame of reference requires that we understand the nature of the individual's perceptual field. Knowing the meanings that exist for a particular person, we may then be able to create the conditions which will facilitate changes in his behavior and personality.

Looking at the problem from this frame of reference, I will attempt, in the pages to follow, to describe the truly adequate, self-actualizing person in terms of his characteristic way of seeing himself and the world. How do such persons see themselves and the world in which they live? What is the nature of their perceptual organization and how does this differ from their less fortunate fellows? I have sought the answers to these questions in psychological research and theory, on the one hand, and from my own experience as counselor, teacher, and observer of human relations, on the other. In the course of this study I find myself brought back repeatedly to four characteristics of the perceptual field which always seem to underlie the behavior of truly adequate persons. These characteristics are: (a) a positive view of self, (b) identification with others, (c) openness to experience and acceptance, and (d) a rich and available perceptual field.

A POSITIVE VIEW OF SELF

Extremely adequate, self-actualizing persons seem to be characterized by an essentially positive view of self. They see themselves as persons who are liked, wanted, acceptable, able; as persons of dignity and integrity, of worth and importance. This is not to suggest that adequate people never have negative ways of regarding themselves. They very well may. The total economy of such persons, however, is fundamentally positive (1). They see themselves as adequate to deal with life. As Kelley has put it, they see themselves as "enough." Adequate persons have few doubts about their own worth and value and have so large a reservoir of positive regard that negative perceptions are unable to distort the totality. They seem able to say, when it is so, "Yes, I have not been as honest, or fair, or good as I should have been," without such self-perceptions destroying the remainder of the personality structure. Negative aspects of self can be taken in stride. Indeed, it is even this essentially positive structure of self that seems to make *possible* the admission of negative self-references.

When we describe the truly adequate person as seeing himself in essentially positive ways, we are speaking of the individual's self concept, not his self-report. We mean by the self concept, the ways in which an individual characteristically sees himself. This is the way he "feels" about himself. The self-report, on the other hand, refers to the way in which an individual *describes* himself when he is asked to do so. These are by no means identical (3). What a person *says* he is and what he *believes* he is may be very far apart. Indeed, the person who finds it most necessary to claim a positive self may even turn out to be the least adequate. When we describe the adequate personality as feeling essentially positive about himself, it is his self concept we are talking about, not his self-report. It is what he *feels* about himself, not what he says of himself, that determines his behavior.

We are beginning to discover that the kind of self concepts an individual possesses determines, in large measure, whether he is maladjusted or well adjusted (10). For example, it is not the people who see themselves as liked, wanted, acceptable, worthy and able who constitute our major problems. Such people usually get along fine in our culture and make important contributions both to themselves and to the societies in which they live. It is the people who see themselves as unliked, unwanted, unworthy, unimportant or unable who fill our jails, our mental hospitals and our institutions. These are the maladjusted: the desperate ones, against whom we must protect ourselves, or the defeated ones, who must be sheltered and protected from life. It is the people who feel inadequate, who succumb to brainwashing, who feel so little faith or strength within themselves that they are fair game for any demagogue, who offers security and strength from without. The movement toward personality health is an expression of increased strength of self, just as bodily health is the product of strength of physique (18). Psychotherapists have repeatedly observed that improvement in mental health is correlated with a stronger, more positive view of self (26).

Positive View of Self Expressed in Action

A positive view of self gives its owner a tremendous advantage in dealing with life. It provides the basis for great personal strength. Feeling positively about themselves, adequate persons can meet life *expecting* to be successful. Because they expect success, they behave, what is more, in ways that tend to bring it about. "The rich get richer and the poor get poorer" (15). With such a basic security, life can be met straightforwardly. Courage comes naturally. Indeed, behavior which seems courageous to their fellows often to very adequate people seems to be only the "normal" thing (21).

Because they feel essentially sure about themselves, self-actualizing persons can feel a higher degree of respect for their own individuality and uniqueness. As a consequence they are less disturbed or upset by criticism (6). They can remain stable in the midst of stress and strain. Positive feelings of self make it possible to trust themselves and their impulses. They can utilize themselves as trustworthy, reliable instruments for accomplishing their purposes. They have less doubts and hesitation about themselves. Small wonder that weaker persons are often drawn to them or that adequate people are likely to gravitate into leadership roles (3).

With a self about which he can be fundamentally sure, a person is free to pay much more attention to events outside the self (5). When the house is in good shape and food is set by for the winter, one is free to go adventuring. A strong self can be forgotten on occasion. A weak self must be forever buttressed and cared for. It intrudes in every situation. With a strong self, problems can be dealt with more objectively because self is not at stake. Solutions can be sought solely as "good" answers to the problem at hand, rather than in terms of their immediate contribution to the enhancement of self. Adequate persons can afford to behave unselfishly because the self is already basically fulfilled.

An essentially positive view of self permits adequate people to be effective without worry about conformity or nonconformity. For them, conformity is not a goal or even a way of dealing with life, but only an artifact of the process of problem solving. They can behave in terms of what seems best to do, and let the chips fall where they may. When the goal is problem solution without the necessity for personal aggrandizement, then, whether one conforms or not is merely an outsider's judgment of what happened, not a governing motivation in the behaver.

Having a positive view of self is much like having money in the bank. It provides a kind of security that permits the owner a freedom he could not have otherwise. With a positive view of self one can risk taking chances; one does not have to be afraid of what is new and different. A sturdy ship can venture farther from port. Just so, an adequate person can launch himself without fear into the new, the untried and the unknown. This permits him to be creative, original and spontaneous. What is more, he can afford to be generous, to give of himself freely or to become personally involved in events (21). Feeling he is much more, he has so much more to give.

Development of a Positive Self

The self concept, we know, is learned. People *learn* who they are and what they are from the ways in which they have been treated by those who surround them in the process of their growing up. This is what Sullivan called "learning about self from the mirror of other people" (28). People discover their self concepts from the kinds of experiences they have had with life; not from telling, but from experience. People develop feelings that they are liked, wanted, acceptable and able from *having been* liked, wanted, accepted and from *having been* successful. One learns that he is these things, not from being told so, but only through the experience of *being treated as though he were so*. Here is the key to what must be done to produce more adequate people. To produce a positive self, it is necessary to provide experiences that teach individuals they are positive people.

It is a common fallacy among many lay people and some teachers that, since the world is a very hard place and people sometimes fail, children should be introduced to failure early. The logic of this position, at first glance, seems unassailable and in harmony with the goal of education to "prepare for life." But the position is based on a false premise. Actually, the best guarantee we have that a person will be able to deal with the future effectively is that he has been essentially successful in the past. People learn that they are able, not from failure, but from success. While it may be true that toughness and adequacy come from successfully dealing with problems, the learning comes not from experiencing failure but from successfully avoiding it. Similarly, to feel acceptable one must experience acceptance. To feel lovable one must have been loved. A positive view of self is the product of fulfillment, of having been given. The product of deprivation is a diminished self, and even, if carried to extreme, a depraved self.

IDENTIFICATION WITH OTHERS

A second major characteristic of the truly adequate personality seems to be his capacity for identification with his fellows. The self-concept, we know, is not confined to the limits of the physical body alone. It is capable of contraction or expansion so that the self may be defined so narrowly as to virtually exclude the physical body or expanded so greatly as to include many other people and things. Psychologists have pointed out that infants are highly egocentric and only with growth and maturity achieve an increasing degree of altruism. Some people, unfortunately, never achieve such feelings and remain to the end of their days capable of concern for little more than their own welfare. Others, among them the most adequate men and women in history, seem to reach a point where they can identify with great blocks of mankind, with *all* mankind, without reference to creed, color or nationality. Truly adequate people have a greatly expanded feeling of self.

This feeling of oneness with their fellows does not mean that adequate personalities are necessarily charming hosts or hostesses or even that they like to be surrounded with people. We are not talking of "togetherness" or a frantic need to be with people. Identification has to do with a *feeling* of oneness with one's fellows. This feeling can exist without demanding that a particular individual be a "hail fellow well met" or "life of the party." It is even conceivable that he might not like parties or might prefer to spend much of his time alone in individual pursuits. Searching for a new cure for cancer all alone in a laboratory, for example, may be a profound demonstration of concern for others.

The feeling these truly adequate persons have has also been described as a feeling of "belonging." Unfortunately, this term has come to mean, for some people, "joining," being a member of, or "keeping up with the Joneses." The feeling of belonging characteristic of these adequate people is a far cry from that. It is a feeling of unity or oneness, a feeling of sharing a common fate, or of striving for a common goal. It represents a real extension of the self to include one's fellows.

Expression of the Feeling of Identification

The feeling of oneness with one's fellows produces in the truly adequate person a high degree of responsible, trustworthy behavior. There is reason for this response. When identification is strong, one cannot behave in ways likely to be harmful or injurious to others, for to do that would be to injure one's self. As a consequence, adequate persons are likely to manifest a deep respect for the dignity and integrity of other people and a strong sense of justice and moral probity. A self which truly encompasses others is incapable of "selfishness," in the usual sense. This is a kind of enlightened selfishness in which the boundaries between self and others disappear. One cannot behave in ways which ignore and reject others when self and others are one. It should not surprise us, therefore, that adequate persons usually possess a deep sense of duty or responsibility or that they are likely to be democratic in the fullest sense of the word (12).

The feeling of identification also seems to produce a deep sensitivity to the feelings and attitudes of others. The motives of adequate persons are much more likely to be others-centered (23). Pity and compassion are far more a part of their daily lives and experience. Warmth and humanity come easily to these people as a logical outgrowth of their feeling of oneness with their fellows. This sensitivity also finds its expression in what Maslow has described as a "non-hostile sense of humor" (21).

Because they have strong feelings of identification, adequate persons can work harmoniously with others in either a leader or follower role (2). Feeling adequate, they do not *have* to lead in order to prove their strength and power. Leadership for them is not a way of proving superiority, but a way of organizing to accomplish desirable ends. The feeling of identification produces such trust in others that adequate persons can lead or not as the situation demands and be satisfied in either role.

How Identification Is Acquired

Identification, like the self concept, is learned. It is the product of the individual's experience and an outgrowth of the essentially positive view of self we have already described. One learns to identify with others, depending upon the nature of his contacts with the important people in his life. As people are friendly and helpful, it is easy and natural to extend one's self to include them or to feel at one with them. As people are harmful and rejecting, on the other hand, one's need to protect himself produces an organization from which such people must be excluded. It is a natural reaction to build walls against those who hurt and humiliate us. On the other hand, it is possible to lower defenses when we can be sure of the friendly behavior of others.

Truly adequate people are able to go further. They can often identify even with those who are antagonistic to them. To do this requires that one feel so strong within himself as to be confident he can withstand the attacks of others. The insecure self can identify only with those who make him feel safe and secure. The more positive the individual's feelings about self, the easier it is to identify with an ever broader sample of mankind. The capacity for identification appears to be a product of an essentially positive view of self and of successful, satisfying experiences in interaction with other people. Here is a place where a child's experiences in school can be made to count.

OPENNESS TO EXPERIENCE AND ACCEPTANCE

Truly adequate persons possess perceptual fields maximally open to experience. That is to say, their perceptual fields are capable of change and adjustment in such fashion as to make fullest possible use of their experience. Truly healthy persons seem capable of accepting into awareness any and all aspects of reality (24, 25). They do not find it necessary to defend themselves against events or to distort their perceptions to fit existing patterns. Their perceptual fields are maximally open and receptive to their experiences.

This capacity to confront life openly and without undue defensiveness has sometimes been called acceptance. Acceptance, however, should not be confused with resignation. The openness to experience we are describing refers to the ability to admit evidence into awareness. One cannot deal effectively with what he is unable to conceive exists. The admission of evidence to awareness is the first necessary step to effective action. Being willing to confront the facts, however, does not mean one is defeated by them. On the contrary, it is the only basis upon which any action can safely be premised.

The capacity for acceptance is directly related to the individual's freedom from the experience of threat (29). We know that when people feel threatened: (a) their perceptions become narrowed to the threatening events, and (b) they are forced to the defense of their existing perceptual organizations. These unhappy concomitants of threat are the very antithesis of the openness to experience we have been describing as characteristic of the truly adequate personality. Whether an individual feels threatened, furthermore, is a product of two factors we have already discussed; namely, the positive self and identification. The more secure the individual's self, the less he will feel threatened by events and the more open he can be in relating to the world about him. Similarly, the more the individual is identified with other people, the less threatened he will feel by those who surround him and the more he will be able to accept his experience with others with equilibrium and profit. Openness to experience and acceptance, it thus appears, are related to the individual's freedom from threat, and this freedom in turn is a product of a positive self and identification.

To this point we have spoken of the adequate person's acceptance of events outside himself. But the openness to experience and acceptance we have been describing refer equally to the individual's perceptions of self. Adequate persons are more accepting of themselves (30). Feeling fundamentally positive about self makes it less necessary to be defensive or to bar from perceptual organization what is true about self. Adequate persons are less likely to be at war with themselves and so see themselves more accurately and realistically.

Effect of Acceptance upon Behavior

A greater openness to experience offers many advantages. It provides adequate people with more data and, with more data, they are much more likely to be right. Maslow found, for example, that his self-actualizing people were not only connatively right, they were cognitively right as well (21). A more open perceptual field can encompass more. Adequate people are thus more likely to include the generic as well as the specific aspects of problems or to perceive events or details that would be missed or would seem unimportant to others. This is another way of saying adequate persons behave more intelligently, for what else is intelligence but the ability to behave more effectively and efficiently?

A broader, more accurate perception of the world permits adequate persons to behave more decisively. Decisions can be made with more certainty when one feels he is in command of the data and feels sufficiently sure of self to be unafraid to commit himself to action. Decisions made on the basis of more data are likely to be better ones. On the other hand, the straightforward, uncomplicated relationship these people have with reality also makes it possible for them to live comfortably *without* a decision when this is called for. They are characterized by what Frenkel-Brunswik called a "toleration of ambiguity" (16). That is, they find it possible to live comfortably with unsolved problems. They do not *have* to have an answer when there is none yet, so are less likely to adopt spurious or expedient explanations.

The accurate, realistic assessment of self resulting from acceptance makes possible the use of self as a dependable, trustworthy instrument for achieving one's purposes. These people do not kid themselves. They can permit themselves to be what they are while working to become the best they can be. They do not have to fight what they are. As a consequence, they are free to devote their energies to what is positive and constructive. With a more accurate conception of self, they can and do set more realistic goals for themselves (7, 9, 17). Their levels of aspiration are more likely to be in line with their capacities. Because goals are more realistic, they are more likely to achieve them. And, of course, the more often goals are achieved, the more positively they feel about self and the more acceptance of and openness to experience become possible for them.

Increased capacity to accept self, we know, permits greater acceptance of others as well (4, 22, 27). Adequate people are, therefore, less disturbed and upset by the errors and transgressions of their fellows. They are able to take them, too, as they are. They can be more sympathetic and less judgmental. Because they do not demand of others that they be what they are not, they can have greater patience and forbearance in dealing with human foibles. With a greater openness to and acceptance of other people, human relationships are likely to be more successful, since they derive from broader, more accurate perceptions of what other people are like. Disillusionment and despair in human relationships are the product of inaccurate assessment of what people are like and what can be expected of them. A clear conception of possibilities and limitations is more likely to produce more realistic goals. These in turn provide the bases for success experience and good morale.

The capacity for openness to experience and acceptance makes life more pleasant and exciting for adequate persons. It permits them to feel a greater wonder and appreciation of events (21). Without the necessity for defensiveness, the world can be met openly and gladly. Life can be experienced and savored without fear or hesitation. It can be lived "to the hilt." Such people experience more of what Maslow has called "peak experiences." What is more, adequate persons seem to remain more imaginative and creative even when well along in years.

Dynamics of Openness and Acceptance

Openness and acceptance are not innate characteristics. They are learned. Adequate persons develop these capacities as a function of an essentially positive self and identification. An essentially positive self and a strong feeling of identification with one's fellows make it possible for adequate persons to operate freer from the inhibiting and crippling effects of the experience of threat (8). What contributes to the child's feelings of security and integrity and to his feelings of oneness with his fellow human beings makes possible a greater acceptance of and openness to his experience.

A third factor contributing to acceptance of and openness to experience is the existence of a value system that prizes openness. Perceptual psychology has presented us with a vast body of research demonstrating the effect of values on the perceptual field. It seems clear that persons who have developed attitudes of valuing new experience, of seeking personal growth, or of the testing of idea against idea are likely to develop perceptual fields more open and accepting. Values of this sort, moreover, can be learned and can be taught. The individual's search for personal adequacy can end, as it does for many, in attempts to protect the precious self, to ring it round with defensive works and to reject or ignore what might cause disruption or change (20). Or, fulfillment may be found in an approach to life which flirts with danger, actively seeks for challenge, enjoys the testing of one's mettle or the satisfaction of achieving a new goal or objective. The kind of experience provided to people in their most formative years will determine which kinds of values they espouse.

Acceptance is learned. Clinical evidence shows that children can accept even the most formidable handicaps if these handicaps can be accepted by those who surround them. Accurate, realistic concepts of self are essential bases for growth and fulfillment and are in turn the products of one's experience. It is characteristic of the neurotic that he is unable to accept either himself or his fellows. In the protocols of psychotherapy one can perceive how neurotics reject themselves and their associates. It is apparent in these protocols, too, that as clients get better, they become increasingly able to accept themselves and the people and events which surround them (14, 19, 24, 26, 27, 30). Apparently one learns to accept himself and others as a function of having *experienced* acceptance. It is not surprising, therefore, that modern psychotherapy stresses the acceptance of the client by the therapist as an essential for progress. But the experience of acceptance is by no means limited to the relationship of therapist and client. Acceptance can be experienced in the relationships of the child with his family, his peer group or his teachers in the public schools.

A RICH AND AVAILABLE PERCEPTUAL FIELD

To this point we have described the adequate personality in terms of his perceptions of self, of others, and of the openness of the perceptual field to experience. In the complex society in which we live one cannot be both adequate and stupid simultaneously. The truly adequate person must also be well informed. Indeed, the minimum level of what everyone needs to know just to exist continues to rise year by year as we become ever more specialized and dependent upon technical know-how. One need not know everything to be adequate, but one must certainly have a field of perceptions, rich and extensive enough to provide understanding of the events in which he is enmeshed and available when he needs them. Adequate people have such perceptual fields.

This does not mean that their perceptions are necessarily of an abstract, intellectual character or gained solely from formal schooling. Rich perceptual fields may be derived from quite informal sources through firsthand involvement in human relations, in business, in recreation, or in performing a trade or occupation. On the other hand, with the rapid rise of specialization and technology in our world, perceptions of a technical and abstract character become increasingly necessary for successful action and are less and less available from informal sources. Whatever their origin, however, the fields of adequate people are rich and extensive.

The mere existence of perceptions within the perceptual field is not enough, however, to assure effective behavior. We have already observed that the fields of adequate people are open to their experience. This facilitates the development of a rich and extensive field. The richest field, however, is of little account unless perceptions are available when they are needed for action. This availability, too, seems characteristic of the fields of adequate persons. They not only possess more information or understanding; they are more able to produce these when needed and to put them to effective use.

Some Effects of a Rich and Available Perceptual Field

Clearly, if behavior is a function of perceptions, then a rich and available perceptual field makes possible more effective, efficient behavior. One can do a better job when he has a fine array of tools immediately at hand than he can when he is limited to the use of a hammer and screw driver for every task no matter what its character. Just so, with wider choices open to them, adequate persons can and do operate in ways more satisfying and productive both for themselves and for the world in which they live. They show better judgment and are more often right in their observations and decisions. This is simply another way of saying they behave more intelligently (10).

How Rich and Available Fields Are Acquired

People get their perceptions, we have seen, as a consequence of their experience. Rich and extensive perceptual fields are a product of the kinds of opportunities an individual has been exposed to. Other things being equal, the richer the opportunity, the more likely the development of a rich and extensive field. It is such opportunities that educators have long sought to provide for children. Unfortunately, other things are seldom equal and, as any teacher is aware, mere exposure to an event is no guarantee that the event will be perceived by the individual or be available on later occasions.

Something more than confrontation with events is necessary to insure inclusion of perceptions in the field and their availability on later occasions. This availability seems dependent upon at least two factors: (a) the individual's discovery of personal meaning, and (b) the satisfaction of need.

The degree to which any perception will affect behavior depends upon its personal meaning for the individual. Perceptions may exist at any level of meaning—from isolated bits of information that pass through our consciousness, like the bits of news we read at the foot of a newspaper column, to those perceptions having deep personal meanings for us, like our feelings about a daughter or son, or those concerned with matters in which we are deeply interested, as a business project, hobby or the like. These varying levels of personal meaning are expressed in the words we use to describe such perceptions. Arranged in order of increasing meaning, we speak, for example, of looking, seeing, knowing; of understanding, belief, conviction. The deeper, more personally significant the perception, moreover, the more likely it is to affect behavior.

Adequate people seem to have many more such personal meanings. As a consequence, much more of their knowing affects behaving. They are less easily swayed and much more precise and efficient because the relationship and pertinence of perceptions are clearer and more available when needed. Such meanings, of course, are a result of the nature of the individual's experience. One learns the meaning of events. Whether perceptions exist as isolated knowings or as deep personal understanding will depend upon the opportunities, stimulation and encouragement a person has had, the values he has acquired, the freedom he has had to explore and discover meaning, and the existence of a positive self.

The availability of perceptions in the field will also be vitally affected by the individual's achievement of need satisfaction. Need has a focusing effect upon perception. We perceive what we *need* to perceive. A more adequate self permits attention to wander far afield from self while the inadequate person, desperately seeking maintenance and enhancement of self, must, of necessity, focus most of his perceptions on events contributing directly to such feelings. Failure of need satisfaction produces narrowness and rigidity of perceptual organization. The adequate individual, on the other hand, with a secure self, has a more fluid, open field of perceptions. It follows, then, that the production of a more available field requires the development of a positive view of self, and a positive self, we have already seen, is a function of the kinds of experiences provided in the course of a child's maturing.

In this paper I have attempted to describe the truly adequate, healthy person in terms of four characteristics of the perceptual field: a positive view of self, identification with others, acceptance of and openness to experience, and the richness and availability of the perceptual field. Since all of these ways of perceiving are learned, they can also be taught if we can but find ways to provide the necessary kinds of experiences. No other agency in our society is in a more crucial position to bring about these necessary conditions than are the public schools. Indeed, the production of such people must be the primary goal of education.

To contribute effectively to the production of such persons, however, is not as much a question of revolution as it is of evolution. To produce adequate persons requires not that we do something entirely new and different, but that we all do more efficiently and effectively what some of us now do only sometimes and haphazardly. Educators have been in the business of effecting changes in perception since teaching was invented. No one knows better than they how to bring such changes about. Our new understandings of the truly healthy personality provide us with new and important objectives toward which to direct our efforts. Who can say what kind of world we might create if we could learn to increase our production of adequate people?

SELECTED REFERENCES

1. G. W. Allport. *Becoming: Basic Considerations for a Psychology of Personality.* New Haven, Conn.: Yale University Press, 1955. 106 p.

2. G. B. Bell and H. E. Hall, Jr. "The Relationship Between Leadership and Empathy." *Journal of Abnormal and Social Psychology* 49: 156-57; 1954.

3. J. Benjamins. "Changes in Performance in Relation to Influences upon Self-Conceptualization." *Journal of Abnormal and Social Psychology* 45: 473-80; 1950.

4. E. M. Berger. "The Relation Between Expressed Acceptance of Self and Expressed Acceptance of Others." *Journal of Abnormal and Social Psychology* 47: 778-82; 1952.

5. R. E. Bills. "Attributes of Successful Educational Leaders." In: R. L. Hopper, editor. *Interdisciplinary Research in Educational Administration.* Lexington, Ky.: College of Education, University of Kentucky Press, 1953. p. 16-38.

6. J. J. Brownfain. "Stability of the Self-Concept as a Dimension of Personality." *Journal of Abnormal and Social Psychology* 47: 597-606; 1952.

7. I. L. Child and J. W. M. Whiting. "Determinants of Level of Aspiration: Evidence from Everyday Life." *Journal of Abnormal and Social Psychology* 44: 303-14; 1949.

8. Bernard Chodorkoff. "Self-Perception, Perceptual Defense, and Adjustment." *Journal of Abnormal and Social Psychology* 49: 508-12; 1954.

9. L. D. Cohen. "Level-of-Aspiration Behavior and Feelings of Adequacy and Self-Acceptance." *Journal of Abnormal and Social Psychology* 49: 84-86; 1954.

10. Arthur W. Combs. "Intelligence from a Perceptual Point of View." *Journal of Abnormal and Social Psychology* 47: 662-73; 1952.

11. Arthur W. Combs. "Phenomenological Concepts in Non-Directive Therapy." *Journal of Consulting Psychology* 12: 197-208; 1948.

12. Arthur W. Combs and Donald Snygg. *Individual Behavior; A Perceptual Approach to Behavior.* Revised edition. New York: Harper & Brothers, 1959. 522 p.

13. Arthur W. Combs and D. W. Soper. "The Self, Its Deviate Terms and Research." *Journal of Individual Psychology* 13: 134-45; 1957.

14. Dorothy Conrad. "An Empirical Study of the Concept of Psychotherapeutic Success." *Journal of Consulting Psychology* 16: 92-97; 1952.

15. Charles W. Eriksen. "Psychological Defenses and 'Ego Strength' in the Recall of Completed and Incompleted Tasks." *Journal of Abnormal and Social Psychology* 49: 45-50; 1954.

16. Else Frenkel-Brunswik. "Distortion of Reality in Perception and Social Outlook." *American Psychologist* 4: 253; 1949.

17. Edgar Z. Friedenberg and Julius A. Roth. *Self-Perception in the University; A Study of Successful and Unsuccessful Graduate Students.* Chicago: University of Chicago Press, 1954. 102 p.

18. Kurt Goldstein. *Organism; A Holistic Approach to Biology Derived from Pathological Data in Man.* New York: American Book Co., 1939. 533 p.

19. Margaret Hartley. "Changes in the Self-Concept During Psychotherapy." Unpublished Ph.D. dissertation, University of Chicago, 1951.

20. Prescott Lecky. *Self-Consistency; A Theory of Personality.* (Edited by John F. A. Taylor.) New York: Island Press, 1945. 154 p.

21. A. H. Maslow. *Motivation and Personality.* New York: Harper & Brothers, 1954. 411 p.

22. C. J. McIntyre. "Acceptance by Others and Its Relation to Acceptance of Self and Others." *Journal of Abnormal and Social Psychology* 47: 624-25; 1952.

23. E. L. Phillips. "Attitudes Toward Self and Others: A Brief Questionnaire Report." *Journal of Consulting Psychology* 15: 79-81; 1951.

24. Carl R. Rogers. "Some Observations on the Organization of Personality." *American Psychologist* 2: 358-68; 1947.

25. Carl R. Rogers. "The Concept of the Fully Functioning Person." Mimeographed statement. University of Chicago, 1957.

26. Carl R. Rogers and Rosalind F. Dymond, editors. *Psychotherapy and Personality Change; Co-ordinated Research Studies in the Client-Centered Approach.* Chicago: University of Chicago Press, 1954. 446 p.

27. Elizabeth T. Sheerer. "An Analysis of the Relationship Between Acceptance of and Respect for Self and Acceptance of and Respect for Others in Ten Counseling Cases." *Journal of Consulting Psychology* 13: 169-75; 1949.

28. Harry S. Sullivan. *Conceptions of Modern Psychiatry.* Washington, D.C.: William Alanson White Psychiatric Foundation, 1947. 147 p.

29. Calvin Taylor and Arthur W. Combs. "Self-Acceptance and Adjustment." *Journal of Consulting Psychology* 16: 89-91; 1952.

30. M. J. Vargas. "Changes in Self-Awareness During Client-Centered Therapy." In: Carl Rogers and Rosalind Dymond, editors. *Psychotherapy and Personality Change; Co-ordinated Research Studies in the Client-Centered Approach.* Chicago: University of Chicago Press, 1954. 446 p.

Other Publications by the Author

Arthur W. Combs. "The Myth of Competition." *Childhood Education* 34: 119-28; February 1957.

Arthur W. Combs: "Seeing Is Behaving." *Educational Leadership* 16: 21-27; 1958.

Arthur W. Combs. "Personality Theory and Its Implications for Curriculum Development." In: *Learning More About Learning.* Washington, D.C.: Association for Supervision and Curriculum Development, a department of the National Education Association, 1959. p. 5-20.

Arthur W. Combs and Donald Snygg. *Individual Behavior; A Perceptual Approach to Behavior.* Revised edition. New York: Harper & Brothers, 1959. 522 p.

CHAPTER 6

PERCEIVING AND BEHAVING

FROM COMBS

Perceptual psychologists have stated, as a basic axiom, that all behavior is a product of the perceptual field of the behaver at the moment of action. That is to say, how any person behaves will be a direct outgrowth of the perceptions existing for him at any moment. To change behavior in this frame of reference requires that we understand the nature of the individual's perceptual field.

One need not know everything to be adequate, but one must certainly have a field of perceptions rich and extensive enough to provide understanding of the events in which he is enmeshed and available when he needs them. Adequate people have such perceptual fields.

These varying levels of personal meaning are expressed in the words we use to describe such perceptions. Arranged in order of increasing meaning, we speak, for example, of looking, seeing, knowing; of understanding, belief, conviction. The deeper, more personally significant the perception, moreover, the more likely it is to affect behavior.

FROM KELLEY

One of the most revealing facts about perception is that it is *selective.* We do not see everything in our surroundings. There are thousands of coincidences in the situation in which we find ourselves at any point of time. To perceive them all would cause pandemonium. We therefore *choose* that which the self feeds upon.

The additional element which appears to determine perceptive intake is purpose. There is ample evidence now to show that all living tissue is purposive, and, of course, in man this purpose is partly, but only partly, on the conscious level. In perception it operates automatically most of the time. And so, just as we do not eat everything, our psychological selves are particular as to what they feed on. What they take in has to suit their purposes, and fit onto their past experiences.

FROM MASLOW

To the extent that perception is desire-less and fear-less, to that extent is it more veridical, in the sense of perceiving the true, or essential or intrinsic whole nature of the object (without splitting it up by abstraction). Thus the goal of objective and true description of any reality is fostered by psychological health. Neurosis, psychosis, stunting of growth, all are, from this point of view, cognitive diseases as well, contaminating perception, learning, remembering, attending and thinking.

Science and education, being too exclusively abstract, verbal and bookish, do not have enough place for raw, concrete, esthetic experience, especially of the subjective happenings inside oneself. For instance, organismic psychologists would certainly agree on the desirability of more creative education in perceiving and creating art, in dancing, in (Greek style) athletics and in phenomenological observation.

FROM ROGERS

It is this tendency toward existential living which appears to me very evident in people who are involved in the process of psychological health. It means discovering the structure of experience in the process of living the experience. Most of us, on the other hand, bring a preformed structure and evaluation to our experience and never relinquish it, but cram and twist the experience to fit our preconceptions, annoyed at the fluid qualities which make it so unruly in fitting our carefully constructed pigeonholes.

I find such a person to be sensitively open to all of his experience—sensitive to what is going on in his environment, sensitive to other individuals with whom he is in relationship, and sensitive perhaps most of all to the feelings, reactions and emergent meanings which he discovers in himself. The fear of some aspects of his own experience continues to diminish, so that more and more of his life is available to him.

THE PERCEPTUAL FRAME OF REFERENCE

In the preceding chapters our four invited authors have described the fully functioning, self-actualizing, truly adequate personality as they see him. It is time now to turn our attention to the question of what these ideas mean for schools and education. In the remaining chapters of this book, therefore, we will ask what these ideas mean for the development of fully functioning, self-actualizing people in our public schools. What practices do these concepts tend to support? What educational practices do they question? What new directions for education do they suggest? These are the questions we shall ask.

Reading our four invited authors, one is struck with the "sweet reasonableness" of much of what they have to say. One is carried along with them. Their ideas about adequate persons and how they come into being are challenging and exciting. They have also given us a number of clues as to what our schools might do to produce an increasing number of such people. However, before looking at the implications of the specific ideas they have about the truly adequate person, we need first to look at some of the fundamental assumptions these authors have made about human behavior more generally. Concentrating on the specific comments they have to make about the fully functioning person, we may overlook the fact that all four of these authors have taken positions about the nature of human behavior, in general, that are themselves laden with great meaning for education, even without reference to the question of the adequate personality.

The point of view they have taken is not the usual picture which many of us learned in a more orthodox psychology. All four of these authors are at the forefront of a movement in psychological thought which has sometimes been called the "new look" or "third force." Actually, the point of view has now been in existence so long it can hardly be considered new any longer, but it is a psychology which seeks to understand man in dynamic terms. It looks at human beings, not only through the eyes of an outsider but also in terms of how things look from the point of view of the behaver himself. It is concerned with more than the forces exerted upon people from the outside. It seeks also to understand the internal life of the individual: his wants, feelings, desires, attitudes, values and the unique ways of seeing and understanding that cause him to behave as he does.

The point of view underlying the work of all these authors is a frame of reference which has variously been called the "phenomenological," "perceptual," "interactional" or "existential" approach. This way of looking at human behavior provides the basis for the descriptions these four authors give to the truly adequate personality. Yet these basic ideas, themselves, are fraught with significant implications for educational practice. This is particularly true with reference to four basic principles. These are:

1. Behaving and learning are products of perceiving.
2. Behavior exists in and can, therefore, be dealt with in the present.
3. All people everywhere have a basic drive toward health and actualization.
4. Much of a person's behavior is the result of his conception of himself.

BEHAVIOR AND LEARNING: A PRODUCT OF PERCEIVING

The perceptual view of human behavior holds that the behavior of an individual is a function of his ways of perceiving. That is to say, how any person behaves at a given moment is a direct expression of the way things seem to him at that moment. People do not behave according to the "facts" as they seem to an outsider. How each of us behaves at any given moment is a result of how things seem to him. What a person does, what a person learns, is thus a product of what is going on in his unique and personal field of awareness. People behave in terms of the personal meanings (perceptions) existing for them at the moment of action.

There is a vast difference between facts and meanings. Combs,[1] in an earlier article, pointed out that education has done well in gathering facts and in making them available to people, but has done much less well in helping people discover the meaning of such facts so that behavior is affected. Kelley,[2] in his book, *Education for What Is Real,* has made a similar point. An educational system that hopes to change behavior must do more than provide facts; it must deal actively with meaning or personal perceptions. The learning of "the facts," it must now be recognized, is but the first and simplest phase of the educative process. Bringing "the facts" into the meaning world of the child is a teaching activity which will make a difference in the lives of students.

Teaching has often been seen as a process of assigning subject matter to be covered, of setting up tasks to be accomplished, of demanding compliance and conformity. If behavior is seen as a function of knowing facts, such an approach naturally follows. So long as behaving was equated exclusively with knowing the facts, teachers pounded away at students in a vain attempt to have them remember all of the facts in the textbooks as well as those tossed out in lectures. But students have persisted in behaving contrary to facts. They have continued to cheat on examinations after they have memorized the rule, "honesty is the best policy." They have persisted in using the wrong personal pronoun after they have memorized the rules of grammar. "Knowing" the rules or the facts has frequently not found its way into action. Much education, however, has continued to pour facts into children, hoping that chance or fate or future situations would somehow translate them into behaving. Even now we are under pressure from well meaning critics to pour on even more facts. The process of building up stores of unrelated information within the child continues, even though it is generally observable that something is wrong with the basic assumptions.

If behavior is a function of perception, as our invited authors seem to suggest, the preceding conception is inadequate. If behavior is a function of personal meanings, then perceptions must become the center of the teaching-learning situation. If we accept Kelley's statement that perceptions are the stuff of growth, the basis of intelligent behavior, then personal meanings become the stuff of learning, the material with which we must

[1] Arthur W. Combs. "Personality Theory and Its Implications for Curriculum Development." In: *Learning More About Learning.* Washington, D.C.: Association for Supervision and Curriculum Development, a department of the National Education Association, 1959. p. 5-20.

[2] Earl C. Kelley. *Education for What Is Real.* New York: Harper & Brothers, 1947. 114 p.

work. Perceptions must take their place as a vital part of the curriculum if knowing is to be effective in the lives of students.

The idea that behavior is to be understood as a matter of perceiving, of personal meanings, is quite different from the point of view we most often see expressed in action around us. It is different, too, from what many of us learned in a more orthodox kind of psychology in our training days. That approach usually described behavior as a function of the forces exerted upon the individual. Looked at in that way, the explanation for what people do was sought in the circumstances surrounding them, the pressures upon them, or the facts they knew. In such a point of view, furthermore, the child is regarded as something to be made, to be molded in the "proper" fashion. Teaching in this frame of reference becomes a matter of setting goals for children and then attempting to create the proper conditions to make sure that they reach them. Learning was a matter of "knowing what was so." It was primarily a matter of "facts." The task of the school, it followed, was to gather facts and transmit them to the child. The assumption was that when people know differently they will behave differently.

Seeing behavior as a problem of the forces exerted upon the individual, teaching becomes primarily a matter of controlling these forces. This is done by telling, showing, rewarding, punishing, directing, guiding, making, arranging, manipulating, and even, when need be, forcing and coercing. It will be recognized that this point of view is the underlying assumption about human behavior which forms the basis for many of the current demands to make children work harder, tell them more facts. Most experienced teachers, however, especially of young children, have long since become disenchanted with this approach, for a quite simple reason—it does not work very well. Even when we can demonstrate that the student can repeat the facts on demand, it is still, unhappily, no guarantee that learning has really taken place.

Perceiving and Learning

Seeing learning as a function of meaning calls for a quite different approach. It is easy to deal with facts. These can be gathered and presented in hundreds of ways. But if learning is a matter of meaning, this is only the beginning of the process; learning has not really occurred until some change takes place in the child's own personal and unique perceptual field. If learning is the exploration and discovery of personal meaning, we have a quite different problem—one that calls for different methods as well.

Meanings lie inside of people and cannot be directly manipulated and controlled. Learning only occurs when something happens inside the learner and this is, for the most part, in his, not the teacher's, control.

To a child, the words *New Delhi* may be a symbol for a dot on a map or the capital of a country (whatever the word *capital* means to the child) to be associated with a name of the country and memorized in association with it for a test. It may, however, come to have much more meaning as a place where people live and work and strive for satisfaction from life; it may become peopled with those who seek the same things that students seek for themselves. Students may come to see these people as human beings who have developed different ways of satisfying their needs, but people who share the same world and who are coming to terms with it in the only way they know. As a result of exploration, students may come to see an East Indian quite differently from the original perception they had of him. They may come to see the Indian as a person. As a result of seeing the Indian as a person, an important part of the human race, the child's behavior in the presence of an Indian would be quite different than if he were seen as a statistic or as a foreigner with odd, alien or ridiculous customs.

The classroom must become a place where the exciting experience of exploring and discovering meaning is the central activity. If the objective of instruction becomes that of perception building, students may become aware of, or sensitive to, the importance of meaning. In this way they learn about learning. They learn how perceptions or meanings are broadened or changed and how they are built. They learn how to learn.

If behavior is more directly a function of human meaning and perceiving, rather than the forces exerted upon the individual, then the methods by which people are taught and the role of the teacher in the learning process become quite different. Meanings lie inside of people and cannot be dealt with directly. It follows that the teacher's role must not be that of a director, a maker, a manipulator, but he must be a person who assists, helps, aids, ministers to a growing, living, dynamic organism already in the process of becoming. It means that teaching must be a process of helping children explore and discover the personal meaning of events for them. To do this effectively requires more than the provision of information. It also calls for skill in the creation of the kinds of atmospheres that make exploration of meaning possible on the one hand and the facilitation and encouragement of the active process of discovery on the other.

Perceptions Are Personal and Private

Perceptions are within the individual and will not be brought out unless the climate outside is safe for them. No one can force them out. They come out only when the perceiver feels that he wants them to be presented, and he will not bring them out in the classroom or anywhere else if there is danger that they will be attacked or ridiculed. So long as the perceiver keeps his perceptions safely within, there is no opportunity for them to be measured against the facts in the case. The classroom climate must be made safe for exploration of meanings if they are to be changed. Its atmosphere must be fundamentally accepting. If the teacher and students accept the perceptions of each person as he currently is, then each student is free to explore his perceptions without fear of ridicule or of feeling attacked. If the teacher accepts student perceptions, other students tend to accept them.

Acceptance does not mean the teacher agrees that a student's meanings are valid, nor does it mean that these perceptions are made a part of the teacher's way of perceiving. It means giving the student the privilege of holding and presenting his meanings without ridicule or attack, the privilege of seeing things the way he does. It is in interaction with others that a student builds his perceptions, the meanings that people, ideas, information have for him. There should be ample opportunity and time for this type of exploration.

Learning—Change in Personal Meaning

Since learning is the exploration and discovery of personal meaning, the learning process itself must be a highly personal one. It has to do not only with what the teacher did, or said, or provided, but also with what this meant in the unique world of the learner himself. Learning is, after all, an individual, personal experience. Since this is so, it is hard to see how mass techniques of teaching, and impersonal, objective ways of dealing with students can effectively produce the kind of learning we must have. People can learn, to be sure, from situations where they are treated as passive sponges, but this is pretty inefficient learning. It is a horse and buggy approach to a twentieth century problem. We can no longer afford the luxury of such inefficiency. To continue to treat the business of learning as though it were not a question of personal meaning, when we know it is, is like baking a cake and intentionally leaving out some of the ingredients you know it requires. It *might* turn out all right, but then again, it might taste awful. We cannot afford to let learning take place by accident. Too much is at stake.

The learning process in a "meaning" oriented classroom becomes that of jointly planned, as well as teacher planned, activities—activities which provide each class member an opportunity to bring facts and information to bear on *his* perceptual world. In a wholesome classroom atmosphere, facts and information are important and are the raw materials for new and exciting ways of seeing the world. This calls for teachers who are keenly sensitive to students—how students are, how things seem to them. It also means helping students find ways of expressing their needs rather than dictating to them what their needs should be. It means finding ways through which students may experience self-expression as well as seeing the need for self-restraint. It means helping to elicit and clarify the purposes of the individual members of the class. It means accepting the aims and goals of each class member. It means searching, with students, for activities which will provide opportunities for self-expression and self-clarification. It means developing learning situations based upon exploring and discovering meaning in place of disseminating or "telling" facts.

Experiences planned for and with children will be developed so that each individual has an opportunity to experience success and to see others as helping him to achieve. Classroom activities will provide opportunities for each member to make a contribution to the project or activity. Each individual will be able to feel that he has made a contribution; that he has developed new meanings as a result of the experience. He will have had an opportunity to see himself as one who can do things, as one who can learn and who has learned. He will have had an opportunity to feel that what he does matters; to feel that he is someone who is important in his own right.

The Key to Human Interrelationships

Much of our misunderstanding of each other and the consequent breakdown of human interaction seems due to a failure properly to understand the importance of the principle that behavior is a function of personal meaning. This seems true not just in the classroom but wherever human beings interact. To deal effectively with other people, whether it be across the lunch table or across the diplomatic conference table, requires a sensitivity and understanding of how things seem to the other fellow. The principle is important beyond its use by the teacher. It is an important understanding for the student as well. It is a subject matter to be included in the curriculum. We need to teach students this way of approaching the human problems they encounter.

The students should also, through exploration, come to see that people change their way of doing things only when they see new or different and better ways of doing them. Through such exploratory activity students may come to learn about learning and about their behavior. In this way they may learn that meanings are individual and that the differences in behavior among their classmates and others may be accounted for because of the meaning each sees in the situation. This, in effect, can change a student's attitude of blaming the person for his behavior to one of understanding why he behaves the way he does. For the student, another individual may come to be seen apart from what he does or does not do. As a result of understanding this concept, the student is able to deal more effectively with his own problems. He is able to understand why he behaves as he does and what must be done to make his behavior more precise and effective.

Organization for Learning

If the environment in which permissive exploration of meanings can occur is developed, it must be planned. Time schedules, teacher assignments, class sizes, teaching tools, and classroom furniture must be planned, determined and provided.

Classes should be large enough so that a student may measure his ideas against those of others and small enough so that he may have ample opportunity to get his ideas before a diverse group. The composition of the group is also important. If students are always grouped homogeneously, there may be small opportunity to explore the different ideas of others. There is small chance for students of one socioeconomic or ethnic group to come to see how other groups feel. Students in a static, homogeneous group do not have an opportunity to explore with other groups their value system, their ways of seeing and behaving.

Not only are size and composition important, but continuity is vital if an atmosphere for optimum learning is to be developed. This is particularly true at junior and senior high school levels. The six to eight shifts per day in group composition do not provide time for a feeling of trust and confidence to develop on the part of the pupils. Nor is there time for more than cursory exploration of any problem. The compartmentalization of time and knowledge is not conducive to broad range exploration to include all aspects of knowledge in problem solving situations.

Class sizes have been developed and standardized upon the basis of a "telling" theory of education. Educators have come to see class sizes in terms of 30 pupils per class in both elementary and secondary schools. These ideas about organization have been written into accreditation standards and have come to be regarded as commandments in education. Libraries have been developed to provide a rather large reading room with little space set aside for small group work or for individual research. Other facilities have been designed to implement the program with which school people are now familiar. New and unique school plants will be needed in the future to provide the special facilities for implementing a new type of program.

In the light of these ideas educators will need to take a look at class sizes and also at the present system of grouping students for instruction.

The traditional Carnegie unit system of awarding credit used in the secondary school may be a stumbling block to effective planning. The practice of using time spent, content covered and facts memorized to determine scheduling practices, credits awarded and graduation requirement policies may need to be changed.

Reorientation of School Personnel May Be Required

If education accepts as its goal the development of fully functioning people, school personnel may need reorientation in the nature of growth and behavior. If the perceptual view of learning and growth is accepted, the classroom will need to deal much more adequately than heretofore with feelings, attitudes, convictions, beliefs, doubts, fears, loves, hates and values. This will not be easy for some teachers, and even some schools are positively frightened at the thought of dealing with values. Feelings are quite often ruled out of the classroom and the "iron will" idea holds forth. Students are taught to control or sublimate their feelings rather than to understand them and to use them constructively.

If the point of view presented in Chapters 2, 3, 4 and 5 is to become effective, teachers need to come to see teaching differently. They may need to be helped to see themselves in positive ways, also to become acceptant and open to their experiences. Teachers, administrators and supervisors will need to see themselves as helping or facilitating persons.

Administrators are in a strategic position to help teachers see the "meaning" of the perceptual approach to teaching and learning. Teachers, too, change behavior only when new ideas about people, about learning and about effective ways of working come to have meaning for them; when they can see these ideas as consistent with their perceptions of self and of their role as teachers. In staff meetings and in individual conferences, the administrator can provide the supportive, accepting atmosphere, which is conducive to personality change. When teachers are accepted as people of dignity and worth, as responsible people, as people who are trying in the only way they see to be adequate teachers, they tend to see themselves in more positive ways and to become more adequate in their relationships with students. Administrators and supervisors may help to provide the quality of experience and the emotional climate for teachers which will help to free them to become their best selves.

To change people's ways of seeing is not an easy matter. Any administrator who has attempted to bring about changes in a school system is aware of the tenacity with which teachers and others cling to their perceptions of how a school should be run and how a class should be conducted. Any young teacher with new ideas may soon become aware of the techniques employed by the "old guard" to bring his perceptions into line with theirs Teachers' perceptions, too, are highly personal. They are not changed by dicta or decrees. If they are changed at all, they are changed in the same way and in the same type of climate that has been described for changing students' perceptions. There must be a freedom to hold what they have and a chance to explore other ways of seeing education, learning, motivation and the like.

There is an increasing amount of research data to support the perceptual approach to teaching and learning. The problem will be that of bringing these research findings into the teacher's world of meaning. The technique of exploration and personal involvement with the meaning of the data as well as with the theory will be helpful in accomplishing this goal. Action research may also prove a very valuable technique to accomplish this purpose. Action research may be used as an instrument of in-service training as well as a means of discovering ways of helping students to behave more effectively. Teacher involvement in research may be a way of enabling them to see the importance of the helping relationship to student growth and learning.

If teachers, administrators, counselors and other school personnel accept the premise that, to change behavior, perceptions must be changed, then education becomes more individual and more personal. The atmosphere within the school becomes more friendly; relationships change from authority figure-subordinate relationship to a person-to-person relationship. The classroom environment becomes less threatening and more facilitating and supporting; less content centered and more meaning centered. Such acceptance implies that classrooms become laboratories where facts, information and the perceptual world of students are brought together in the presence of a catalyst (the teacher).

A PERCEPTUAL VIEW OF CAUSATION AND BEHAVIOR CHANGE

All four authors point out, as psychologists usually do, that adequate persons are a product of their experience. They see human behavior as a resultant of the kinds of experiences that the individual has had in his past. This idea we are used to. They also point out, however, that persons react to events according to how they see them at the moment of action as well. This adds a whole new dimension to the understanding of behavior most of us grew up with. It means there are *two* ways we can look at the problem of causation: we can see it historically or immediately.

These ideas are not mutually exclusive. They are both true. A person's behavior is, indeed, a result of his past experience, his life history. How he behaves right now, however, results from his ways of seeing, learned from his past experience, to be sure, but existing in his present perceptions at this time. The immediate view stresses that it is the way of seeing the situation at this moment, today, this instant, which produces the person's behavior at this instant. This means—if we can understand how a person is perceiving right now—we may be able to help him change his behavior *even if we do not know how he got this way.* That is, if human behavior is a function of perception and if perception exists in the present, then it should be possible to change behavior if we can change present perceptions. This opens vast new possibilities for education.

For several generations we have dealt with problems of human behavior almost exclusively from the historical point of view. While this has been very helpful to us in many ways, it has also imposed upon us some serious handicaps in working with people. The introduction of this immediate point of view with respect to behavior, we feel sure, will come to many teachers as an exciting new challenge. Being able to look at a problem in a new way is always helpful. It adds new dimensions in terms of which we can often behave more effectively.

The *historic* view gives us help in understanding how an individual gets to be the way he is. It provides information about the person's past life and the forces that have been active upon him as well as gives information about the conditions under which he now lives. This is extremely important information, for example, for planning programs or developing curricula. The *immediate* view gives us information about why one does what he does when he does it. These two conceptions are not dichotomous. Each serves a purpose in studying behavior and effecting change in individuals.

The Historic View of Causation

The historic approach is valuable when there is an opportunity to change the conditions under which a person lives—what is sometimes called environmental treatment. For example, if personnel is available to work with the parents of a child, it is important to know something about parent-child relationships. If foster home placement is to be considered, it is important to know the home and community conditions bearing upon this possibility. If we wish to do something about the circumstances surrounding a youngster, information about that situation will have to be obtained. A knowledge of outside situations, however, may be of much less value in working directly with the child.

Much past educational practice has been predicated on the belief that since behavior is tied to individual history and influences outside the school control, this history and these influences had to be fully known if the child was to be helped. Since most of these forces exist in the past, moreover, it has often been felt that schools could do little or nothing about changing behavior since they could do nothing about history. An historic view of causation makes education a victim of forces over which it has very limited control, if any. It implies that the effect of teachers on children can be little more than a "holding operation." Furthermore, a view of causation which sees the child's behavior as almost exclusively a function of the forces exerted by home and community requires that the school seek to exert control and direction over the family and community in order to produce changes in the child. This is an extension of the school's authority that is likely to be strongly resisted.

Seeing behavior as a consequence of outside causes, educational leaders have insisted that teachers and counselors should "know all about" the family and community background of each child. This dictum has deeply affected both teacher training and educational practice. Courses at the college level were developed to show teachers and teacher trainees how to make case studies, how to make the dossier, and how to collect the bits of background information to be included. To carry out this assignment has required large amounts of the teacher's time and energy. If conscientious elementary teachers did the job as they were instructed and made a complete study of each child in the way they were taught to in some teachers colleges, a good portion of the year would be consumed before the task was completed even if they did little else. Difficult as such a task is for the elementary teacher with 30 pupils, for the high school teacher, with 150 pupils per school day, it is patently impossible to know the history of each child.

The job of studying the accumulated data, gathering new information and recording it has often consumed valuable time that might have been devoted to more worthwhile teaching activities. Mountains of records have been compiled and assiduously stored away because they might be needed "someday." Teachers following this requirement to the letter have also sometimes been rebuffed by parents who resented what seemed to them to be "prying." Guidance workers, psychologists, visiting teachers and deans of boys or girls have similarly been caught in the merry-go-round of record keeping and paper shuffling. Too much of their time has been devoted to looking for the forces that caused the behavior and too little devoted to *doing something* about it. In some states parents have been so worried about what went into school records that they have passed state laws opening records to their examination. While this action, at first, was met with consternation by many school people, they have since discovered they have been able to live quite comfortably with the idea. Some records, it turned out, were not very necessary anyhow.

The point of view that outside forces exclusively cause behavior has confronted the schools with a dilemma. On the one hand, there is the notion that you cannot help a child unless you can do something about his parents; while, on the other hand, there is the idea that it is obviously impossible for the teacher to make much of a difference in parents. As teachers have pondered a solution to this problem, they have felt defeated and frustrated and have ended by blaming parents for the plight of the younger generation. This is one very comforting thing about the historical view. It lends itself beautifully to buck-passing. If you did not succeed, it was, of course, because of what somebody else failed to do. Parents, on the other hand, have felt that what the school does *should* make a difference; that children *should* change as a result of school experiences. Was that not what they paid their taxes for? Consequently, blame has been bandied back and forth from public to teachers and from teachers to public in a vicious circle of buck-passing and blaming.

Immediate View Is Hopeful

The immediate view of causation is a more hopeful one for education than is a rigid reliance on historical or external determinism. It adds a new dimension. The acceptance of this idea means that teachers and guidance workers do not *have* to know all the past history of a child in order to effect change in his behavior. This view focuses attention on *knowing children* rather than *knowing about* them. Teachers and guidance workers who operate from the perceptual frame of reference can devote the time formerly spent in learning about children to listening to them and learning from them what it is like to feel as they feel. The immediate view says there is something that can be done for every child in school even though we do not have control over his outside world.

Teachers and personnel workers operating in an immediate frame of reference can be relieved of much of the paper shuffling involved in case studies and devote the time gained to working with students. They can feel that what they do as teachers and guidance workers is as important as what they know. Neither do schools have to bring about a change in parent behavior nor change the environment in order to help children. They do not *have* to be able to describe the child in psychological language; they do not *have* to be psychologists in order to create new ways of behaving, although of course there is nothing wrong with such understandings and they may conceivably be very helpful. What teachers and guidance workers *do* becomes much more important in effecting behavior change than what they *know* about the life history of their students. The opportunities which they provide that enable the students to see self, others, things and ideas more accurately and realistically may be even more important to children's lives. The following example illustrates the importance of teacher sensitivity to pupil feelings.

A Florida first grade teacher illustrated the idea that even housekeeping duties can become growth-enhancing experiences for children. She wrote:

> Sometimes a pupil's confidence in self can be developed through "housekeeping" activities in the classroom.
>
> Daphine wouldn't say a word in class when school began. She would make no attempt to do anything in reading readiness, nor would she attempt any other activity. Since she had to wait for a bus each afternoon, I asked her to help me tidy up the room after school. As we worked together day after day, two things happened. She gained confidence in her ability to do things for herself and she came to see me as a person who cared enough for her to help her. She came to trust me.
>
> She was ready to begin reading much earlier than seemed possible during the first days of school.
>
> Late in the school year Daphine became involved one day in the task of illustrating a story she had made, and missed the bus. I took her home. Since I was there, I visited her mother. At home Daphine was completely sheltered, and her mother treated her as a helpless infant.

This teacher did not need to make a case study of this child to know that she saw herself as one who "cannot do things" (lacked self-confidence). The child's behavior had provided sufficient evidence of her lack of self-confidence. Accordingly, the teacher set about providing experiences which would give the child an opportunity to see herself as one who "*can* do things." Although a chance visit provided the knowledge or understanding of *why* the child was this way, it did not change Daphine. The teacher *did not have to know* the home situation in order to help the child. Daphine's confidence was built by the quality of her experience with this teacher.

Similarly, a very successful remedial reading teacher reports that the big problem in helping poor and nonreaders learn to read, or to read better, is to build a confidence in them that they can read (help them see themselves as people who *can*). To build this confidence the teacher need not necessarily know the history of experiences which have contributed to a child's reading behavior. She does not have to know why, or when, or how the failure to gain confidence developed. Such information, of course, may be helpful. *Any* information may be. The point is that we have a new view of what is *essential* information for helping a child. This teacher reports that she initiates her program by setting up situations in which children experience success. When failures occur they are accepted "without judgment." With some success and the feeling on the part of the child that "here is a person who will let me make mistakes," the child can afford to try. The teacher stated, "Once the 'fear-of-error barrier' is broken, progress in reading is rapid, and behavior in other areas of the child's activities is much improved."

Good teachers have always been concerned about individual children and the classroom atmosphere or climate. They have been able, in some measure, to enter into the kind of relationship with their students described by Rogers in Chapter 3. They have, through experience, developed a feeling for children as children are. These good teachers have developed a sensitivity to what children need to experience in order to change and grow. They have been able to bring facts and information into the lives of students in such a way that these facts have personal meaning for the individual. These teachers have been concerned with the immediate, with changing ways of seeing things, with bringing knowledge and information to bear on the child's world in such a way that things are seen differently or that new ways of seeing are learned. They know that a good present experience is good for a child no matter what he has put up with elsewhere.

Implications for Guidance

The guidance worker who operates as if the cause of behavior is in the immediate present is concerned with how the student is, how he feels, with letting him be what he deeply is and helping him become what he can be Rather than trying to force change through holding out present or future rewards, he seeks intently to know how the child is now. The guidance worker is concerned about the student as he is. The student in turn feels this concern and is thereby enabled to see himself more precisely; from here he may be enabled to move in more positive ways and to see his stake in others. The counselor's job is that of helping students to see themselves and to function more fully and adequately. He can spend less time diagnosing and more time helping. The records he keeps may also become less burdensome, for there is less that seems crucial that others must know.

The guidance worker operating in this frame of reference can be freed from many clerical duties to become what he is trained to be—a counselor. He can proceed more directly to help people rather than record information about them. He becomes more concerned with students as persons than he is with the scores they earn on the increasingly numerous standardized tests that may be administered. He is more concerned with how students perceive their world than he is with a recorded image of the student for the world to see. His concern is helping students to actualize their potential to become.

Teacher Education and the Immediate View

The immediate view of behavior has implications, as well, for teacher education. Most of the educational psychology or human growth and development taught in our teacher education institutions in the past has been primarily from a historical frame of reference. It seems likely that the college of education of the future will need to move more and more toward the use of an immediate frame of reference. This will be true for *what* it teaches teachers and also for the *way* it teaches them. This will not be easy, however. It is much simpler to teach students accumulated facts about human growth and development. There are libraries full of this sort of information and a flood of research to be examined on almost anything from the ossification of the wrist-bones in the infant to typical dating behavior of late adolescence. Training the teacher to know the accumulated facts about behavior in the abstract is comparatively simple. Helping a teacher to understand a child is a quite different matter. *Knowing about* and *being sensitive to* a child are not the same thing at all.

To deal with a child effectively in the classroom, it is necessary not only to know about his past history—teachers need also to know about how he sees himself and the world in which he is living today. We need teachers who are able to perceive youngsters, not only in the historical, but also in the immediate, frame of reference. This is a question of sensitivity to how a child is thinking and feeling as well as an understanding of the factors that may have contributed to his present state.

The production of this kind of sensitivity calls for a somewhat new role for the teacher education institutions; it calls for the development of people who *are* something as well as people who *know* something. It is an easy thing to teach a person to know something. It is far more difficult to teach him to *be* something. The experiences planned at this level should be such that teacher trainees are enabled to become sensitive to how children are, to how they feel, to how things come to have meaning for them. Student teachers should be helped to become conscious of their own needs and of their ways of satisfying them. They must be helped to find ways of satisfying their individual needs in a manner which does not exploit students. This does not mean that college teachers must all turn psychiatrists, but that teacher training programs should be designed to promote *personal* adequacy as well as *content* adequacy. This calls for increased attention to teaching methods as well as to ample counseling service for all prospective teachers. If the suggestion of our four invited authors that adequate people promote adequacy in others is accepted, a goal of teacher education institutions will be the development of personal adequacy in their students.

The immediate view of causation offers hope to teachers that they can be more effective in changing the ways students behave. It suggests that even disturbed children can be helped by what teachers do in the classroom. It offers relief to teachers who have felt that their hands were tied by the past and by forces over which they had no control. It offers teachers the satisfaction of feeling that what they do, how they behave, the experiences they plan are really important in changing behavior. This view of causation also means that schools must accept responsibility for changing behavior. They do not have to be responsible for changing parents or society in order to help children to become better people. They do, however, need to accept the responsibility for what they can do and if the immediate view of causation is accurate, what they can do is far more than they have believed. Educators can contribute to changing perceptions and building new ways of seeing, to bringing new facts and information into the child's world of meaning. Teaching, it appears in this view, is more important than many of us have thought.

CHAPTER 7

MOTIVATION AND THE GROWTH OF SELF

FROM KELLEY

The self has to be achieved; it is not given. All that is given is the equipment and at least the minimal (mother and child) social environment. Since the self is achieved through social contact, it has to be understood in terms of others. "Self and other" is not a duality because they go so together that separation is quite impossible.

The additional element which appears to determine perceptive intake is purpose. There is ample evidence now to show that all living tissue is purposive, and, of course, in man this purpose is partly, but only partly, on the conscious level.

For the development of a fully functioning self, a person needs to have opportunity to live the life good to live. This life, or his world, needs to be populated by people whom he can view as facilitating. It is almost entirely a matter of people, not things.

FROM MASLOW

In the normal development of the normal child, it is now known that *most* of the time, if he is given a really free choice, he will choose what is good for his growth. This he does because it tastes good, feels good, gives pleasure or *delight*. This implies that *he* "knows" better than anyone else what is good for him.

Capacities clamor to be used, and cease their clamor only when they *are* well used. Not only is it fun to use our capacities, but it is also necessary. The unused capacity or organ can become a disease center or else atrophy, thus diminishing the person.

This force is one main aspect of the "will to health," the urge to grow, the pressure to self-actualization, the quest for one's identity. It is this that makes psychotherapy, education and self-improvement possible in principle.

This inner core, or self, grows into adulthood only partly by (objective or subjective) discovery, uncovering and acceptance of what is "there" beforehand. Partly it is also a creation of the person himself.

FROM ROGERS

I have little sympathy with the rather prevalent concept that man is basically irrational, and that his impulses, if not controlled, would lead to destruction of others and self. Man's behavior is exquisitely rational, moving with subtle and ordered complexity toward the goals his organism is endeavoring to achieve.

As I have observed individuals who appear to have made important strides toward psychological health, I believe they may be thought of as moving toward an implicit goal—that of becoming a fully functioning person.

I find such a person to be a human being in flow, in process, rather than having achieved some state. Fluid change is central in the picture.

FROM COMBS

The self concept, we know, is learned. People learn who they are and what they are from the ways in which they have been treated by those who surround them in the process of their growing up. This is what Sullivan called learning about self from the mirror of other people. People discover their self concepts from the kinds of experiences they have had with life—not from telling, but from experience. People develop feelings that they are liked, wanted, acceptable and able from having been liked, wanted, accepted and from having been successful. One learns that he is these things, not from being told so but only through the experience of being treated as though he were so. Here is the key to what must be done to produce more adequate people.

The accurate, realistic assessment of self resulting from acceptance makes possible the use of self as a dependable, trustworthy instrument for achieving one's purposes. These people do not kid themselves. As a consequence, they are free to devote their energies to what is positive and constructive.

A NEW VIEW OF MOTIVATION

Much educational practice is now based almost exclusively upon the idea that man has to be prodded or moved into action by an external force or stimulus. This notion that man is at the mercy of the external forces exerted upon him has led to a system of education that seeks to provide the forces necessary to move students from inertia to prescribed activity. The organism has been seen as a sort of inert mass of protoplasm or object to be molded—made into something. In this view, teachers cannot afford to trust the organism. Indeed, they need to be constantly on guard against its reverting to some base animal character. Certainly students cannot be trusted to decide what is good for them. It is assumed that someone (curriculum makers) must decide what is "good for them" and then some others (teachers and administators) must decide what forces should be exerted to keep children moving through this "good experience." Children are regarded as a kind of enemy of schools. They are certain to go wrong if we do not look sharp to our business and keep them straight.

Unfortunately, however, for those assigned the task of forcing students through such an assembly line, some students have ideas of their own about what is "good for them." They have managed to wriggle out of line to find their own ways to self-fulfillment. These students have learned that the only way to escape the dies designed to cast them into conformity is through rebellion or escape. Rebellion, however, does not always take a creatively constructive direction, nor does escape or running away develop productive or creative people. Such students often create problems for schools and society.

This static view of human motivation has been with us a long time. It tends to see the human organism as basically untrustworthy and certain to move in the "wrong" direction unless carefully supervised and controlled. Motivation in this view is a matter of controlling the external events to assure that students will arrive at the prior and "proper" determined ends. It is basically a question of force, coercion, control, management, direction, aimed at molding the child in "the way he should go."

A More Hopeful View of Man

The view presented by our four authors suggests quite a different approach. They point out that all of us have a basic, internal, *given* need to grow that does not have to be imposed; it is there already. This view of man and of learning offers a new and challenging idea about children's motives. Each of the four authors predicated his view on the idea that man has a built-in thrust or will to health; a *need* to become fully functioning or adequate—a psychologically healthy person. This dynamic, Maslow says, is characteristic of the inner core or nature of man. It strains for expression, and through expression and need gratification the individual may ripen and mature to become the self-actualizing or fully functioning personality. Maslow also points out that this inner core or inner nature may be thwarted or perverted unless it is provided the right environment for expression. Thus, he sees adequacy as a function of the development of this inner nature and he sees growth emerging through expression and need gratification rather than through repression or inhibition. He views man as moving toward self-actualization unless growth is thwarted by need frustration. In other words, he sees man achieving adequacy through need gratification and inadequacy through need frustration. This point of view about man's motives is generally shared by our other authors as well.

This is, indeed, a refreshing and hopeful view of man. Generations of teachers have been raised on the concept that children must somehow be *made* good. Motivation was seen as a matter of stimulus and response, of direction and control. In the view of our four invited authors, however, the problem of motivation even disappears. According to these authors, people are *always* motivated; in fact, *they are never unmotivated.* They may not be motivated to do what we would prefer they do, but it can never be truly said that they are unmotivated. What is more, according to our four authors, the direction of this motivation is toward health. This means that, basically, students are "on our side." They want the same things for themselves that we want for them, namely, to be adequate, fully functioning people.

Here is an optimism about humanity that is reassuring in this age of gloom. Its promise is that education can be of more account than the prophets of doom believe; that it can assist mankind toward a path of fulfillment rather than toward a path of destruction. Education does not have to convert the beast or tame him; the task does not call for directing, controlling, remaking and molding an innately antagonistic organism. Rather, learning becomes, in this new view, a matter of working with, rather than against, the organism. Teaching consists of facilitating, helping, assisting, aiding and encouraging an organism which seeks the same eventual aims as teachers themselves seek.

This seems but a simple shift in our thinking, but its implications are tremendous. What view we hold about human motivation is important. We can, after all, behave only in terms of what we believe is so. It makes a great deal of difference, therefore, how we go about dealing with children if we believe they are fundamentally opposed to us or if we believe that they are basically seeking the same ends we are. We do not behave the same way toward our friends as we do toward our enemies. A teacher who respects his student's ability and believes he "means well" behaves quite differently from one who believes the pupil is mean and unable. Whatever our basic ideas about the nature of children, they will have vast implications for every aspect of our behavior in dealing with them.

The teacher who disapproves of and distrusts the fundamental motives of his students cannot permit them the freedom to seek what they need. His view of himself as a responsible teacher requires that he use coercive methods of control and even, if necessary, to use force. It should not surprise us, if such a teacher sees pupil-teacher planning, group decisions, spontaneity, self-determination, and the like as puzzling, fuzzy minded or downright dangerous. This evaluation is inevitable if one begins with distrust of human motives. Obviously, a teacher who believes that students are basically motivated toward evil ends and permits such self-expression to go unchecked could not live with himself or hold up his head in his profession. He would feel he had betrayed everyone. No wonder he is threatened by new curriculum ideas, based on a different view of man. They may even seem to him to be evidence of sheer irresponsibility in his colleagues. With his views about human motivation, students and teachers are forever on opposite sides of the fence and "never the twain shall meet." They are sworn enemies interested in and motivated by directly contrary forces.

Many of the modern critics of our schools hold a similar view of human motivation. Believing it is "natural" for children to loaf, to misbehave, to avoid learning, they advocate making schools tougher, increasing the rigors of assignments, examinations, regulations, discipline and the many demands which schools make of students. They believe, "If it's hard, it's good for them."

The Teacher's View of Motives

What a difference it makes when one can trust the persons with whom he works! A trust in each individual's motivation toward health helps teachers to become more human and schools far pleasanter representations of the society they hope to advance. A student seeking to become the best person he can be is seeking the same thing for himself that teachers want for him. Teachers and students are not antagonists (although to be sure, they *can* be). Rather, they are co-workers, cooperating people seeking the same ends. Student involvement in choice and decision making becomes not only possible but desirable. Methods of guidance, facilitation, cooperation, exploration, assistance and help become natural devices to carry out the educative process in place of force or coercion.

The natural thrust of motivation can be clearly seen in beginning first grade students. There is an almost limitless desire to "know," to find out about things. Those who have worked with first graders are familiar with their requests: "Let me see it"; "Let my try"; "Let me taste"; and so on and on. Here the whole world of things and people is their subject matter and they research it in their own way. They are aware of their limited experience and are eager to use all of their natural resources to "see" what the unknown is like. The attitude of many kindergarten or first grade teachers reflects this excitement. Their subject matter is usually found in the concerns of children, and primary pupils are encouraged to explore the meaning of the many things they find in their world.

Something happens, however, as students move through school. Teachers tend to assume more and more responsibility for deciding what is to be learned, how the child shall be motivated, and the way he shall learn. Less attention is given to what children think and feel and believe, and increasing emphasis is placed on factual textbook content. C. W. Hunnicutt once remarked, "As students progress through school and become increasingly able to make choices, they are given ever decreasing opportunities to make decisions." It seems that children are given the greatest opportunity to make decisions when they are least able, from the standpoint of experience, to make them. Succeeding school years, instead of increasing opportunities for choice, prescribe more and more the children's learning experiences. Too often the attitude of the school seems to move from the "Let's find out" in primary classrooms to an exclusive "What are the facts?" concern in the upper school grades.

One first grade teacher states that her class spends the first few months of the school year exploring the world which is so new to six-year-olds—exploring the world that is the school. The teacher feels that school may be a very threatening place for many children. "During this time," the teacher explained, "through reading such stories as 'Epaminondas' and 'The Twelve Sillies,' we explore the humor of mistakes. In this way, students learn to see that mistakes can even be fun." The teacher states that she laughs at her mistakes and purposely brings her errors to the attention of the children. From her experience the teacher has verbalized the following principles or guides for herself:

1. Accept each contribution a child presents. Never "belittle" anything a child cares to relate to his group or the teacher.
2. Provide each child with an opportunity to make an important contribution to the activity in which the class is engaged.
3. Search constantly for ways of expressing the care I feel for each child in my group.

This teacher has been accused by her colleagues of wasting time during those first weeks of school, but second grade teachers enjoy teaching her former students. One teacher states, "Miss Johnson's students read as well as any others and they are such nice students to work with." Parents, too, want very much to have their children in Miss Johnson's first grade. Her students can afford to try, since errors are not considered sinful. They all have a chance to be successful, to see themselves as important; they all are cared for; they can all be themselves. As a result of taking the time necessary to create this atmosphere, tests show that her students equal or excel the pressured ones in much less time than is required in classrooms where more pressure is exerted on students to read and count.

Miss Johnson, whether consciously or unconsciously, utilized the motivation that is *within* the children she teaches. She does not resort to the artificial, externally imposed motivating devices that so often are harmful in their effects. No child in her classroom can come to see another as a threat to him because another can gain teacher approval quicker than he. Each child comes to see the teacher as a helping person—one who cares in a nondemanding way. No child in Miss Johnson's classroom sees learning as a threat to him—he is not condemned nor is he made to feel that he is not acceptable because he makes mistakes. Every child is allowed to have his likes and dislikes—to be his deeper self and to experience his self from time to time as he relates to his teacher, to other students and to classroom material.

All this is possible because Miss Johnson is not afraid of her students. She trusts them. She believes they can and will learn. As a consequence she can be more relaxed. Not everything has to be dealt with. Much can be ignored. Learning can even be fun. This is possible when the basic motivation of pupils is seen as essentially positive.

People Are Trustworthy

The four invited authors see man as essentially dependable and trustworthy. His innate impulses must propel him toward actualization if he is free to move. They see each person with a built-in desire to be the best person it is possible for him to be. They see him with an inherent need to use his capacities in a constructive fashion, with a built-in thrust toward health, toward actualizing his abilities to *become*.

Ill health, on the other hand, is described as a falling short of growth. Our authors see the main source of illness as frustration of the basic need to develop the idiosyncratic potential, of the expression of the self and of the tendency of the person to grow in his own style. Some high school students, for example, have often built around themselves what Kelley calls a "defensive screen." A student who has been unsuccessful at school oriented tasks or has found himself condemned for his errors may develop many defenses for the tender inner core—the self. It is easier for the student to take the punishment imposed for not trying than it is to be ridiculed for being wrong. It is easier to appear not to care than it is to allow others to know that they have scored a hit when he has not performed as demanded of him.

For the student who has not been given the opportunity to experience the growth described by Maslow, sickness results—the sickness of not growing. Kelley calls it "perceptual malnutrition." The growth potential has been stymied, covered over so it can no longer progress. What the counselor does with such a person, as described by Rogers, is to uncover the inner nature and potentials for growth. Counseling, according to Kelley and Maslow, is a process of "peeling off" the defensive layers so that the imprisoned self may again become expressive and exert its thrust toward adequacy—toward self-fulfillment.

The task of school people is similarly to create conditions which are conducive to actualizing the inner core or nature of students and minimizing the situations which inhibit or stop growth. Much of our educational practice is predicated on a conception of human beings as static, inert. The function of schools in this frame of reference is to make people what they are not. The view presented here is quite different. It sees people in process—not static but moving, not inert but becoming. This calls for a quite different approach to the learning problem. It means, for example, that teachers may take a more relaxed attitude toward their work and the outcomes of education. If students are motivated toward health, teachers do not have to feel duty bound to force students to take what they (the teachers) feel is good for them. Teachers and students are playing on the same team. They are both working to accomplish the student's purposes: to achieve his goals, to satisfy his need to become a fully adequate person. The tensions, conflicts and frustrations that teachers and students experience as a result of conflicting goals and purposes will be absent. Both can experience the satisfaction of moving toward a common goal.

The Encouragement of Becoming

The concept of becoming calls for schools and classrooms which see students as growing, dynamic and creative processes. In this sense a school is not a place where you do something to children, but a place which makes something possible. That "something" is the most efficient possible growth of the individual toward self-realization. This makes of the teacher not a director or coercer, but a situation provider; a kind of friendly representative of society, skilled in understanding people and able to create situations that set them free to become the very best they can. This calls for teachers who are more than manipulators of children; it requires people who can enter into meaningful and productive relationships with students—a teacher must, himself, be first and foremost a person.

Students will select what is good for their growth if they have a wide enough field of experiences and the opportunity to do so. This means more than the opportunity to elect a course, a club or activity. Opportunities will have to be carried into every aspect of the classroom so that the curriculum comes truly alive. It means freedom from threats, rewards and punishments developed to move the student toward the school's goals for him. It means a classroom environment and a school atmosphere in which the student feels free to have his own ideas and express himself, to explore what he basically is and make his own selection of the stuff of growth in terms of what he finds.

Traditional approaches to motivation dependent upon various forms of reward and punishment, grades, honors and the like may often have effects directly contrary to the view of motivation we are discussing. Honor rolls and special privileges for conforming often simply restrict growth. These devices tend to fence-in students and force them into a status seeking situation. Students quite often elect courses which they see as "crips" so that they can keep their average up, stay on the "honor roll" or gain "time off" at the end of grading periods or whatever artificial status accrues to getting "A's." This stops growth and produces the illness discussed by Maslow. It moves people away from searching for the "real me" and for the "stuff" which moves one from "me as I am now" to "me as I become." They are left floundering around at a static level of development in search of status symbols. These become a substitute for the more important status gained in interaction with self and others and, through the development and use of one's general and unique capacities, the self-status gained from a knowledge of self-growth.

If all people are insatiably engaged in a process of becoming, then whom shall we blame for what? If persons are always motivated toward becoming the best they can be and if they will move in such directions if they can, it becomes clear that most of our "blaming" of people is futile and unrewarding. It is perhaps comforting and enhancing to the "blamer" who can divest himself in this way of responsibility or feel superior for a moment to those he blames. But if all people are desperately seeking to become the best they are able, blaming gets us nowhere, and we had better use our energies helping them become more able. There is also a widespread assumption that guilt is somehow good for people. Accordingly, it is frequently used as a device for controlling behavior by shame, ridicule and humiliation. According to our authors, however, these feelings are not motivating; they are stupefying.

It is only as teachers develop a faith in the student's ability to make wise decisions and to direct his own life that an atmosphere of mutual confidence evolves which is growth enhancing. When there is trust in and respect for the inner core, the self of the student, there can be a nonpossessive, nondemanding caring. There is a feeling that each is a person of worth and importance. An emotional climate evolves which Combs, in Chapter 5, describes as a condition essential for the development of an adequate view of self. In such circumstances both teachers and students experience growth toward adequacy.

In this type of atmosphere the student finds himself supported through the behavior of his teachers. The teacher is aware of the importance of the feelings and attitudes he communicates to students by both word and action. He is sensitive to the impact of his own actions in facilitating and encouraging the growth of self.

Teachers will evaluate their behavior in terms of its effect upon the self concept of the child. The importance of teacher behavior in this regard has been studied and reported by J. W. Staines.[1] What teachers say to students, the feelings they communicate by facial expression and

[1] J. W. Staines. "The Self Picture as a Factor in the Classroom." *British Journal of Educational Psychology* 28: 97-111; June 1958.

posture, etc., affect not only how children feel about themselves but the amount of knowledge acquired in the teacher's class. Staines found that in classrooms taught by teachers whose words and actions were enhancing to students, more learning occurred. Students scored slightly higher on mathematics and word recognition in classes of supportive teachers than in control situations where teachers used conventional motivational techniques. A faith in children is required for a good learning atmosphere to prevail in a classroom.

In such an atmosphere, mistakes have value. Students are not made to feel that they have failed because they have made a mistake. From mistakes, students may gain new insights and derive new and more realistic directions. In a supportive classroom environment one can afford to make mistakes; he can afford to try. He can afford to take part in class discussions; to put forth a tentative answer; to advance a proposal for the solution of a problem. He can afford to be a part of a group which has for its goal exploring ideas and possible solutions to problems.

The guidance worker can also see students as able to solve their own problems. He sees his task as providing an accepting atmosphere in which students may unwind the layers of "protective screens" that they have built up; of giving the "inner voice" a chance to speak clearly and distinctly. The counselor comes to see the student as knowing better than anyone else what is good for him.

The ideas presented in Chapters 2, 3, 4 and 5 are based upon a fundamental belief about the nature of people. The position is that people can be trusted to do the things that are conducive to their growth if they are given the freedom to do so. The four authors see people as searching for ways to actualize the abilities which are common to all people as well as those which are unique to the individual. It is also evident from these papers that these abilities, both unique and generic, need to be expressed; they are needs that press for expression. If given free expression, the uniqueness develops into free flowing creativity. People are involved in a process of becoming. Our problem is not to fight them, but to help them. If these abilities are actualized and given an opportunity for expression, the person moves toward total self-actualization.

ADEQUACY—A FUNCTION OF A DEVELOPING SELF

Combs, Kelley and Rogers, in their discussions of the nature of the adequate person, stress the importance of the individual's conceptions of self, the self concept. They point out that the adequate person is very largely determined by the ways in which he comes to perceive himself.

This emphasis upon the self concept and its importance in behavior seems to be shared by many other psychologists in these times. The self concept, they tell us, is one of the most important factors affecting the way in which an individual will behave. If this is true, then any educational program which hopes to make a difference in its charges must be concerned with the nature of the self and its development.

The Self Is Achieved

The healthy self concept is achieved. It develops from the relations which an individual has with others. It is influenced by the quality of these relationships; first with family, then with peers in unstructured situations, then with teachers and peers in more structured situations. The people around the individual form the climate and the soil in which the self grows. If the soil is fertile and the climate is wholesome, there is vigorous and healthy growth.

If the climate is unwholesome and unkind, growth is stunted or stopped, and illness occurs. There is either growth or nongrowth—and nongrowth, Kelley says, is illness. Kelley also states that one who has been subjected to an unhealthy climate and is forced to build defenses actually closes out the stuff of healthy growth. Knowledge then is distorted or closed out and growth is stopped. Learning under these circumstances is in terms of self-*protection*, not in terms of self-*growth*.

The self, our invited authors tell us, is achieved. It is learned as a consequence of the kinds of experiences individuals have in the years of their growing up and this, of course, includes the school years. What is more, the self concept is involved and modified by every life situation in which the individual moves, not just those labeled, "Self Concept 236." People learn who they are and what they are from *all* their experiences, not just those directed at teaching them the nature of the self. Like character and values, the self is learned from every human experience This kind of learning used to be called concomitant learning. One cannot rule the self out of a classroom. One can only learn to deal with it more or less effectively.

Factors Barring Self from the Classroom

The inclusion of an honest concern about human meanings, feelings and understandings in the curriculum is not an easy matter, because our schools are representatives of the society we live in and much of that society has made a fetish of objectivity. Our society is proud of its productivity and magnificent control over the things of the world. We glory in our high standard of living and our achievement of material wealth. It is natural, therefore, to jump to the conclusion that the principles governing the control and production of the "things" of our world which have served us so well apply equally to our dealings with people.

Another factor in more recent years which has led to this fetish of objectivity is the tremendous impact of physical science upon the world we live in. On every hand we can observe the tremendous accomplishments of science. To describe a thing as "scientifically" discovered is almost to close it forever after from any question whatever. Science is a sacred cow in our world. We marvel at it, revel in it; we even attempt to teach the scientific method as a way of life. Science is wonderful. Science is objective. *Ergo,* "objectivity" is the road to salvation. So goes the reasoning. But people are not objective and a school which operates entirely with a preoccupation for the objective deals with less than half a man.

Still another factor making many teachers wary of the inclusion of subjective experience in the public schools is the time honored separation of church and state. Many teachers are so thoroughly ingrained with the importance of the clear-cut separation of church and state that they are prevented from considering questions of morality, human feelings or questions of right and wrong in the classroom. They cry, "How can I deal with questions of morality and ethics, of human feelings and attitudes, when I am expressly forbidden from considering religion in the public schools?" Such a misunderstanding makes many teachers deeply fearful of excursions into the realms of feeling, believing and values. Such a dichotomy need only exist, however, if belief, morality and values are equated with a given religion. But surely this is not so. No religious group has a mortgage on understanding of morality and values. These things lie in the public domain and as a consequence are the legitimate business of the public schools. Indeed, schools which do not deal with these problems are not living up to the responsibilities society created them to fulfill.

Still another factor which lies in the path of the school's consideration of attitudes and feelings in the classroom is the crowded conditions existing everywhere. Feelings, attitudes, beliefs, values and understandings are individual and unique. They exist as personal matters within the peculiar personality of a particular person. But, crowded conditions, teacher shortages, building inadequacies and poorly trained teachers encourage operating in the quickest, easiest fashion. The most expedient fashion, moreover, is to deal exclusively with subject matter. Facts can be set before people by steam shovels. But unfortunately people feed themselves by the spoonful. Certainly there is a place for the mass dissemination of data. We would be amiss if we did not take advantage of all the communicative devices the marvels of modern science are capable of giving us. To stop at this point, however, is to rob the young people of our world of a large portion of their birthright.

The Self Must Be Admitted to the Classroom

The self concept begins with awareness at infancy and, as Rogers puts it, is in a state of flow, in process. It is important, therefore, in working with students, that the feelings about self be given an important place in the classroom program. This does not call for units and assignments and lectures about *how* one should see himself. Rather, it grows out of the normal conditions of teaching. It is possible for a teacher to see his educational goals in terms broad enough to include the self concept while simultaneously achieving high academic standards.

If a positive view of self is so important in the development of creative, productive people, then the self must be admitted to the classroom and provision made for its development. Since teachers, like others, tend to behave in terms of what they consider to be important, the teacher who believes the self concepts of his charges are important will do something about them. Teachers who do not believe the self concept is important, or who are unaware of the nature of the self concept and its effects upon behavior, will be less likely to be effective in encouraging and assisting the development of more adequate selves.

Teachers Must Be Facilitating

The teacher who brings the self of students into his classroom must be a facilitating person. He must see his role as that of a helping person rather than a driver, a pusher. He must be willing to search for ways in which students may find themselves experiencing success. He must create situations in which students can find themselves needed and wanted by others. He must develop situations in which he can show each child that to his teacher and to his fellow students he matters, that he is accepted as he is. As individuals within the group begin to see themselves in positive ways and to share in group tasks, they, too, become facilitating. Facilitating, helping people tend to produce helping people. In a classroom where the climate is one of acceptance and warmth, students may tend to help each other to grow—to become a process, i.e., a person in movement from old "me" to new "me."

The school can do much to help in the development of the growing, developing self. Much of what the school does will be done as a result of the type of emotional climate or atmosphere that is provided or developed within the classroom, in the counselor's office and in other areas where groups of students are brought together under the supervision of a a person charged with the responsibility for their growth. Since it is in the classroom that students spend most of their school life, however, it is the classroom which bears the major responsibility for creating the environment where healthy emotional growth and maximum intellectual growth can occur.

Warmth Is Characteristic of the Adequate Classroom

Greatest growth of the self occurs in an atmosphere in which the student feels that he is respected. The teacher who genuinely cares for students as individuals and does not fear letting the students know he cares is one most likely to produce a warm emotional climate.

In such a classroom, extreme value is placed upon the individuality of students and upon the relationships that exist within the group. The problems of each individual are important to the teacher and each individual is heard in terms of how he feels rather than in terms of what he should do about his feelings.

The words that a teacher uses, the way he looks at children, become important. A word, a look, a bit of sarcasm or ridicule can be very humiliating, a crushing experience for a child, and although such tactics may subdue the child or the group, it may have a traumatic, negative effect on the feelings that students have for themselves.

The warm classroom climate is developed through the use of warm, emotionally toned words. There is an informal, friendly atmosphere that helps students feel relaxed and content and feel that "in this classroom is a friendly haven, a place from which the world of people, things and information may be explored in safety."

Acceptance Is Characteristic of the Adequate Classroom

For the self to be freed for growth, it must be accepted as it is currently structured. The atmosphere of acceptance can be created under the guidance of an accepting teacher. As students are accepted by the teacher as persons of dignity and worth, the individual moves toward acceptance of self, which is requisite to acceptance of others. And as peers accept each other, growth is further facilitated.

To accept a student, the teacher must accept his values and standards as a part of him, i.e., the teacher must be willing for him to hold these values. It does *not* mean that the teacher accepts the student's values and standards as his own. Combs, Kelley and Rogers state that an individual is free to change his values only when he is free to hold them. When he is free to hold them he is not forced to defend them. When he feels that his values are *not* condemned or categorized as "bad," he can then allow them to be explored (explored, not judged) by himself and by others. Out of exploration can come change and the development of new values based upon facts and upon new ways of seeing or perceiving. This is the free atmosphere in which perceptions and behavior patterns are changed.

The Adequate Classroom Atmosphere Is Permissive

Permissiveness is often taken to mean freedom to create physical chaos, to upset or destroy property and the decorum of the classroom. Permissiveness, as used here, means the freedom to have ideas, beliefs, values—permission to be oneself and to pursue interests and curiosity in search for meaning in life. A recent advertisement sponsored by a large corporation which manufactures electronic equipment states that "for scientists to be creative and productive they must be free to follow their curiosity." It seems reasonable that children will be most productive when they are similarly allowed to follow their curiosity. This means teaching becomes an individual matter in which the curiosity of the student is considered in deciding what the subject matter will be. The teacher is a facilitating person who assists the immature person to find effective ways of getting the information he needs to satisfy his curiosity about the world in which he lives.

The adequate classroom, then, must be a facilitating environment. It is an environment in which the student finds himself accepted with warmth and friendliness and in which he is helped through planned experiences to satisfy his need to know about himself and his world. It is a safe fortress from which he may venture into unknown and hitherto dangerous (to him) areas. It is an environment in which vigorous and healthy growth toward adequacy can be achieved.

Adequacy Is an Achievement, Not a Gift

From the descriptions of the adequate personality given us by our four invited authors, it becomes clear that adequacy is an achievement, not a gift. People *become* adequate; they are not born that way. Society's problem is not to find and coddle adequate personalities. Rather, we need to get about the business of *producing* them as fast as we can. What people have to learn, they can be taught. Adequate personalities are not a gift. They are the crowning achievement of teaching—the product of our best efforts.

This is a good thing to know. For much too long our educational system has lived in the shadow of a belief that human capacities were strictly limited by heredity. Consequently, we have often been encouraged to pass the buck for our failures to parents or other forces in our society. A conception that all good things in human personality arise from heredity also means that, at best, our public schools can be little more than a holding operation, preventing children from slipping backward, but with little hope of raising them, and hence future generations, to higher levels. It is good to know, then, that the adequate personality is learned, for this opens a whole new vista of possibilities for us in the teaching profession. It means that we are not merely guardians of the present, limited forever to producing a new generation entrenched in our own ruts. Rather, we have it within our means to produce an even finer generation than our own.

To contribute most effectively to the production of more adequate persons through our education institutions, it would seem clear that we need, first, to define the nature of the adequate person. This is what the four invited papers of this yearbook have attempted to begin for us. Following that, we need to understand the dynamics of how such self concepts are brought about. With these understandings in hand, we have the criteria in terms of which we may judge whether the classroom experiences we provide are contributing what they should to the development of ever larger numbers of truly adequate personalities. In the years to come we will no doubt find many means by which this end can be accomplished. But we do not have to wait for that. From the descriptions of adequate persons we already have, we can see interesting hints as to ways in which we can improve our practices so that more such people can be produced. In the chapters to follow, let us look more closely at the nature of fully functioning persons and at how they can be more effectively produced in our public schools.

CHAPTER 8

THE POSITIVE VIEW OF SELF

FROM COMBS

Extremely adequate persons seem to be characterized by an essentially positive view of self.

Negative aspects of self can be taken in stride.

A positive view is learned from the ways people treat the learner.

People learn that they are able, not from failure, but from success.

FROM KELLEY

The perceptive process is the only avenue by which the self can be fed. We choose that which the self feeds upon. The direction of growth of the self depends upon those choices.

Confidence opens the barriers so that the perceptive stuff of growth can be received.

Optimism is the natural outcome of an accepting view of self and hence of others.

The fully functioning self is motivated by the value of facilitating self and others.

FROM MASLOW

Every person is, in part, "his own project," and makes himself.

Growth forward . . . requires courage and strength in the individual, as well as protection, permission and encouragement from the environment, especially for the child.

The "better" culture gratifies all basic human needs and permits self-actualization.

FROM ROGERS

The individual moves toward more acceptantly being a process, a fluidity, a changing.

Self and personality emerge from experience.

If they are open to their experience, doing what "feels right" proves to be a competent and trustworthy guide to behavior which is truly satisfying.

He is unified within himself from the surface level to the level of depth. He is becoming "all of one piece."

THE IDEAS

Adequate people, according to our four invited authors, seem to be people who view change and adjustment to circumstances as opportunities for renewing and revitalizing their sense of adequacy. Their positive view of self has been achieved through an accumulation of success-experiences and an attitude toward problems as challenges to a strong self rather than as threats to a restricted self they cannot trust.

In contrast, people who are relatively inadequate tend to hold a low estimate of their capacity to cope with problems. As a result, such people develop even more negative perceptions and feelings about self. They focus on their incapacities to the extent that change or adjustment becomes threatening in a degree far out of proportion to the realities of the situation. They seem to lose touch with their own strengths and concentrate on their weaknesses as they seek to maintain a cherished, though rigid, self-image. These people also lose touch with others who are their greatest resource for helping them in their exploration and understanding of self. They are doubtful of themselves as individuals of worth and dignity and unable to see themselves as liked, wanted or able.

Those fortunate people who have developed some degree of self-actualization have positive views of self. They tend to see themselves as liked, wanted and worthy. They tend to see themselves as "able to." According to our invited authors, adequate persons, feeling able, can more effectively assess their strengths and weaknesses; act on their needs for self-improvement; handle their feelings constructively; initiate change as well as accept change; assess situations and design approaches to them; revise their values and establish new value-goals; cope with problems inventively as well as realistically; stockpile successes as guides to future self-direction; accept and set reasonable, realistic situational limits; keep growing steadily in their desired or chosen ways; and reach out and up for peak experiences.

THE POSITIVE SELF: A YARDSTICK FOR JUDGING PRACTICE

It is the function of our schools to produce an ever larger number of adequate personalities. This is our reason for being, the charge of our society. If a positive self is so important to the development of the truly adequate personality as our four authors have suggested, then our success in the production of positive views of self in the students we teach must stand as a major criterion in terms of which we judge our success or failure. We will need to ask ourselves, with regard to every aspect of public education, "How does this building, this policy, this organization, this method, this teacher, supervisor or administrator contribute to the production of more positive experiences of self?" The positive view of self, it appears, must serve as the criterion by which we judge the effectiveness of our practices.

How shall we behave? What experiences shall we provide to help people feel about themselves in positive ways? How shall we help people feel liked, wanted, acceptable, able, dignified, worthy? The answers lie in the descriptions themselves. What each teacher, administrator, supervisor, counselor can do to develop more adequate personalities may be found in his individual ways of thinking and behaving in answer to these questions:

How can a person feel liked unless somebody likes him?
How can a person feel wanted unless somebody wants him?
How can a person feel acceptable unless somebody accepts him?
How can a person feel able unless somewhere he has some success?
How can a person feel important unless he is important to someone?

In the answers each of us finds to these questions, we shall find the solutions to what we need to do to produce more adequate persons, whether it be in the classroom or from our position of vantage as supervisor, administrator, counselor, school board member or private citizen.

A POSITIVE VIEW OF SELF CAN BE LEARNED

According to our four consultants, the sense of self is learned through experience; a positive self is teachable. If the self is learned as a function of experience, then, whether we are aware of it or not, children learn about themselves in the classroom. They learn about themselves from the kinds of experiences we and they provide. If the self is as important as our four authors suggest, moreover, then it behooves those who have responsibility for the educative process to be aware of its importance and of the contribution that teaching can make in the development of a positive self.

The self is learned. What is learned can be taught. What can be taught is fair game for the public schools. The question is not one of whether we approve of teaching for a positive self in the public schools. We could not avoid affecting the self if we wanted to. We may ignore the self in our teaching. We cannot, however, escape the fact of our influence upon the self or our ultimate responsibility with respect to whether the effects of schooling are positive or negative.

If the public schools accept the responsibility for their effects upon the self, it is clear that the self must be recognized in the classroom. The effect of schooling upon the child's self must be seen as equally important with the acquisition of subject matter. In recent years many citizens, and some teachers, have become deeply disturbed at what has seemed to them a continual drift of the public schools toward too much concern with the adjustment of the child. For many of these people this growing concern for the child's adjustment seems to be a betrayal of the traditional purpose of the school for producing learned people. The question has been stated as an either-or. They ask, "Shall our schools teach for adjustment?" or "Shall our schools teach for knowledge?" Such a dichotomy is, of course, ridiculous. As Earl Kelley once pointed out, whenever ideas seem to lend themselves to being stated as a dichotomy, it is almost certain they are both wrong. The plain fact of the matter is we need *both* well adjusted people and people who know something. As Arthur Combs once said in a speech, "Clearly, we do not want from our public schools either smart crooks on the one hand or well adjusted dopes on the other!"

Despite the public clamor, it is clear that our public schools must accept a greater rather than lesser responsibility in this area. Fortunately, we do not have to make such unhappy choices as seem to be implied by the critics. Children can and will, if given the opportunity, explore their personal feelings and concepts about even the most difficult events. What is more, positive feelings about self can be acquired simultaneously with the general curriculum of the school. The experiment by Staines [1] has shown that self-actualization can be achieved in regular classrooms with no loss of learning in traditional subject matter. He experimented with two matched classes at the fourth grade level, with one teacher operating in usual fashion and another teaching the same things, but simultaneously attempting to help children explore and build self concepts. At the end of the year the two groups were on a par in academic matters, but mental health scores of the children taught in traditional style decreased. Those taught by a teacher concerned about self concepts increased their scores significantly. Like character or discipline, the self is learned in *every* class no matter what its title or level.

If schools are going to make a contribution to the adequate personality, it is clear that they must be much more concerned than they have been traditionally with the unique experience of the individual as he confronts the subject matter provided by the school. Teaching must deal not only with the acquisition of subject matter but with what subject matter *means* to the person who is exposed to it. Learning, we now know, is much more than the acquisition of subject matter. Whether or not learning has *really* occurred can only be measured in terms of the peculiar meanings ideas have in the private world of the individual. This private world extends far beyond a mere knowledge of fact. It is a world of feeling, believing, understanding, hoping, wishing, dreaming; a world of aspirations, desires, wants, needs. To strip a human being of such concepts is to strip him of his humanity itself. These aspects of human experience may be regarded by some as of no concern to the school. To see them so, however, is to rob

[1] J. W. Staines. "The Self Picture as a Factor in the Classroom." *British Journal of Educational Psychology* 28: 97-111; June 1958.

the school of its meaning and make it for most children, "a place where you learn about things that don't matter."

THE CLASSROOM AS A LABORATORY FOR SELF-DISCOVERY

Conceptions of self are not cold hard facts. They are deep personal meanings, beliefs, values, attitudes and feelings about one's self. These are not the traditional curricula of the schools. Indeed, in many places there exists a feeling that such concerns are spineless matters for schools to "truck with." If, however, the nature and development of the self are as important as our invited authors imply, we shall have to do far more with meanings and values than we have heretofore.

Self-Discovery Takes Time

Even though we may occasionally note sudden flashes of insight, changes in self-perception are more likely to be gradual. It takes time to produce important changes in self-perception. It takes values and purposes that encompass the dynamics of interaction, on a person-to-person basis or a person-to-group basis, to produce the kind of vital experience that noticeably changes self-perception.

The self, we need to remind ourselves, is affected as a consequence of an individual's experience—not just by the words we use. Changes in the self-perceptions of children can best be facilitated in situations which provide freedom for exploration within limits which are comfortable and not too confining. It serves well to remember that positive views of self are caught more so than taught. Caught from the reactions of others to the person, the self becomes a mirror reflecting its positive enhancing experiences. Or the opposite may occur and the individual may come to see himself in negative terms.

The classroom as a laboratory provides, as do most laboratory situations, freedoms as well as limitations. In the past we seem to have emphasized the limitations at the expense of being imaginative about how to use the freedoms, even though each of us values particularly the freedom to learn. Self-learning, learning about self, now is known to be an essential element if other learning is to progress. This has been made rather clear to us through studies of children who have had blocks to learning. As children are given help in understanding self and in developing more positive self concepts, they can more readily exercise self-help in overcoming their difficulties.

If positive self concepts are important, then it means for the classroom:

1. The teachers must be aware of this importance.

2. They must be willing to admit concern about the self concept into the classroom as a legitimate part of the educating process.

3. They must find ways of creating a climate in the classroom that will permit the exploration and discovery of the self.

4. They must find ways of actively encouraging the discovery of the student's self in a positive fashion.

CLIMATE OF THE CLASSROOM

To produce the kinds of adequate personalities our four authors have described, it will be necessary for us to see the classroom as a laboratory for self-discovery. Schoolrooms will need to be places where process and content can dynamically assist people to become more knowing about both self and the world. Such a laboratory must provide, upon the one hand, a climate that facilitates and assists the process of self-discovery and, on the other, provides positive experiences through which people can discover more adequate relationships between themselves and the world in which they live. What kinds of climates shall these be?

The classroom can become an important laboratory for the discovery of self when teachers are sensitive to feelings and values and are alert to help children examine both themselves and others with candor. Even the most distressing events can often be explored with good effects when teachers know how to use such experiences as are shown in the following example:

Connie is a brain-damaged child with severe speech problems. The children in her class asked, "Why can't she talk good? We can't understand what she says."

The teacher replied, "Talking is hard for Connie. Every person has something that's especially hard for him. For some children it's tying shoes. For others, it's learning to ride on a two-wheel bike. For others, it's managing their tempers. For Connie, talking is especially hard. Let's listen for words we can understand and help her."

Later that morning Debbie said, "Listen! I've helped Connie learn to say *Kleenex!*"

This would seem to suggest that, even in the very young child, "hard" things can be looked at. A positive view about his own growing adequacy and an honest understanding of how people differ enable the child to reach out to help others learn to cope with their inadequacies.

When these same five-year-olds were confronted with death, through the loss of a classmate, their teacher did not impose adult conceptions. She helped them explore their feelings and personal meanings.

Johnny is dead. How can a teacher help a group of five-year-olds accept and, to a degree, resolve feelings about the death of a classmate? To most of the children, it is a verbalization with no strong feelings, yet.

To an insecure child, the fearful question repeated over and over is, "Will I die? How do you *know* my heart isn't bad like Johnny's was?" To Tim, who is under pressure to take care of his clothes, to keep them clean, to save money, the concern is, "Did they bury him in all those good Sunday clothes and ruin them?" From happy-go-lucky, kind Mark comes the response, "Maybe he was a blue baby and couldn't run like we could, but now he can fly and we can't."

Classroom laboratories must be places which facilitate the business of looking at self and the world. They must provide a climate which encourages exploration and discovery. Whatever produces defensiveness, rigidity and inability to look at self or the world in any form inhibits the process of free discovery and exploration. This calls for classroom climates which are high in challenge and low in threat. Children need to be challenged, but the negative effects of threat in narrowing perception and forcing individuals to the defense of existing positions is clearly antithetical to the kinds of open exploration and discovery essential for the development of the truly adequate self.

Respect for Uniqueness

Such a climate calls for a deep respect for the uniqueness of the individual. The discovery of self is a deeply personal matter that does not come about in blanket ways. Each individual, in the final analysis, must discover his own unique being in his own unique and highly personal ways. This is unlikely to be affected in classroom situations where everyone is treated alike and where differences are regarded as bad or improper. The full discovery of self as a unique individual of dignity, value and worth can only be found in an atmosphere where uniqueness is encouraged and difference is valued. The atmosphere conducive to positive self-discovery must also provide a kind of protection from negative experience during the process of exploration. Negative, self-damaging kinds of experience force people to crawl deeper into their existing positions, to build shells around themselves and do not permit the open, outgoing exploration and discovery required for the production of a fully functioning positive self.

The classroom must be a kind of microcosm of the society in which an individual will move. This little society provided for the child, however, should be one which protects him during his growing and developing phases from the harsher, more negative and destructive forces that work in the society at large. As Kelley and Combs both point out, the belief that people are strengthened by threat and failure is a fallacy. The best guarantee we have that people will be able to deal with the exigencies of the future is that they are essentially successful in the present. It follows that the kind of world we should construct in the classroom is one in which youngsters are protected from the more violent forces of the society at large. They need a world of positive things, people and events. Such a world makes it possible for them to develop the kind of strength out of which they may be able to deal more effectively with the negative events in the broader world. This calls for classroom situations in which destructive competition, prejudice, bigotry and the vicious dog-eat-dog behavior of vested interest combating vested interest is reduced to a minimum. It calls for teachers who behave as friendly representatives of society and for social experiences for each child that show him that he *is* acceptable, liked, wanted, able, a person of dignity, worth and importance.

Open Communication

The fostering of self-actualization requires open communication. It demands the acceptance of values, feelings and personal meaning as valid data for getting an education. Almost anyone knows how important it is to listen to the other person in order to keep communication open and mutually meaningful. But because it is a time-consuming business, one often feels like the old farmer who, long familiar with a certain countryside, spoke impatiently to his young companions who were seeing it for the first time: "If you'd have followed the creek, you'd have been there an hour ago!" he said. Obviously, the interesting things to see along the circuitous route no longer held the promise of adventure for the old gentleman that they did for his young companions. So it often happens that those who have been over the ground tend to overlook the excitement and the important learnings involved in making one's way more slowly.

A classroom which is to serve as an effective laboratory for self-discovery must provide positive kinds of experience. This means that children must be treated *as though they were* positive people. They must be helped to see themselves as people who *can*.

Both self- and content learnings can be inferred from this boy's remark, "I discovered I can do it myself," or from this girl's remark, "Of course I can't do it—I'm only five years old." Such remarks enlist the kindly understanding of the teacher, but each alerts her to an individualized kind of responsive action. With the boy, the teacher can share his celebration of a success experience that furthered his sense of adequacy. With the girl, she can explore some things to do in keeping with her individual "five-year-oldness" and her need for success that will have a positive self-reference by adding to her feeling of "can-ness." Thus, the process, to be dynamic, must be interactive and subject to sensitive innovation in child-teacher relations. In short, teachers can help children explore themselves even as they deal with content. Accepting a child as being just as he is from the first second of the first day of school is extremely encouraging for any student. The assumption that a child *can do,* and that *what* he can do is good enough, will give any child a shot in the arm. One of the main themes in Marie Rasey's book, *What We Learn from Children,*[2] is the value of "can-ness." Unfortunately, too many teachers today spend almost all their time discovering students' past and present mistakes and emphasizing what students should not or cannot do rather than what they *can* do. Teachers who wish to encourage students to become fully functioning must find the courage to begin by accepting students as being good enough as they are. After that, they may help them to move forward to what they can become.

EXPERIENCES THAT ENCOURAGE ADEQUACY

Individualizing Instruction

Experiences of adequacy cannot be provided for children in situations where all are treated alike. Psychologists have repeatedly assured us that, if there is anything we know about children, it is that they are different; each is a unique and individual personality. If this is so, it is hard to see how the stockpiling of success experience required for the development of feelings of adequacy can occur in schools and classrooms organized in lock-step fashion. The "average child" is a statistic, not a person. Schools organized to teach the "average" child, then, must surely be out of touch with most children most of the time. Since students by their nature are unique and individual, the experiences which contribute to their growth and development must "fit" the people they are. This calls for increasingly individualized kinds of learning experiences.

Unfortunately, the pressures of mass education have often militated against individualization of experience in the public schools. Our society has been vastly impressed with the mass methods of production which have so successfully turned out material goods for our population. As a consequence we have often been led to apply the same methods and techniques to the problems of human education. Now there is not a shadow of a doubt that the magnificent decision to educate everyone imposes difficult problems upon us. However, the existence of these problems has sometimes been used as an excuse for practices that are convenient or easy. We loudly proclaim that we cannot possibly individualize instruction in our classrooms today like the one-room country schoolteacher of a previous generation because, like the old woman in the shoe, "we have so many children we don't know what to do!" This,

[2] Marie Rasey and J. W. Menge. *What We Learn from Children.* New York: Harper & Brothers, 1956. 164 p.

in spite of the fact that we still organize our schools in classes of 30 just like the one-room school. In addition, we have far better equipment to work with and teachers who are much better selected and trained for their jobs. It is simply not true that the demands of teaching many people require us to teach badly.

There are other forces in our society tending to push us ever further and further away from the concepts of individualization of instruction which also need to be examined with great care. Sometimes in reaching out for one thing it is possible to lose another so that "what we make on the oranges we lose on the bananas." One place where this is so, for example, is in the continual pressure to enlarge the size of the school unit, ostensibly to provide children with more and varied curricula. Sometimes this worthy motive has produced schools of such vast size that students get lost, both literally and figuratively. In many a modern high school, individual students are often little more than faces drifting through classrooms. Certainly we need schools large enough to provide a rich curriculum. Surely it must be possible, however, to organize such schools so that *somebody* on the faculty is in touch with a child long enough to know him as a person.

We face a similar problem with respect to the great new techniques we have developed for mass communication. Television and the public address system have placed in our hands marvelous devices for the imparting of information to large groups of people. These new devices enable us to bring the broad world into the classroom in a fashion never before possible. There is a real and important place for such devices in our educational program. They are not, however, panaceas, nor has it yet been demonstrated how they can take the place of the individualization of instruction required for the provision of adequate experiences for every child. There is certainly a place for improved mass instruction, but not at the cost of further inroads upon the already inadequate provisions for individual, personal experience.

Pacing and Readiness

Ways of pacing individualized instruction so that learning can become increasingly rewarding and self-directive are not so difficult to find when children have a strong sense of adequacy to support their striving. When teachers value individuality and uniqueness, they recognize the importance of pacing materials and instruction so that many successful experiences are possible. Children find such experiences enabling and supportive for their own personal organization of learnings. Our authors tell us the experience of success is important to the development of adequacy. If this is to be effectively accomplished in the public schools, it means that we must learn more effectively how to pace our teaching to the rate and the readiness of the individual.

If the self is to be affected we need to organize for it. We need to question the kinds of practices that tag children with failure when they need guidance and room for growth. Instead of prodding and pressuring to meet unrealistic, perhaps unexamined, expectations, we need to see that children are grouped and then regrouped according to their changing needs and purposes. We need to recognize the timing and pacing for individualized help. Just how do teachers go about stockpiling personal meanings as resources for guiding individualized development in positive directions? Since individuals do not grow and develop or learn at the same rate, it is clear that a lock-step organization cannot be productive of the kind of success experience that pupils must have. Indeed, it is likely that any fixed organization must necessarily miss many pupils much of the time. It is clear that we need a great deal more flexibility in organization and methods if we are to achieve the goal of success experience for all children.

Expectancies and Goals

People measure their success by the degree to which they are able to meet expectancies and reach the goals they have established either for themselves or from others. To provide the kinds of success experience out of which a feeling of adequacy is produced, children need to feel they are reaching goals and meeting expectancies continuously. This means the goals and expectancies created for children in the classroom must be accurate and realistic and within the capacities of the child.

It is the concern of education to produce excellence. It is possible, however, for a preoccupation with excellence to produce precisely the opposite effect. There is a widespread belief that schools must set high standards, expectancies, goals for children. This is fine as far as it goes, but it is possible to set expectancies and goals too high and this destroys the very effects we hope to achieve. What produces adequacy is achievement, not failure. Goals which are out of reach do not stimulate or motivate; they only discourage and disillusion. Since the feeling of achievement is a purely personal matter, the setting of goals and expectancies must be an individual matter as well.

Lest it be thought we are advocating a "soft" school program, let us hasten to say that it is possible to set goals and expectancies for children which are too low as well as too high. Goals and expectancies set too low do not provide experience of success and achievement—only experiences of boredom and apathy. Success experience is a function of challenge, not repetition. The feeling that one is important, able, worthy and successful arises from the successful solution of important problems; not just any problems, but *important* problems. Adequacy is the product of challenge. But what challenges an individual, it must be recalled, is what challenges *him,* not his teacher.

Adequacy—A Function of Interaction

Opportunities for interaction provide clues for positive guidance. When people have the opportunity to interact freely with their environment, they provide teachers many clues for fostering positive feelings about themselves in learning situations. Teachers who can "read" these clues can also develop ways to help individuals find secure levels of participation and commitment. If teachers are people who can maintain a positive view in their approach to building emotional readiness, they interact with children in ways that are supportive and enabling. This seems to help children focus on adjustment and improvement instead of succumbing to negative feelings of guilt and failure. Thus, teachers become an integral part of the big steps that children take in response to an idea or suggestion that carries personal meaning. They become increasingly aware of feeling tone as a reliable guide to their positive helping roles.

Barbara seemed to get the most pleasure in nursery school from running away and being "found" by college students. On the first morning of kindergarten she announced with pride, "Do you know what *I* do at school? *I* run away!"

The teacher said, "Barbara, I don't think you'll run away from kindergarten. Little girls come to kindergarten to play and have fun. You'll like the puzzles, and the records and many other things."

Barbara returned several times to ask, "Tell me again why I won't run away." She never did!

Here Barbara got hold of an idea for self-management even though she had to have repeated reinforcement from her teacher in order to be able to think about "why I won't run away." In the next account Tommy, too, needed reinforcement from an adult. His teacher's suggestion that he delay his decision about "not reading any more," until he gave himself more of a chance to know his real feelings, seems to have been a very wise one.

"I can't do it good," is Tommy's usual response to new situations. "I can't read good," he told his teacher. "I'm in a big, hard-cover book now and when I finish it I'm not going to read any more."

The teacher replied, "Tommy, let's not decide now. You read this one and then see how you feel about reading."

Two books later, when he seemed to be having a delightful experience with reading, the teacher said, "Tommy, do you remember what you said when you read *Little White House*?"

Tommy replied, "Yes! But I didn't know then that it would ever be fun!"

Tommy's discovery that "reading can be fun" will likely serve him as earned adequacy for finding out that other kinds of learning, too, can be fun.

The experience of adequacy, we have seen, is a function of the individual's interaction with the physical world on one hand and with the world of people on the other. The self, we are told, is largely learned in the "mirror of other people." We learn who we are and what we are from the actions and interactions we have with the significant people in our world. The self is constructed primarily through these relationships. Classrooms, therefore, which set children apart fom one another, which place them in competition with each other, or which insist upon feelings of separateness may actually be robbing children of valuable opportunities to discover themselves as more adequate human beings. The self is not learned in isolation and it is important that the classroom be a social situation in the best sense of the term. Children need to be given positive experiences of interaction with teachers, supervisors, counselors, other pupils, everyone in the school, including janitors and other nonacademic personnel.

Evaluation and Assessment

An important part of the laboratory process is assessment. Usually some formulation of a status report is developed and used as the basic framework for the study of a problem. In the classroom, teachers can help children learn to see themselves in formulating group undertakings. This often opens the way for assessing self, at first on fairly superficial levels, but ultimately facing up to more deeply personal understanding. There is no better way to make clear to children that you are genuinely "interested in them as persons." This is also the teacher-quality most often rated at the top of the list by children who have been asked to indicate desirable teacher traits.

In the process of assessment, teacher and pupils have the live, meaningful data for charting directions for learning about self, and for setting goals that incorporate their needs and values—be it in arithmetic, reading or science. Such procedure carries a very different feeling tone and enlists a greater sense of personal involvement than does determination of content by various other means, more or less remote from the learners involved. Even the standardized tests of measurement can become less of an evaluative threat and more of a diagnostic assessment in an atmosphere where people are learning to look at self openly and unafraid. Children have a chance to see that everyone has needs, some in common with others, some highly individual, and that needs and values can give meaningful direction to goal setting and to exciting hard work. Perhaps some blocks to learning could be prevented by early confrontation and assessment and by positive approaches to improvement in self- and content learnings. In any event, more positive views of self are possible when one is able to feel and know his needs and values more precisely. He can then begin to take charge of experiences for changing them. Thus the individual can begin to move away from an inadequate concept of self toward a sense of "can-ness."

Some interesting and illuminating illustrations of self-assessment in reading were written when a group of eleventh graders were looking at their needs for improvement during their final years in high school. From the "reading evaluation" included here, one can get an impression of a boy who was able to take charge of his reading experiences and to do so with good humor.

Since the start of the tenth grade, when my teachers began to stress the importance of reading, I have been trying to read better books by some of the authors mentioned in literary circles. Until that time, my reading consisted of books that never would be found at an auction of great books. I mean the type of book like *Tom Swift and His Motorcycle*—not noted for its literary excellence.

In my eyes (I say "eyes" because, contrary to popular belief, I do use them in reading), a program to get, or shall I say prepare, oneself for after high school should be well rounded. I should include some of the classics, some best sellers, plays, poetry, and newspapers and magazines. I have been trying to follow this course and, although I have hit a few navigational snags, I have made progress. I have read some classics such as *A Tale of Two Cities* and *Madame Bovary*. I have read some best sellers: *Tobacco Road, Ben Hur, The Ugly American*. Last year I tried two plays, one by O'Neill and one by Coward. Through reading poetry I have found a great liking for verse I didn't know I had. Last year I read, among other things, *The Rubaiyat of Omar Khayyam*. Every day I try to read something out of the newspaper. This summer I found fun reading the short stories out of the *New Yorker*.

So you see, I hope that I have a start at my rounded reading program, but I still have some flat sides. I will try to round them out this year. To do this I will continue reading along the lines I have mentioned before. I have a list given to me by a member of the family who is off to college this year. This list has five books on it that she was told by the school she would be wise to read. She read them, was tested on their content and didn't have to take first semester English. I would like to talk to you about this list, as someone once said, in the "fear nuther" (near future).

Looking up the other day I found that college time is coming up fast, so I must start right now. I don't want to be like the man who was having trouble with his love life and thought he would get a book on the matter. He went to a little bookshop to have a look around. After a long time he came upon a book called, *How to Hug*. "This is it," he thought, so he paid the price and went home with high hopes. When he got home, his hopes vanished like the mist before the rising sun. The man had purchased one volume of an encyclopedia! Reading is becoming very important to me and I don't want my hopes burned away by the heat of some mistake.

Coping with problems that have been formulated through interactive processes seems to be especially challenging to creative thinking and, in turn, productive of creative solutions. Whether solutions are tentative—the best at this point—or final, in terms of situational limitations, such interactive processes also tend to free people to act in "the best way we know at this point" rather than to block them with frustrating indecision.

It is also important for teachers to assess themselves. When teachers turn to their own self-assessments, they, too, need to value possibilities and limitations, for teaching style seems to be an elusive combination of qualities. It is surely self-determined and somewhat modifiable. At the same time, it is the most powerful force in each child's learning experiences. We have been reminded that "the teacher's interest in me"—the student—is the most important teacher-quality in the student's eyes. The teacher faces real challenge to keep his self-styled teaching under scrutiny, subject to flexibility and change, open to new knowledge, and selective and creative with procedures that are in tune with this working group of students, individually and collectively. At stake, at least in part, is each child's right to create the design of his own becoming—his own best possible unique self. Enabling and facilitating teacher-roles become the strong right arm of good instruction. This is a goal worth striving for.

TEACHER ATTITUDES AND GROWTH

The Importance of Teacher Attitudes

Children discover who they are and what they are as a consequence of experience. The school's contribution can be positive, negative or of no account, depending upon what teachers make it. The experiences children have can be controlled and designed with an eye to these inevitable effects, or they can be regarded as of no importance while attention is given to other values and so be left as matters of chance. Teacher behavior is important because the teacher determines to a great degree the positive or negative effect of his teaching, especially when he is aware of the impact of the school on the student. Teachers, like everyone else, behave in terms of what seems to them important. If schooling is to have positive effects on the child's self, then a concern for this self and the effects of classroom experiences on it must be admitted to the classroom as a legitimate and important part of education. Whether or not this goal is achieved will depend on how successful we are in selecting and training teachers who have this kind of sensitivity and understanding.

The kind of sensitivity required for the facilitation and encouragement of adequacy in students is not solely a question of knowing subject matter or even a question of knowing "about" students. Rather, what is required is a sensitivity to how things seem to the young people with whom the teacher is working and an ability to behave in ways that deeply and importantly affect those ways of perceiving. It is a matter of *understanding students* instead of *understanding about* students. It includes a sensitivity to and a concern for human values, attitudes, beliefs, convictions and unique ways of perceiving. If teaching is to affect the self of the student, then teachers must be aware of the student's self, on the one hand, and of the impact of the teacher's own self on that of the student, upon the other. What is more, if this process is to be more than a haphazard, catch-as-catch-can matter, it will be necessary for us to select teachers who have promise in this direction and to train them further in this kind of sensitivity.

Teachers Can Find Opportunities To Learn About Self

Teachers can avail themselves of opportunities to learn about self as well as others in the process of "their own becoming," with each teacher striving to discover and accept his very best possible self and his own individual teaching style. Jersild puts it in more forceful language in the following statement: "The teacher's understanding and acceptance of himself is the most important requirement in any effort he makes to help students to know themselves and to gain healthy attitudes of self-acceptance." [3]

For a teacher to gain understanding and acceptance of self, it would seem important that he, too, have many experiences in being treated as a likable, wanted, accepted and knowing person. Research shows that self-acceptance is contingent upon having been accepted by others, which in turn makes it possible for the person to accept others. This should serve as a reminder to administrators and supervisors in working with their staff members. For a teacher to teach for adequacy in others, there must be some feeling of adequacy in the teacher himself.

Teachers, like all adults, have more or less established patterns for handling their emotions with varying degrees of openness. But being

[3] Arthur T. Jersild. *When Teachers Face Themselves.* New York: Bureau of Publications, Teachers College, Columbia University, 1955. p. 3.

teachers, they need to stretch for deeper understanding of emotional readiness through examining the emotional investments of their own lives. Too often the public image of the teacher is one that pictures a creature of stoic self-control with feelings hidden as though they are extraneous to the events of learning situations. But in reality, the teacher is fortunate, indeed, who has come to realize that most problems are to a great extent emotional in nature, and thereby has set out to become a healthy handler of his own feelings. As he becomes more trusting and, hence, more spontaneous and adequate in handling the emotional impacts of his own experiences, he can become an enabling person, alert and relaxed about helping children experience the fullness of their emotional growth instead of becoming victims of emotional impoverishment.

Through exploring their own capacities for self-directive growth, teachers become better instruments for transaction. They learn to harmonize their efforts with children's interests and purposes instead of "soloing" to a captive audience in a starved classroom environment. Realizing that the impact of people is the strongest influence in developing and modifying concepts of self, teachers risk the problems of permissive, exploratory learning instead of demanding of the students self-control in teacher-planned pursuits. They cultivate a "sixth sense" for guidance toward growth in self-directive behavior. Here the measure of success originates from a different base. Teachers are sensitive to perceptual meanings and indications of needed growth. They become builders of bridges from the learner's interests and aspirations to what the teacher believes will be his needs as an adult.

Strong affiliations with others concerned with education are important to teacher growth. They develop through continuous communication about common problems and in turn contribute to the lifelong process of self-discovery. Actually, education needs to be concerned with such development for supervisors, principals, administrators, board members, bus drivers and custodians, as well as for teachers. For if the process of discovery of self is really to contribute to the adequacy of children, it would seem to indicate that each level of the education structure in the classroom and out must be concerned with the development of positive selves. Fortunately, there are already many school people working at their respective levels along these very lines, as evidenced in the following account.

Sometime after a particularly rewarding three-week workshop, an experienced teacher's evaluative reflection was, "Did you ever see such a variety of people get together so energetically on their common problems?" She went on with thumbnail sketches about the backgrounds and interests of the various working members of the group—the administrators, teachers, supervisors, guidance personnel and psychologists among them. She was expressing admiration for individuality and diversity, for zestful commitment to productive learning and her own forceful realization of the dynamics of interactive learning. Would it not seem likely that this teacher could convey to children in classrooms something similarly satisfying through implementation of personal meanings gained? These people, adults in this case, seem to have gained new insights about shared values as a working base. Many of them had had a new experience with the feelings of commitment and the obligations entailed. There was opportunity for exploration and mutual learning about self and others which can be the basis for thoughtful revisions in self-organization and consequent modifications of behavior and methods. Such modifications of teachers' behavior could make a profound difference in the lives of the several hundred children with whom they work.

TEACHER SELECTION AND TRAINING

The process of teaching for adequacy begins with teacher selection. It is teachers who work at the grass-roots level with children and it is through teachers and the experiences they construct that student self concepts are built or destroyed in the classroom. The kinds of teachers we provide will be crucial in the production of positive selves in students. Some teachers have the kind of sensitivity and skill that helps young people develop positively to start with. They seem to have acquired it by a kind of "osmosis" from their own living and growing. Others achieve it only after careful training and experience. Still others seem so deeply fixed in another frame of reference that they are unlikely ever to develop relationships with students that produce positive effect. The first two of the above groups we need to recruit as rapidly as possible into the the profession; the third had better be helped to new goals elsewhere.

The process of teacher selection may be designed to help students build a more positive view of self. If scholastic grade average and purely intellectual prowess are the only criteria for admission to programs of teacher preparation, we shall be unduly handicapping ourselves in finding and educating the teachers we need. Teacher selection should consider many more factors and assist the prospective teacher in assessing his potential for teaching. The admission process should consider such factors as health, interest in teaching, ability to communicate, his present store of information and potential for succeeding in college, and the kind of positive self which will enable him to free others to learn.

Adequate personalities have positive effects upon their fellows. It follows that we need to recruit the largest possible number of adequate people to our profession. It would be good, indeed, if it were possible to assure that all teachers were so. Until that millenium, we need to select the most adequate we can and help them thereafter to become even more so. The less promising we need to help find places in other vocations which do not require such personal qualities.

Once selected, teacher education institutions must develop the teacher's self to the utmost. This calls for the acceptance of responsibility for self-development of students by our teachers colleges. Teacher education programs must be concerned with helping students explore and discover more adequate selves. They must also help students become well acquainted with content. We need to strengthen the individual's ability to deal with content and to improve his skill in making it available to students in the future. By paying more attention to the nature of the developing self, teacher education institutions can help students in preparation gain the advantages of great personal strength and security which follow when feelings about self are positive. Just as we expect teachers to become more concerned about the selves of children, teacher education institutions will need to be more concerned about the personalities and selves of teachers in training.

In recent years colleges of education have been under severe criticism for the so-called "frills" in their programs. This criticism has been particularly negative with respect to the study of methods, human relations, child growth and development and the like. The directions pointed by the papers of our four authors, however, would seem to call, not for less concern about human relations and personality growth, but for more, much more. Learning only occurs in people, and an understanding of people is not a frill, but a necessity for the skillful teacher.

Teacher selection and retention should become a continuous process extending beyond preservice selection through in-service self-evaluation on the job. People who are uncomfortable with boys and girls or who are unable to create an atmosphere which makes it possible for children to develop more positive selves should be helped to become interested in other occupations. Teachers who destroy the selves of children need to be helped to behave more positively or be removed from the system. Decisions are difficult but must be made. Supervisors and principals need also to be aware of differences in teachers and recognize that they, too, are in process of becoming. Teachers, too, can be aided to greater adequacy in an atmosphere wherein they have success experiences which foster a positive view of self.

CHAPTER 9

ACCEPTANCE AND THE ACCURATE VIEW OF SELF

FROM MASLOW

Coordinate with this "acceptance" of the self, of fate, of one's call, is the conclusion that the main path to health and self-fulfillment for the masses is via basic need gratification rather than via frustration. This contrasts with the suppressive regime, the mistrust, the control, the policing that is necessarily implied by basic evil in the human depths.

To the extent that perception is desire-less and fear-less, to that extent is it more veridical, in the sense of perceiving the true or essential or intrinsic whole nature of the object (without splitting it up by abstraction).

FROM ROGERS

Individuals are able to trust their total organismic reaction to a new situation because they discover to an ever-increasing degree that if they are open to their experience, doing what "feels right" proves to be a competent and trustworthy guide to behavior which is truly satisfying.

When a person is open to experience there is a maximum of adaptability, a discovery of structure in experience, a flowing, changing organism of self and personality. It means discovering the structure of experience in the process of living the experience.

And as he lives and accepts these widely varied feelings, in all their degrees of intensity, he discovers that he has experienced *himself,* that he is *all* these feelings.

FROM KELLEY

The growing self must feel that it is involved, that it is really part of what is going on, that in some degree it is helping shape its own destiny, together with the destiny of all.

The perceptive process is the only avenue by which the self can be fed.

The self "looks out" upon the surrounding scene largely in terms of its own enhancement or defense.

When the fearful person withdraws within his psychological shell, the self becomes less adequate and the whole person loses its ability to do, to venture, to create.

FROM COMBS

Open people are free to devote their energies to what is positive and constructive. They can and do set more realistic goals for themselves. Their levels of aspiration are more likely to be in line with their capacities. They are more likely to achieve their goals because those goals are more realistic.

Openness to experience and acceptance refer not only to acceptance of events outside the person's self but equally to the individual's perceptions of self. The adequate person is less defensive and does not bar from perceptual organization what is true about self.

The accurate, realistic assessment of self resulting from acceptance makes possible the use of self as a dependable, trustworthy instrument for achieving one's purposes.

THE IDEAS

Our authors are in agreement that adequate persons are characterized by openness to events. That is, they are willing to confront reality, to permit data into awareness. This readiness to confront the world, psychologists also call "acceptance." As psychologists use the term, however, acceptance should not be confused with resignation. An accepting person is willing to look at data. This does not mean he is beaten by it. Nor does it mean that adequate persons always agree with what is going on. They do not find it necessary to avoid life or to pretend it is nicer than it is.

Since effective behavior can only begin from reality, adequate people must have an accurate, realistic understanding of themselves and the world in which they live. They need to be open to their experience, including perceptions about themselves. The more open the individual and the richer his experience, the better able he will be to deal effectively with life. Inadequate persons, on the other hand, must defend themselves against the world and reject data that are unhappy or inexplicable. As John Greene, of our committee, stated, "They are like the terrapin who can't go anywhere until first he comes out of his shell, and who dies if he is never permitted to come out!" In order to achieve adequacy, people need to have accurate, realistic, nondefensive concepts of self. Such a self concept makes openness more possible and is at the same time validated or changed by openness to the world.

Accurate, realistic conceptions of self are learned. Since they are learned, they are teachable. As our four authors have indicated, the self is a product of the individual's experience; that is to say, his real experience, not how it seems to someone else. There may be a world of difference between an event as it is experienced by the behaver and as it is observed by an outsider, like a teacher or parent, looking on at the event. Personal experience requires much more than just telling. For the most part, learning about self is a product of interaction with human beings. Acceptance and openness are a function of the quality of the individual's experience with the significant people in his world.

Can We Encourage Realism and a Positive Self?

We seem, now, to be confronted with a dilemma. In a previous chapter we have seen that it is essential to give children a positive view of self. In this chapter we are saying that an adequate person must see himself accurately and realistically. At first glance these seem like mutually antagonistic concepts. These principles do not mean that the teacher praises indiscriminately or protects a child from unflattering evidence or gives inaccurate information in an effort to build a child's positive feelings. Rather, the production of adequate self concepts requires the teacher to assume the equally important responsibility of assisting the child to see himself accurately and realistically. That children require assistance to feel positively about themselves and at the same time to see themselves in a realistic and accurate way are not mutually antagonistic concepts.

It is only as individuals build reservoirs of positive self-perceptions that they are able to accept and evaluate honest, realistic information about themselves. Feeling self-confident, they can take criticism, can admit shortcomings, can handle unhappy events or attacks. They feel positively about enough important aspects of self to be able to balance at least a certain number of negative concepts. They are comfortable with themselves; seem almost to say, "I get along with people at school, my family thinks I'm okay, I'm good at games, and kids like me, I can do all of the arithmetic—so what if right now I'm having trouble with reading?" These are the children who can admit realistic, even negative, truths about themselves without being overwhelmed or disorganized. Indeed, through acceptance of accurate information, it is possible for a child to become more adequate and consequently more secure in a positive view of self.

It is the child who feels unwanted and unable who cannot afford to be accurate in self-assessment. It is the child who is afraid no one likes him who needs to defend himself against all criticism—the one who is sure he cannot achieve, who cannot enter into a new learning situation or profit from new information. These are the children who most need the teacher's unconditional acceptance, who must learn, from being accepted and respected, to accept and respect themselves. They must be helped to see very honestly what they can do and what they can become. With this sure and positive knowledge they are able to admit data and so to work toward satisfying their needs. But basic to their self-discovery must be the teacher's absolute sincerity and her clear goal of helping children see themselves accurately and realistically. Only with an honest view of self can reliable and enduring positive self concepts be built.

Accepting Self and Accepting Behavior

Fortunately, the solution to the above dilemma is helped by the fact that it is possible to distinguish between accepting an individual and accepting his behavior. This is what the parent does who conveys to the child that he is loved and wanted, even though his behavior may at times be disapproved of. This is what the teacher does, also, who helps the child feel a respect for his own dignity and integrity, while at the same time making clear to him the errors in his approach. What this amounts to is a matter of helping people discover they are acceptable *as persons*, even if their behavior is not.

The teacher who cannot accept the child makes it impossible for the child to accept himself. One learns that he is acceptable only by being accepted. Acceptance cannot be learned in a vacuum. Without feeling he is, himself, acceptable, the acceptance of others is difficult or impossible. The child who feels he is unacceptable must defend himself against his experience by rejecting or distorting it. He lies, cheats, explains, excuses, dissembles. All these, of course, are defenses against what is so and strictly antithetical to an accurate, realistic conception of self.

The individual's capacity for acceptance is intimately affected by the degree to which he has developed positive feelings about self. Our four authors have pointed out that a positive view of self makes it possible for the individual to be less defensive, so he can afford to accept a great deal more of his experience. The factors, therefore, which we have discussed in the previous chapter as affecting the positive self have an equally important bearing upon the matter of acceptance. In general, what helps individuals feel positive increases the likelihood of acceptance. On the other hand, whatever diminishes the individual—what degrades, humiliates, undermines or subtracts from his respect for self—at the same time increases his difficulties in accepting what is new and different.

PRACTICES THAT HINDER ACCEPTANCE

Among the factors that interfere with the growth of acceptance is the preoccupation of much schoolwork with "right" answers. Our whole educational structure is built upon "right" answers. Such a preoccupation is likely to produce in the individual a lack of trust in himself and his beliefs and give him the feeling that the only good things are those which he is not. Worship of what others think destroys the capacity to accept one's self. There are few right answers, anyhow—only better or worse answers.

Schools and teachers may become so obsessed with "facts" that meaning and creative thought are ruled out of the classroom. Overconcern with "right" answers teaches children that one cannot depend upon himself for the solution of problems. Relying solely on "textbook" answers or solutions is, in effect, saying to the child, "You do not have the ability to think"; or, "What you think is not at all important"; or, "You should not or you cannot think"; or, "It is only what others think that is important." Students who come to feel that what they "are" or what they "think" is unimportant look for answers in some other place. They copy their reports from reference books. They are unable to work a mathematics problem unless the textbook has a specimen problem for them to follow. In writing sentences for an English assignment, they are lost unless the "book" has an example which they can imitate. If a student comes to see that there is only one way to solve a mathematics problem or do a science experiment—if there is only one right answer—and this answer is in the book or within the teacher, his world is closing in. He is being taught a rigid approach to life which makes acceptance difficult or impossible.

We have seen in the four papers that whether or not learning is effective is largely dependent upon the individual's discovery of the personal meaning of ideas. Nevertheless, a great deal of schooling in some places seems to be expressly designed to eliminate personal reference from the classroom. Overconcern with right answers, with objective tests, with ritualistic procedures, with problems solved by the rules, all take personalness out of learning. In some places, opportunity to experience and explore feelings toward others is frowned upon. Feelings of altruism, love, fear or anger are firmly squelched. It is as if, by suppressing these feelings, one believes they will go away, and the individual, like the mathematics problem or the "cookbook" science experiment or the objective test, will become standardized and then the problems of teaching will be solved. All will learn the same thing at the same time. In such a climate the self of the individual is growing toward dependence, toward inadequacy rather than toward adequacy.

Some classroom atmospheres seem almost to be afraid of permitting feelings to enter the classroom situation. The concept of love, for example, although it is probably one of the most important conceptions in human life, is a topic rarely discussed in the average classroom. Worse still, it may be discussed only with embarrassment or ridicule. In many classrooms the attitude is, "What you feel is not important; we are here to deal with hard facts. Let's keep our feelings out of it."

In one school, after a discussion about love, a fifth grade boy wrote: "I was surprised when we talked about love. I learned a lot from it, but it surprised me to talk about it in school. I didn't know we could talk about things you didn't get grades for!" Whatever restrictions we place upon what can and cannot be looked at build attitudes of acceptance or its lack, in spite of ourselves.

Disciplinary Measures Can Be Constricting

Experiences which tend to make a student feel unworthy, unimportant, unable or unwanted are, in Kelley's words, crippling. In an effort to "maintain control" of a classroom situation or gain conformity, teachers sometimes resort to "crippling" devices. Students may be made to feel guilty when they have violated relatively unimportant rules or failed to obey implicitly the teacher's instructions. An individual overly burdened with guilt feelings cannot feel worthy or important. The practice of making students feel guilty because they do not know or have not performed at the teacher's level of expectation may also develop within the child a feeling that mistakes and evil are synonymous. Whatever closes and offends the self makes acceptance ever so much more difficult.

In our zeal to motivate children there is often a very real danger that we may teach the child that he is never acceptable as he *is*. Setting ever higher and higher goals seems very desirable until we are aware of how this may seem to the child involved. Some of the traditional techniques used by teachers to "challenge" students may become *threats*. A challenge to perform a task which the student feels unable to accomplish may only succeed in discouraging.

Teachers too often fail to see things through the child's eyes. They are unwilling to accept the student as a child with a child's limited experience, a child's set of values, a child's immaturity. In many classrooms there is insistence upon the child's being a little adult. Too often he is judged by adult standards or by the standards of a particular adult teacher. Activities within the classroom are developed upon the basis of how they seem to the teacher rather than of how they seem to the student. Under a steady diet of this sort, the student may become a person who looks to others for direction. Subjected to such an environment year after year, students may come to see themselves as people who are unable to make decisions about what is right or wrong for them to do. They can only ape the values and standards of others. They may become the kind of people Maslow mentions, who are living by a set of "values" which are not worth fighting or dying for. In a classroom where there is constant judging of behavior by adult standards—blaming, condemning, criticizing and punishing—the self of the child may become withered and stunted like a plant in a room where the temperature is severely low.

PRACTICES THAT HELP ACCEPTANCE

To produce students who are able to accept themselves accurately and realistically, we need open, accepting school situations. This requires teachers, administrators, supervisors who are accepting of children as they are and who can treat them as persons of dignity and integrity. People learn acceptance from being accepted. Of primary importance in this task will be the kind of atmosphere we create, whether it be in the school as a whole or in some more limited place like a particular classroom, playing field or laboratory.

From the time a student enters the campus, the school atmosphere needs to communicate acceptance. In such an atmosphere students need have no fear of being themselves. They should sense that they are accepted as persons by all around them. Students should be involved in formulating rules and regulations and thus will have no fear of such rules or desire to sabotage them. Students should be encouraged to be active without fear of making mistakes.

The relationship the teacher has with each individual pupil is crucial in establishing acceptance. It is not too hard to accept the "good" child and to be patient with his immaturity. However, accepting an actively misbehaving child who is constantly on the move may be much more difficult. Lecturing, punishing or coercing will certainly not result in self-acceptance; nor can the child see himself as being accepted when the teacher becomes a doormat. Teachers must learn how to deal with a misbehaving student in such a way that he comes to see himself as acceptable. The teacher's problem is to create a way of behaving which does not encourage the annoying behavior while at the same time maintaining a friendly, accepting atmosphere. This calls for ways of behaving that neither attack nor appease, but which recognize and respect the fundamental dignity and integrity of the individual.

People, Rather Than Things, Are Important

To create an effective and lasting atmosphere of acceptance, *people* rather than *things* must be valued as important throughout the entire school system. This means all people, including custodians, cafeteria helpers and patrolmen, should be accepted as worthy and dignified human beings. Only when they so see themselves can they contribute to children's feelings of acceptability.

In our "materialistic" culture, which often seems to value things more than people, it is crucial that school be a place where students see themselves as well as others as important. All the adults in the school must make sure that their concern for property does not result in rejection of children. The security provisions in some libraries, for example, often communicate the idea that books are more important than people. The fuss over a broken window or a mark on the floor has convinced many students that glass and varnish are more important than they.

In an atmosphere where people are important, there is invariably a feeling of friendship and belonging. People are recognized as being unique and different, yet they are accepted because they belong to the human race. We should long since have rejected the shibboleth that "familiarity breeds contempt." The teacher who is truly accepting develops a friendly relationship with students and so serves as a friendly representative of society. Regardless of the behavior of students, every attempt needs to be made to maintain a friendly atmosphere.

The Atmosphere for Acceptance

It would appear that the capacity for acceptance is most likely to be learned in atmospheres which encourage openness and personal involvement. This calls for classroom climates which—

1. Encourage self-revelation rather than self-defense. Threat to self must appear at a minimum so that personal feelings, attitudes, ideas, doubts, wonders and concerns may be openly brought to light and examined. It means giving each individual the feeling that he can try his wings, even fail if need be, without fear of humiliation, embarrassment or the diminution of self in the process. Where the self cannot be safely ventured, it cannot be subject to much exploration. Students must be encouraged and helped to commit themselves. Teachers, meanwhile, must make every effort to assure that the consequences of such commitment are positive rather than negative.

2. Give each person a feeling of belonging. Without a feeling of being a part of what is going on, there can be no personal involvement, no learning to accept or to be accepted by others. Children who do not feel they belong feel no responsibility for those who reject them. Whatever contributes to making a child feel he is apart from or inacceptable to his fellows makes it just that much more difficult for him to accept either himself or anyone else.

3. Create the impression that difference is good and desirable. This means that both teachers and students must show acceptance of difference, whether it be of opinions or of people. Where difference cannot be accepted, individuals cannot be, either. Learning situations which emphasize too much the "one right answer," or the "one good way" to be, or to think, or to believe, necessarily restrict and limit exploration. Uniqueness, originality, even breaking with tradition and questioning the most strongly held concepts of our society, must be permissible if children are to learn to look at themselves and others fearlessly and intelligently.

4. Encourage children to trust their own organisms. Classroom atmospheres must give children the feeling it is "all right to be me"; "my ideas can be looked at." Without some trust in one's self, that self cannot be invested. Where students are continually reminded that who they are or what they are is not enough, there must eventually result a closing up of self and a reliance upon authority. Acceptance requires an atmosphere

which teaches the individual that he can trust his own organism and his own ideas. This calls for situations which make it possible for students to depart from the rules and to determine action on the basis of trust in self. This is basically democratic practice rather than blind trust in rules or the dicta of other people. When students are involved in making policy and evolving rules, the rule or policy loses its power to threaten. They obey because it is "our" rule or "our" policy. Obedience then becomes an enhancing experience.

5. Emphasize the existential, ongoing character of learning. This means an atmosphere that gives all concerned a feeling that all that is to be learned is not "out there." It means emphasizing and appreciating the worth and contribution of each individual, giving each child the feeling that there is something he can contribute, that his meanings, his feelings, his ideas have value and pertinence.

6. Finally, acceptance requires the establishment of an atmosphere which is generally hopeful. Such an atmosphere gives the child the feeling that he *can* be more than he is rather than a feeling that he *must* be more than he is—the feeling that he has something to bring to this business of education rather than the feeling that all of education means acquiring something from somewhere else for some unpredictable time in the future.

Teacher Attitudes and Relationships

We know acceptance of others is related to acceptance of self. Teachers who are highly self-critical tend to communicate this criticism to others. To provide an atmosphere of acceptance of others, we must begin by helping teachers achieve a greater acceptance of self. We need teachers able to identify with others, to have a feeling of oneness with others. The teacher cannot compartmentalize his attitudes. If he feels identity with persons in various age groups, of different skin colors, from different cultural backgrounds, he will be more likely to feel a oneness with children. Although he cannot enter into the world of childhood, he can identify with the needs of the growing human organism.

We know the capacity for acceptance is also related to freedom from threat. When an individual feels threatened he must erect defenses which prevent acceptance of others. The teacher who feels that his status depends upon the achievement test scores made by his class will find it difficult to accept the children who do not achieve well. Their very presence represents a threat to his status as a teacher. The teacher who works with a principal who believes that "merit" teachers are those who have quiet classrooms will find it hard to accept the child who is exuberant or noisy. Such attitudes are communicated to children. The child who feels threatened by the competitive reading chart which shows the number of books each child has read will not experience acceptance despite the teacher's *words* that it is good he has completed two books. What the teacher *really* believes is shown by his approval of the person who *reports* he has read 30 books.

A fearful teacher will inhibit the development of an atmosphere of acceptance in a classroom. He will tend to limit experiences instead of opening the field of experience. If school administrators are afraid children may get hurt or misbehave and bring criticism to the school, they will prevent field trips. If teachers are afraid children will be injured in handling tools, such as hammers and saws, children will be denied experiences in making things and in problem solving. When teachers are afraid "something might happen," children are not left alone to develop self-discipline. Shielding children from mistakes and from hurts narrows experience and may in the long run have the effect of teaching children that the world of things is very dangerous.

Superficial gestures and sentimental phrases such as "dear," "honey," "sweetheart," are often used by primary teachers in addressing pupils, but these words do not indicate acceptance. It is the little things a teacher *does* in his ways of working that say so much to children. A group of 10-year-olds were working in the art room, trying a new method of painting. The art teacher frequently told one boy to get busy, to stop annoying others, and finally said that he had to make one picture. After he finished a desultory attempt in the last few minutes of the class, the teacher gushed, "Now, that's a lovely design, dear." A classroom teacher who worked with the children during the next period had a different approach. Once again the boy wandered about and seemed uninterested in experimenting with new media. His teacher said, "John, apparently you don't want to try these materials today. Choose something you would enjoy here or you may go to the library or just rest if you need to." She did not nag or scold, she did not allow him to disturb others, but his right to make a decision, to feel "out of sorts," was accepted. What teachers believe shows in the minute-by-minute decisions they make in creating an environment for learning.

Teachers and Pupils Live in Different Worlds

A teacher of six-year-olds reported her sudden awareness of the difference in the worlds inhabited by children and adults. She recalled saying to a child, "Really, Jimmy, you have caused trouble all morning. There is surely enough chaos and trouble in the world without your adding to it." Jimmy replied, "Well, Miss Allison, I think the world is sunshiny—it's not so bad." The adult looks out upon the world of tension, but the child's vision usually does not encompass the ideological conflicts or mushroom shadows of an atomic era. It is difficult for the teacher to realize that he cannot enter the world of childhood. The child's world is not without tensions or worries, but they are of a different sort. We cannot enter this world, but we can accept the child's right to it and attempt to grasp his perceptions of it.

The conflict of values held by middle class teachers and those of children from lower or upper class homes has often been described. There is still a need, however, to be more aware of the importance of accepting children with differing values. A junior in college was shocked on her visit to a school in a low socioeconomic neighborhood. She said, "I've just never been near children who were dressed in dirty and ragged clothes. Some of these children even smelled! I'm not sure whether I can do this or not, but I know I have to know more about them." Entering upon a program of reading stories and playing games with children who were different, this student grew in understanding and later wrote, "When we are laughing at a story or planning to dramatize a scene, I forget the gray line of dirt at the wrist and the smell of unwashed clothes and bodies."

In addition to differences in worlds of time and social conditions, there is a wide variation between the teacher's out-of-school roles and life space and those of the child. The teacher may come to school from a quiet, well ordered apartment or from her own household where there are children to feed, mittens to find, a husband to encourage. When 25 to 35 youngsters surge into a classroom, it is difficult to consider the environments they recently left—nagging mothers, crying babies who were getting all the attention, fathers too immersed in the newspaper to listen to the son or daughter—the variety is endless. Remnants of these worlds surround each child as he comes to school. The writers of the four papers suggest that it is not essential to gather all the details about the home background; the essential element in the teacher's relationship with children is recognition of these different worlds and acceptance of the child *as he is* at the moment.

The teacher's basic function is to accept each child as a worthy individual. Such a relationship would mean fewer comparisons, less competition, and no capsule descriptions such as, "He is lazy"; "She has no interests"; "He's from a broken home—what can you expect?"

Acceptance of a particular class may deeply influence behavior and achievement. A supervisor told of a group of children who were considered "very difficult" by a first grade teacher. The second grade teacher was frequently ill during the year, and labeled the group "hard to manage" and "slow learners." This reputation continued with the class until fifth grade, when a new principal and a new teacher decided to try to change the attitudes toward this class. Opportunities to contribute to a total school project, success experiences, development of varied interests, and continued reassurance that this was a good class initiated change. By the time the group reached the junior high school there were definite improvements in behavior, leadership and achievement. Value judgments about "oughts" and "shoulds" are likely to prevent the individual from accepting himself or others.

Teacher Attitudes Toward Handicaps

The school which is concerned with development of an attitude of acceptance of self and others provides experiences which help the child accept and deal rationally with his handicaps. The common practice of teaching the child to compensate frequently does little more than emphasize his weakest point and actually serves to prevent acceptance.

Some schools are finding success in placing physically handicapped children in "regular" or "normal" classrooms. In one first grade, for example, a blind child reads from her Braille book as she works in a reading group with children having normal vision. When she spilled pegs from a peg board, the teacher remarked, "Judy can pick them up by herself." All the children in the group are becoming more accepting of a person with a handicap and Judy is learning to accept her own capacities and limitations.

In an effort to spur a handicapped child to success, some teachers use stories of such people as Edison, F. D. Roosevelt, Steinmetz, Milton or Beethoven. This may make the child feel that the only way he can become acceptable is through being a genius. This means that his handicap is unacceptable in itself, that he must devote his life to atoning to society because he happened to be the way he is. This must be pretty discouraging to the blind child who can never hope to be a Milton, but who must still go through life unable to see.

Teachers can usually accept the child who shows less talent for singing or painting or catching a ball; but overemphasis upon the value of reading, writing and number skills seems to lead to nonacceptance of the child who has difficulty developing these skills. The fallacy, "if you work hard on it, you can improve," too frequently leads only to increased feelings of failure.

Acceptance in School Helps the Child Deal with Problems

In the light of present understanding of human behavior, desperate acts are the consequence of desperate feelings. People behave desperately in anger and hurt or they express hostility when they perceive such a threatening situation that this seems the only way to defend the self. A truly accepting teacher, counselor or friend can make the crucial difference between an accepting youngster open to his experience or a rigidly defensive young person fighting back at his world.

The child who at home is considered far inferior to an older sibling may find at school the acceptance necessary for his well being and ability to deal with the world. Teen-agers who have no place in society, who are often denied the opportunity to be accepted as members of the community, may find acceptance in a school which provides genuine self-government and significant work experiences. The student who expresses a creativity which makes his work unusual or "different" needs acceptance from teachers, for he often finds himself estranged from parents and peers. We should not discount the importance of an accepting school situation for the child in trouble. It may be the one rock to which he can cling while riding out the storm.

The school principal who sees persistent "troublemakers" year after year has a deep responsibility to communicate a feeling of acceptance of the individual, despite the clear disapproval of the particular behavior. He will need to work with teachers and parents to help them distinguish the behavior which cannot be condoned from the essential core of the individual which is accepted as worthy. With current knowledge of child development it would seem needless to comment on corporal punishment, but it is still practiced in many schools. Some principals still believe they can beat "respect" into children or "this is all they know from home," so a slap or a paddling is the only effective way to deal with problems. Nor is this helped any by the common travesty of making the paddling a public event by administering it in the presence of a witness as a "legal protection."

PROVIDING ACCURATE, REALISTIC INFORMATION

The adequate personality requires accurate, realistic information about himself and the world. He needs dependable data, correct facts, sure knowledge and a broad perspective on which to base his behavior. Without such information he is not able to act efficiently, to make wise choices, to judge accurately or to predict the results of his action. Indeed, information true to reality and not distorted by personal fears and anxieties is the only basis on which an individual can make a sensible adjustment. One cannot move from what he is not; one can only move effectively from the facts. Effective behavior can begin only from reality.

If, therefore, schools are to produce more adequate personalities, it is necessary to provide ways to help children face facts about themselves. This cannot be a mere telling operation. A child becomes informed about himself first as he has opportunities to interact with his environment. As young children react to one and all the stimuli which a rich school environment can provide—water play, squishy clay, finger paints, new sounds and melodies, ladders to climb, things to touch, smell and view—they are defining not only "what is out there" but "what I sense and feel and know." As children become older and more sophisticated, learning continues with opportunities to explore more deeply the satisfactions of music and art, dance, sports, tools and models.

A child may learn further about who he is as he reacts to the experiences of others as if they were his own. Vicarious learning, important in its meaning for the individual, occurs as boys and girls become personally involved with books and the many other media—television, recordings, films and pictures—which portray people and events in other places and at other times. Interaction with peers; the opportunity to be with friends; time to talk through experiences, extend indirect learnings about self. While such learning must be highly personal for each individual, the social setting of the school and the give and take of living with others are important if a child is to learn to group his experiences, to know that in these ways he is like others, in these ways he is his own unique self.

Much of what a child knows and feels about himself is learned through the reflected appraisals of others, a kind of mirror image. Such appraisal, however, must be honest; no sugar-coating, no false praise, no attempt to disguise the facts. The child who is secure in the knowledge that his teacher does trust him and is on his side can accept and build constructively upon the truth about his achievements and his needs, his strengths and weaknesses. Children deserve the truth. To know the truth is the only sure way they can touch bottom, assess where they are and know the progress they have made and have still to accomplish. This kind of confrontation with reality needs to pervade all aspects of the school situations.

Free Access to Information

As the adequate personality requires accurate and realistic information, so, too, does he require full and complete information. Indeed, there is no information a well adjusted person ought not have about himself. Gaps in knowledge of self, like false information, can hinder acceptance. This raises a series of interesting questions about many school and student personnel practices. For example, for what purposes are test scores noted and facts filed in cumulative records? And for whose benefit? Is the information which is passed on to the next teacher, to the receiving school or to the prospective employer available also to the student? How can the facts, the school records, be shared with individuals who are the subjects of such extensive record keeping? Might not more of them be used to help children and young people in self-discovery?

Since acceptance and understanding of self are based upon complete and accurate knowledge, the school is responsible for making available to the individual all of the facts he needs to acquire that knowledge. But what facts does he need and how should they be provided? These are two questions to which the school must give thoughtful consideration if the free access to the information it provides is to be something other than irresponsible telling.

Information Which Is Wanted

First, it seems to us, information which is made available to an individual at any level should be information which he wants. Wanting to know implies a need and a purpose for facts which have personal meanings. It may be a need which is expressed directly, as when a student seeks vocational counseling or help in choosing a particular program of study or the college to attend. All needs for information, however, are not expressed so directly or sought so openly as may be the case in vocational or college counseling. They may be conveyed only indirectly.

The child who sets too high standards for his performance or who plans in terms of unattainable goals may profit from help in understanding where he is at present in terms of strengths and weaknesses and what intermediate steps must be taken before he can achieve his goal. The boy or girl who depreciates his own ability, whose performance does not measure up to his capacity to learn, who is so often labeled the "underachiever," may need the evidence and the reassurance of new information about himself, information which says "he can." The desire for knowledge of self may be read in many facets of behavior—overdependence, fear of new learning activities, noncontribution, retreat from testing situations, fabrication, compensation, cheating or the various defensive mechanisms. Each may indicate to the discerning teacher that this child needs help in self-appraisal. Whatever information is available or can be obtained from school or community resources should be provided.

Any information, including achievement and intelligence test ratings, which contributes to the accuracy of his view of self should be available to the student. Withholding records of performance, test results, inventories or other data which can be made available means withholding information important to decision making.

This is not to imply that the school should distribute test scores and the like on a wholesale basis. We too often give students information about themselves that they do not either want or need. Indiscriminate distribution of facts about either ability or achievement may represent a threat to some children and serve only to block self-exploration and discovery. Schools need to make a clear distinction between free access and forced learning. Records need to be open, but the individual's freedom to use or not use those records must also be respected.

Information Which Is Meaningful

A clear distinction needs also to be made between simply handing out test scores and helping people to understand what they mean. The problem of *how* to report test scores so that they may be meaningful to the individual needs to be faced. Unless they are properly interpreted, scores may develop or reinforce feelings of complete inadequacy on the part of some students; for others they may result in undesirable attitudes of superiority.

The challenge lies in the teacher's or the counselor's ability to help students understand the meaning and the implications of test results. Handing out scores, alone, is not the answer; it is not the fact, but the *meaning* of the fact for the individual, that is important. In light of the more than one hundred million standardized tests being administered every year in American schools and of the emphasis that both school and community place on test scores, it is essential that teachers and guidance personnel re-examine the uses made of test results. The trend toward more complete interpretation of test results to pupils and to parents needs to be extended. There should be no secret information, no mystery surrounding a testing program. No one is more entitled to complete and accurate information than is the student himself; to make that information meaningful is the responsibility of the school.

Labeling and the Use of Tests

A fundamental idea advanced by each of the invited authors is that children learn their self-concepts from experience. As children are grouped and classified, assigned learning tasks, tested and evaluated, praised and blamed, they are developing self-definitions. Schools must, therefore, be concerned about the kinds of labels pinned on children. If a child is called stupid and he comes to believe it, he behaves as though he were. If a teacher tells a youngster by her impatience, her admonishment, her unspoken labeling that he reads poorly, he remains a poor reader, for as he views himself, so he behaves. To the extent that children are treated as untrustworthy, dependent, incapable of making decisions, they will learn to live up to those labels. How many children have been taught that they cannot write or spell or sing or dance because their first efforts were not accepted? How many children have been labeled, "just like his father," "no head for arithmetic," "a typical—" and have had to carry in school the burden and blame of community prejudices? How often have segregated schools, rigid track programs, and labeled groups corroborated the negative concepts children have learned about themselves?

But not all labeling is necessarily negative. There are children, too, who in some classrooms learn they are always right, always smartest, always the best. These are children who may also suffer. By accepting early definitions of superiority, they may find it impossible to profit from the mistakes which are an important part of learning. Their need to be correct, to measure up to adult expectations and to the high standards they set for themselves, leaves no room for exploration, no zest for trying the uncertain, no daring to test their ability when success is not assured. Praise, like censure, can be damaging when it closes the doors to self-discovery.

Unfortunately, in the effort to be objective and to obtain accurate, statistically reliable information about children's abilities and achievements, schools have sometimes done little more than refine the labels. Intelligence quotients, grade equivalent scores, percentile ranks, and stanines are more sophisticated labels, but may be pinned to children in the same damaging way. This is not to deny the value of testing. Used wisely and well, tests can contribute to the school's evaluation and improvement of its instructional program. They can add to the teacher's understanding of individual children and with proper interpretation may help students to see themselves accurately and realistically. They are devices convenient and easy to use, though not infallible. Problems arise, however, when overemphasis is placed on test results, when they are used in isolation or authoritatively in counseling pupils or parents. They require a vast measure of sound teacher judgment and must always be interpreted in the light of all that is known about human variability.

The whole process of testing should be re-examined to discover new approaches which might permit the individual greater freedom to express who he is and what he is becoming. Instead of the true-false, multiple choice kind of testing, children might be encouraged to explore questions in greater depth. Questions need to be asked for which there are no sure right answers, but which challenge children to test and develop their full potential. Instead of limiting responses, tests might be constructed to extend meaning, to stimulate intellectual curiosity, to encourage expression of personal convictions. The use of questions which are open-ended, which demand problem solving methods, which encourage creative response, and which allow divergent as well as convergent thinking might contribute to more satisfying self-evaluation. Granted, such tests would be more difficult to grade and to standardize—the results would not yield as exact grade equivalents or as specific scores of intellectual ability; nevertheless, they might produce fewer test-anxious, labeled children.

Implications for Evaluation and Grading

Testing is only one aspect of the total process of evaluation, but questions concerning the use and misuse of test results may be applied as appropriately to other school practices. The basic question of purpose needs to be raised. If the purpose of evaluation is seen as setting standards and measuring children's progress and achievement against them, then it is appropriate to define course content and grade level learnings, to set minimum requirements for the skills to be learned and the content covered, and to assign specific tasks to be mastered in a particular grade or course sequence. Children can then be expected to conform to requirements, and their progress can be evaluated in terms of the standards set. Grades become convenient devices for expressing the percentage of content covered or skills mastered and, as reward or punishment, for providing motivation for learning. Add to grades the prize of the honor roll or the threat of failure, and motivation can be increased. Retention and acceleration, special class assignments and track systems may be necessary adjustments, but in general the logic of the set curriculum can be served by this view of evaluation and grading. Education then becomes a process of defining the subject matter to be taught, presenting the information, setting the standards, doing the evaluating, and awarding the grades. And, unfortunately, this is the pattern in many schools today.

If, instead, the purpose of evaluation is helping each child discover and develop his full potential, evaluation and grading assume new meanings. Evaluation becomes a process, not of teacher measurement against predetermined standards, but of helping each child test and extend his own skills. It is a process of creating opportunities for children to evaluate their current needs, to develop immediate purposes for learning, to set realistic individual standards. Teachers do this as they help pupils see themselves accurately and plan with them the learning tasks suited to the particular needs of the individual. Self-selection of reading materials, personal spelling lists, individual projects, exploration of interests, and self-testing devices are but a few of the methods which allow the child to discover and to satisfy his own learning needs. This is not a downgrading of standards; indeed, many of the standards which schools set restrict learning and underestimate children's full potential. Children who are helped to know their own needs and to find personal meaning in learning experiences raise the standards for their own performance and increase their learning pace.

Grades in this sense are seen realistically—not as reward or punishment or as motivating devices. Without such purposes, however, they turn out to be pretty meaningless. They may help a child evaluate himself, but more often are found to be inadequate or inappropriate devices. They rate, but do not give sufficient information, do not specify strengths or weaknesses. They become little more than labels. They define, but are not appropriate measures for the child involved in the very personal learning of self-discovery. Children need evaluation but not labels.

Implications for Learning Experiences

When classroom programs are expanded to actually teach acceptance of self, opportunities are created for children to participate in a wide variety of activities. Experiences are planned so that children have the time, the space and the materials to follow their interests and satisfy their needs. Time, too, is made available for the incidental, on-the-spot learning; schedules are made flexible and do not limit the pursuit of the immediate study important to children. Since individuals perceive themselves, their needs and their readiness for new learnings differently, activities are structured so that each child may select experiences in terms of his unique purposes. This means children sometimes work alone with the individual teacher's support and guidance which they may require. At other times children engage in group activities, in team games, or committee work where they can communicate personal learnings and react to the experiences and values of others. Interpersonal relating may be limited to a small group or may be extended to include children and resource people from outside the classroom.

There is recourse to both direct and vicarious experience as children are encouraged to find answers to their questions and to clarify and test meanings. There are opportunities for the testing which children seek as they acquire new skills and new learnings. There are both social and physical challenges to be met and the intellectual stimulation which encourages children to question established theory and formulate new opinions. Each youngster is helped to accept the reality he finds, to discover who he is and where he wants to go, and to find his own "magic mountain" to climb.

Schools which encourage acceptance provide creative activities of all kinds which allow children to express their reactions and their feelings. Music, dancing, painting, drawing, clay modeling, dramatizing, puppets and construction work—all help children to gain insight into their own feelings and behavior. Literature, which encompasses reading, listening and their own creative efforts, also enables children to relate to the experiences of others and to test in words the sense of what they know and believe, what they feel and imagine. Perceptions of self and others can be learned in a very real sense as a child takes the part of another in role playing situations, as he incorporates other roles in his play activities and "let's pretend" games. Here children can test unfamiliar roles and new concepts of self in the security of action "as if" these were true.

TEACHERS, TOO, NEED TO BE ACCEPTED

Adults, as well as children, learn to be acceptant by having been accepted. If teachers are to become accepting people, they must experience acceptance as individuals. Teachers, also, need to feel that their work is important; that they are members of an accepted and respected profession.

The Community Provides a Climate

Attitudes and feelings toward teachers reflected in the actions of members of the community influence teachers' feelings about self. The teacher image that prevails in many communities is reflected in the behavior of individuals toward teachers. If the community members see the typical teacher as a stern, grim, forbidding person, they are apt to behave toward each individual teacher as if this were so. Teachers may be seen in some communities and by some people as "different," as people with whom another must be careful—must be "on guard." These perceptions inhibit acceptance. In situations where these perceptions prevail, the teacher cannot feel accepted as he really is. People in communities where such perceptions prevail need to become aware that teachers, too, are persons who may have the same interests, needs and aspirations as others; they may enjoy the same things, share the same sense of humor, love and be loved as persons rather than as preconceived symbols.

The community can express its respect for teachers collectively (the profession) through the activities of its agencies. Recognition given to groups of teachers or to individuals for a job well done is reflected in the *esprit de corps* of the group. When teachers are consulted—as are other professional groups—in community planning conferences, when their knowledge is sought by planning groups, when they are made members of planning and advisory boards, they feel that the community accepts them as important members.

The community attitude toward education and toward teaching as a profession is reflected in the buildings provided to house the educational program, the equipment provided to do the job of implementing the program, the salary schedule provided, welfare benefits such as sick leave, retirement benefits, health insurance and the like. In American culture the importance placed upon any profession or its members is often measured in terms of dollar values. When a community offers its teachers salaries below those of other employed groups, it is saying to the teachers, "We don't feel that you or what you have to offer is very important." It is not surprising if the teacher drawing a bare subsistence wage may feel, "I'm not a very important person and what I have to offer is not very important." These are also the people who, when asked their profession, reply apologetically, "I'm just a teacher." In a supportive community climate, teachers are better able to see themselves accurately and realistically and to accept what they see. This, in turn, has its effects upon the children they teach.

School Administrators Influence Self-Acceptance

Administrators, because of their status position, are able to help teachers develop a feeling of self-worth. The principal who is able to work with his teachers in such a way that they feel they can afford to make mistakes provides an atmosphere in which teachers may grow personally as well as professionally. The administrator who is able to accept the right of teachers to hold opinions which differ from his, who encourages faculty groups to make decisions regarding school policy, who does not use his position to squelch new and different ways of working or thinking, helps teachers to become self-acceptant and to be open to new ideas and ways of working. When other persons accept a teacher, the teacher is more able to accept himself.

The principal or superintendent who enters a faculty or departmental meeting without "knowing" what decisions the faculty or department should make is able to say to the group, by his behavior, "I'm willing to trust your judgment"; "You are able to make sound decisions"; or, "You are important people and I accept you as such." It is in such meetings that teachers have the opportunity to explore the meaning that education, with all its ramifications, has for them. In such an atmosphere the teacher is able to examine his philosophy, his techniques, his strengths and weaknesses, to make a realistic appraisal of himself as a teacher. In such an atmosphere the teacher is free to accept what he finds and to search for ways to improve himself as a teacher and as a person.

An administrator who drops into a teacher's classroom may be saying by the visit, "Your work is important to me as well as the children"; or, "I'm very much interested in what you are doing." On the other hand, by facial expressions and other behavior while in the classroom, he may be saying, "It's my duty to observe you, but I'm terribly bored"; or, "Since I have to rate you, I must visit your classroom." Principals, in many ways other than words, may express interest in the work that teachers do.

Supervisory Practices Play a Part

Johnnye V. Cox, Director of the Georgia Program for the Education of Supervisors, stated in *Educational Leadership:* "Today's concepts of educational supervision are characterized by such phrases as clarifying values, changing attitudes . . . providing security, and changing perceptions." [1] Accepting this role of the supervisor means that supervision must be concerned with effective ways of helping others modify and improve their perceptions.

A very brief description of some of the results of a particular supervisory program will illustrate a vital source of experiences for teachers in the initial stage of self-assessment. In a discussion of some of the values of a cooperative faculty study based on their concerns, a number of teachers stated that the opportunity to exchange ideas, information, techniques and methods was valuable. The following are some of their reports:

Mrs. C.: "I thought the study stimulated new ideas and methods of teaching."

Mrs. R.: "Yes, and it resulted in a growing realization of a real need for sharing information and for working together in order to improve the quality of teaching."

Mrs. G.: "I thought that many valuable teaching aids were gained from the 'This Is How We Do It' phase of the study."

Miss W.: "Sharing techniques led us to try new things and has given us something practical to work with."

It is easy to visualize the feelings of acceptance experienced by the teachers who had shared ideas and techniques. At the most, with regard to part of their professional qualifications—their teaching—they had seen others accept and try their treasured techniques.

Teachers in another faculty group expressed more profound feelings. Their statements, which follow, are more personal in nature. These statements are excerpted from an evaluating discussion session by a school faculty whose members were completing a year of cooperative professional study.

Mrs. P.: "Feelings of satisfaction grew out of working cooperatively on a worthwhile study."

Mrs. Y.: "We also believe that a greater understanding and appreciation of other teachers' problems was achieved."

"Yes," said Mrs. A., "the study has made us a more closely knit group."

"Our greatest gain," claimed Mr. B., "has been a friendly, professional relationship with each other and an appreciation of each other and of our principal."

Without doubt, the four people above are engaged in what they consider a worthwhile venture as expressed through their "feeling" statements. Further, the appreciation for one another is being openly

[1] Johnnye V. Cox. "Educating Supervisors in Changing Concepts." *Educational Leadership* 16: 467-71; May 1959.

expressed in a friendly and professional way. The feeling of belonging, of being an important part of a worthwhile whole, and the opportunities for being understood and appreciated surely contribute to self-acceptance, with subsequent more realistic self-assessment. Cooperative study of common concerns can create the climate and opportunity for acceptance, and for openness to new experience. Such study can provide a setting for persons to assess themselves more accurately and realistically.

CHAPTER 10

CREATIVITY AND OPENNESS TO EXPERIENCE

FROM ROGERS

Time and again in my clients, I have seen simple people become significant and creative in their own spheres, as they have developed more trust of the processes going on within themselves, and have dared to feel their own feelings, live by values which they discover within, and express themselves in their own unique ways.

A fully functioning person is a creative person. With his sensitive openness to his world, and his trust of his own ability to form new relationships with his environment, he is the type of person from whom creative products and creative living emerge.

I find such a person to be sensitively open to all of his experience—sensitive to what is going on in his environment, sensitive to other individuals with whom he is in relationship, and sensitive perhaps most of all to the feelings, reactions and emergent meanings which he discovers in himself.

FROM MASLOW

Creativity has its roots in the nonrational.

Science and education, being too exclusively abstract, verbal and bookish, do not have enough place for raw, concrete, esthetic experience, especially of the subjective happenings inside oneself. Esthetic perceiving and creating and esthetic peak experiences are seen to be a central aspect of human life and of psychology and education rather than a peripheral one.

FROM COMBS

With a positive view of self one can risk taking chances; one does not have to be afraid of what is new and different. A sturdy ship can venture farther from port. Just so, an adequate person can launch himself without fear into the new, the untried and the unknown. A positive view of self permits the individual to be creative, original and spontaneous. What is more, he can afford to be generous, to give of himself freely or to become personally involved in events. With so much more at his command, he has so much more to give.

Truly adequate people possess perceptual fields maximally open to experience. That is to say, their perceptual fields are capable of change and adjustment in such fashion as to make fullest possible use of their experience.

A greater openness to experience offers many advantages It provides adequate people with more data and, with more data, they are much more likely to be right.

FROM KELLEY

Since life is ever-moving and ever-becoming, the fully functioning person is cast in a creative role.

He sees that creation is not something which occurred long ago and is finished, but that it is now going on and that he is part of it.

When the fearful person withdraws within his psychologica shell, communication is shut off. It is just as difficult for such a person to give as it is for him to receive. The self then is denied that which it feeds on. The psychological self feeds on ideas, which come from other people. Without the stuff o growth, the self becomes less adequate, and the whole person loses its ability to do, to venture, to create. The individua comes to see himself as impoverished, but he is not able to d much about it by himself.

THE IDEAS

Creativity has long been regarded as a special endowment bestowe on a chosen few. There has been an aura of the mysterious connecte with creativity. The word *creative* has also been subjected to myria interpretations. It has often been used to describe the commonplace the ordinary, the usual. Traditionally, creativity has been associated wit products—paintings, inventions, literary masterpieces, music. Tangible evidence was the criterion—something to see, hold or hear. Not too muc thought was given to the process. We still search for and encourage th tangible, but the concept of creativity has been enlarged to include idea decisions, relationships, problem solving—results of man's cognitiv powers. The product, whatever form it may take, would not evolve with out the process. The growing realization of the universality of creativity of man's heretofore unsuspected capacity for creativeness, of the unique ness of every individual, places the idea of creativity in new perspective

It is evident that there is agreement among our four authors regardin the creative person, the creative process and creativity, even though th frames of reference from which they view creativity may be differen They have used the terms *creativity* and *adequacy* almost synonymousl They have pointed out that there is a capacity for creativeness in ever person. They state two basic premises: (a) Creativity is necessary for fully adequate personality, and (b) every person has the capacity fo creativity. From these premises we can derive a fundamental purpose fo education, namely, the development of creativity in every individua

Creativity is in each of us, psychologists seem to be saying. This ide is comforting in that it gives us a measure of hope as we work with ind viduals; it is disturbing in that it points up how much we have yet to learn about this intangible, illusive phenomenon. It is commonly agreed that children start school with eagerness, curiosity, capacity for wonder and puzzlement, spontaneity, spirit of adventure, imagination, sensitivity to and fascination for the world in which they live. One need but watch a nursery school or kindergarten in action to perceive the living proof of this. We all begin, it would seem, with the raw stuff of creativity. It may often be observed, however, that adults are not creative; many are passive, conforming and fearful. What happens on the way to adulthood? The challenge is obvious.

If it is true that creativity exists in all of us, the problem for education becomes not the production of creativity, but the releasing and encouraging of the creativity already there. The basic direction of the organism itself is with us rather than against us. We are not involved in a task in which a perverse organism must be coerced into becoming. Rather, it is in the nature of the organism itself to become, if we can find the ways to make it possible. As one of our committee stated, "Man will become the best that he can be, when we have found the ways to set him free." What blocks do we put on creativity when we "squelch" the imaginings of children? Granted that these imaginings may be sheer delightful childlike fantasy—but is this bad? It is just this gift of imagination which is responsible for much of human advancement. Through encouragement and guidance we can develop the habit of imagining and an attitude of readiness toward the novel, the unknown and the original.

CREATIVITY AS A FUNCTION OF OPENNESS

According to our authors, creativity and the development of an adequate personality are associated with two things, openness and drive. The basic drive toward adequacy is characteristic of everyone. Its particular expression, however, may be quite different from person to person. This "difference" is largely responsible for the creative production. How creative the individual is likely to be will depend upon the degree of freedom that is provided for this fundamental drive toward adequacy to operate. This degree of freedom is what is meant by openness.

The individual who is open to his experience has a much wider source of data from which to select his perceptions. Yet openness, as we have seen in Chapter 9, is learned from experience, and what is learned can be taught. Education can help people to learn to be more open to their experience. A basic goal of education itself must be the production of increased openness. What narrows and rigidifies human experience is antithetical to education. The progress of human affairs is not the product of smug satisfaction with what is, but the joyful, even painful, exploration of the unknown.

The conditions which support the emergence of creativity do not require that we effect drastic innovations in our educational system. The conditions for creativity are the same conditions that need to exist for effective learning of any kind. The problem for teaching, therefore, is not so much a question of learning to do something completely novel. Rather, it is a question of discovering those things which many good teachers already do implicitly; then to encourage their further use, making them *explicit* so that they can be more widely utilized in the work of all teachers. Creativity can be fostered through careful planning and implementation. Our authors tell us that creativity is a product of: (a) rich experiences, (b) trust in self, (c) openness to data, (d) attitudes that value change, (e) freedom from threat and (f) willingness to be and to become.

FACTORS THAT HINDER ACCEPTANCE

Conformity and Creativity

Experiences which inhibit the individual's freedom to be and to express his deeper *self* reduce his ability to be creative. Creativity is not learned from restraint. It is a product of the lowering or removal of barriers. It is a matter of being different, of daring to change, of venturing forth.

Schools may have conforming pupils or creative ones, but whichever choice is made, teachers, parents, administrators, all of us, need to be prepared to pay the price. For conformity and creativity are essentially antithetical—what produces one tends to destroy the other. Conformity calls for restriction, order, direction, control; creativity for freedom, experimentation, expression and facilitation. Teachers who want creativity can count on it—their classrooms will not be neat, quiet and orderly. Administrators who demand rigid conformity can count on it—their students will not be very creative, except possibly in devising ways to circumvent controls. The public, demanding more genius and creativity, on the one hand, and more rigid control, less "frills" and less expense, on the other, must also face the fact it cannot have both simultaneously. Whatever choice we make is going to cost us something. The choice will be hard, for some of the things we must give up are dear to our hearts and our pocketbooks. Nevertheless, a choice has to be made either for institutional order and dogmatism or for flexibility and freedom. Both conformity and creativity cannot grow in the same school atmosphere or classroom climate.

The very belief mentioned previously, that only a few are creative, tends to limit the degree to which teachers encourage creativity. Like everyone else, teachers behave in terms of what they believe to be so and a belief that creativity is a highly limited capacity must, necessarily, have its effect on the kinds of situations they provide for children and the tasks they set them.

Maslow points out that creativity is in large part an irrational, rather than a rational, activity. Yet, most of our school programs are predicated almost exclusively on the rational. The cognitive aspects of man's existence are stressed throughout the curriculum, while the sensory, conative aspects are left to shift for themselves, and in many classrooms are even frowned upon if they appear. This is not to argue that our schools should give up their concern for the ordered and logical exploration of knowledge. We are questioning only the perspective taken on the matter that makes the curriculum of many schools almost exclusively intellectual, while practically ignoring the very aspects of human beings that make them human—their subjective nature.

Noncreative Influences

We shall not stop here to explore in detail the factors preventing our schools from fully encouraging creativity. Instead, we will list only a few of the kinds of practices that seem to inhibit creativity and openness. We will then move on, in the remainder of this chapter, to look more positively at things the schools may do to nurture these precious qualities.

Among the factors that stand in the way of openness and creativity seem to be the following:

1. A preoccupation with order. Much of our practice seems to worship order, categorization, classifying, description and pigeonholing of one sort or another. Such a preoccupation is likely to discourage breaking loose and finding new solutions.

2. Overvaluing authority, support, evidence and the "scientific method." Such rigid, tight concepts often permit no question or exploration. They are, by definition, *so*.

3. Exclusive emphasis upon the historical point of view. This seems to imply that those things that have been discovered in the past are always good; change or the present is bad.

4. Various forms of "cookbook" approaches—the "filling in the blanks," "color the picture correctly" approach. This is an ever-present danger of teaching machines, also, if they permit only "given" answers.

5. The essentially solitary approach to learning often emphasized in some classrooms—creativity is very highly dependent upon communication.

6. The elimination of self from the classroom.

7. The school which is ruled almost entirely by adult concepts.

8. Emphasis upon force, threat and coercion. The use of "guilt" and "badness" as means of control; also severe forms of punishment, ridicule and humiliation. Anything which diminishes the self interferes with openness and creativity.

9. The idea that mistakes are sinful and that children are not to be trusted. Where mistakes are not permitted, there can be no experimentation. Teachers who fear youngsters and the possibilities that they may get out of hand cannot permit the kind of movement and freedom required by creativity.

10. School organizations which emphasize lock-step approaches, rules and regulations, managerial and administrative considerations, rather than human ones.

THE ATMOSPHERE FOR ENCOURAGING CREATIVITY

If creativity is to be valued and encouraged, administrators and teachers need to create situations in schools where it is possible to produce open people. Much creative behavior has its beginnings in sheer fantasy. Students need to perceive school as a place where imagination, brainstorming and even daydreaming are encouraged. No idea, regardless of how fantastic it may appear, need be unworthy of consideration or subject to reprimand. Whether it be classroom, hall or playground, school should be a place where students can express ideas even in jest. The total school atmosphere needs to be seen as one in which fun and play are truly welcomed and in which students can feel comfortable while imagination is given rein. When students are accepted as basically active, responsible and trustworthy human beings, they are given hope that they are fully capable of creative behavior.

Provision of Choice

In our attempts to encourage students, we must distinguish clearly between challenge and threat. Essentially, students are challenged when they are confronted with problems they feel able to deal with and are threatened when they are confronted with problems they do not feel able to cope with. Students need to feel involved and feel that administrators and teachers trust them and are behind them. One of the most effective ways of assuring that the school atmosphere will be challenging rather than threatening is to provide maximum opportunity for choices.

Creative behavior is encouraged where differences and flexibility are made possible. Schoolmen certainly need to resist the many pressures, at all levels at which school attendance is compulsory, to increase the number of requirements and to decrease the number of free electives. Even in college it is becoming more and more difficult for a student to find many truly free electives. If the school atmosphere is to be perceived as one in which there is concern for and interest in students as well as subject matter, then students must be involved in making more choices. It is particularly imperative that programs in teacher education provide maximum choice if prospective teachers are to learn to value difference and flexibility.

A teacher must trust and respect each individual student as he is, regardless of his behavior. A child finds it extremely difficult to trust himself or others until he knows that someone cares for and trusts him. Until he trusts himself and others, he will participate in few if any creative activities. The ultimate aim is a classroom atmosphere in which there is mutual trust and respect between the teacher and each student as well as between students. Here a student can take the risks required in being creative.

The classroom climate must support cooperative interaction. Here the teacher plays a key role in determining how authority is used and the kind of group procedures adopted. If competition is used as the spur to learning, pressure is exerted on children to achieve specific objectives, and learning itself becomes little more than a competitive performance. To win the prize—the grades, the scholarships and the recognition—can become the goal of learning. The climate of anxiety engendered does not help children to develop an openness to experience. Instead, students tend to select only those activities which the school chooses to reward and to avoid the experimental, the exploratory study.

Cooperation and the Feeling of Belonging

Cooperative procedures free children to learn, to become their best and most creative selves. Relieved of the pressure and anxieties of competition they can use their fullest potentialities, and optimum involvement and progress are possible. But cooperation is learned and must be taught. Children must have opportunities to practice the skills of cooperative procedures. They need the freedom to define goals, to learn to plan, to interact and to try group management. Beginning efforts require teacher support and guidance and the security of defined limits, but not adult rule. The teacher who uses authority and power *with* children and *not over* them, who is sincere in his consideration for children, their feelings and their way of working, who himself values cooperation, creates the social environment which supports the cooperative learnings necessary to a democratic society.

In like manner, a feeling of belonging makes possible the security from which experimentation and creativity can occur. A feeling of belonging, however, comes from more than mutual trust and acceptance. It requires also that the child be given sufficient responsibility that he may have the feeling that people really count on him. Then one can feel that he is carrying his share of the load. It is at this point that a child in a classroom or in a family can say, "we." Not only can he then dare to try, but he can say "let's try," to others. This is quite different from the behavior of people who do not feel that they belong or do not trust themselves. People who are secure can say, "Let's *do* it and see what happens!" With this courage, even mistakes or failure are no threat but rather an invitation to evaluate and try to do better next time.

A classroom atmosphere which encourages creativity not only respects and values difference, it *encourages* difference. If people should have the opportunity to become their unique selves, it follows that people should become more different rather than more alike. Teachers need, therefore, to encourage difference and uniqueness in the classroom. Kelley has stated that it is the function of the school to produce people who are increasingly unique. Here is a challenge for teachers who are still employing methods of mass teaching and mass testing, yet are dissatisfied with the growth and development of the students. Serious questions need to be raised about the value of ability grouping, large lecture classes and mass media teaching in light of their effect on creativity and uniqueness.

Encouraging Communication

Very closely associated with the encouragement of difference is the establishment of an atmosphere which encourages communication. Communication which encourages creativity depends upon contributions from people with different ways of looking at things. Teachers, therefore, need to welcome different perceptions and to help students develop appreciation for different ways of seeing things. Students should be given freedom to raise questions about *anything*.

Teachers should learn to accept questions even when the questions seem nonsensical or useless. Through the nonsensical kind of question, students at least discover whether their questions will be taken seriously. Students are seldom skilled at asking questions which will give them and other class members the information they seek. They have to experience acceptance while they make mistakes before they will have the courage to be more creative and responsible. Where difference and creativity are highly valued, change is perceived as normal and desirable. It is expected; it is welcome. Teachers need to help students understand that change is normal and to be expected. Prospective teachers, too, need to learn that answers based on the *status quo* are of less and less value in our dynamic, changing society.

Creativity depends on problem solving rather than static answer finding. As changes occur and people become increasingly unique, each human problem is different from those of the past. To find the most effective solutions for the here and now in which we behave, we need every ounce of creative problem solving we can muster. This requires people with courage and a hopeful outlook and who are open to their experience. In teacher education this means that we encourage students to trust themselves as trustworthy organisms. We need to help them find the courage to develop their own best methods of teaching rather than the best methods decided by someone outside themselves.

TEACHER ATTITUDES AND CREATIVITY

Teacher Attitudes Are Important

The atmosphere for encouraging creativity is derived from the expression of teacher attitudes that value self and others. The teacher's behavior results from his perception of the purpose of the school, the role he should play, and the values he holds. Bricks, glass, books, desks—the space, facilities and materials in the school are important, but it is the teacher's attitude toward their use which makes the difference. Although he may not be aware of it, the teacher, himself, is creative in that he is creating an atmosphere as he arranges, organizes, interprets, questions or directs. To produce an atmosphere which facilitates creativity, the teacher must begin by recognizing the differences between his world and that of the child. He must be aware of the effect of his own attitudes and behavior in helping children create their own self concepts.

Openness and Flexibility Must Be Valued

Openness to experience has been emphasized as a prerequisite to creativity. The teacher who values openness is willing to pay the price for it. When openness to experience is valued, there is likely to be more noise, less order, more materials, fewer times when all students are doing the same thing. This does not mean banging or clattering or racing around. It does mean students are working for longer periods of time on their own projects. They may frequently be out of the classroom. They will be using a much wider range of materials than textbooks. It will take more teacher time to procure materials. It will require a new orientation to use of time.

Openness calls for an attitude on the part of the teacher which sees his role as that of a helper rather than a director. His function is to help the learner identify problems, develop interests, satisfy curiosities and seek solutions to problems. These problems cannot be the teacher's problems; they must be sincere concerns of students if openness is to be fostered. The teacher helps the learner delimit his area of study at one time, but he does not say to the pupil, "You are too young to try that"; or, "No, we cannot study that topic now for it will be a part of the work in the next grade." He will help the learner realize there is always more to be learned about a topic, still more to be explored. The "right time" to study a question is when interest and enthusiasm are high.

Teachers and administrators who value openness must also be able to tolerate ambiguity. They must be ready, willing and able to live with unsolved problems. It is often easier to adopt a wrong answer because it is more comfortable to have any answer than to have no answer. When we cannot take time to explore many solutions, when we feel uncomfortable without an answer, when there is more concern for "right" answers rather than "good" answers, we are expressing intolerance of ambiguity. Such intolerance leads to rigidity and defensiveness instead of openness.

Teachers who value openness are concerned with larger rather than narrower questions. They emphasize "big ideas," larger concepts, rather than details. This does not mean that learners do not seek specific information. They do use many sources to gather data, but the teacher helps them see new relationships and helps them formulate their own generalizations.

Individuality Is Valued

Openness and creativity are most likely to be promoted when teachers truly respect students. They view students as trustworthy persons capable of developing creativity. When one feels he is unworthy, his creativity is diminished. These papers emphasize the idea that one learns to trust himself because others trust him. We can become creative only if we learn to trust our own feelings, our own values and our own ways of self-expression. If children are to gain this trust in self, they must experience such trust from their teachers.

Teachers who view themselves and others in the process of becoming recognize the value of process rather than product. All experience becomes creative because each experience is part of the process of creating self. Emphasizing the value of process, these teachers plan fewer dramatic and musical "productions." More time is given to creative dramatics, music and dance in which more, rather than fewer, students experience the process of creative interpretation. There are more science projects in which pupils carry out experiments to learn what they want or need to know; there are fewer projects for competitive science fairs. Children need to be turned loose, rather than held down.

When the emphasis is upon process, children's stories or poems are not returned with unsightly blotches or red markings. If the product is to be shared with others, or if the writer wants help in expressing his ideas, individual help will be given by the teacher, or small groups will work together to evaluate and improve the form, style or vocabulary of the writing. Criticism is accepted and welcomed because there is an atmosphere of friendly interest in improvement. Children should have many opportunities for writing and developing skills of writing, but teacher marks and unsought criticism from teacher or peers may only serve to inhibit written expression of ideas and feelings.

The attitude of trust extends to trust of the senses and encourages openness to experience which emphasizes all the senses. Emphasis upon verbal learning from written and spoken words has led us away from awareness of our daily environment. Value will be placed upon feelings of the whole body. There would be more opportunities to touch, taste and smell, as well as see and hear. School experiences should sharpen the observer's awareness of his environment. Openness can be fostered by providing new experiences in using the senses. Tasting new and different foods and listening to oriental music are examples of ways teachers can extend experiences. The use of the body in expressing ideas has been far too limited in our schools. Dance, for example, which was once an important mode of expression, has been all but eliminated in our society. Freedom to create patterns of movement and to trust feelings expressed in movement can encourage creativity.

To develop creativity, the teacher also values spontaneity. The twist of a phrase to make a joke may bring a reprimand. It could also bring a smile of shared fun. If children are developing respect for others, there is little danger that someone will be hurt. A spontaneous interest which leads a group away from the main study for a time may open new doors. It is this element of spontaneity which so often seems missing in our book-oriented classrooms.

Valuing the uniqueness of each person is basic to release of creativity. Differences are accepted and welcomed. Informal statements express this attitude:

"We learned another way of solving the problem when you helped us see it differently."

"What different ways can you use the chalk on wet paper?"

"Your hunch may not be foolish. How can you test it?"

Children learn it is not threatening to be different when there is acceptance and opportunity to express differences.

The Teacher's Self

To facilitate creativity the teacher himself must be a person who is becoming more creative and open to experience. In a nonthreatening school atmosphere he feels trusted. He has experienced enough successes to feel adequate in meeting the daily challenges of teaching. He finds joy in the process of becoming. With a rich store of information and a keen curiosity about his world, he is continually seeking more knowledge and finding new ways of working with children. Such attitudes toward self make it possible for the teacher to try new approaches which free children to be creative. These teachers share with children their own sense experiences. They create with children—working with them instead of directing. They may paint while children paint, dance with them, share their own writing and evaluate their own products with the group. They take delight in new experiences and share these experiences with their students.

The teacher who fosters creativity helps the child establish his personal values. He disciplines his own values so they do not seem to be the only values permitted in the classroom. When there is mutual respect the child does not feel the teacher has no values. Rather, the student feels the teacher is allowing him to build his own values. The teacher helps the child discover values held by others in other times and societies. He helps the learner realize the way values influence behavior. The teacher communicates his own values by everything he does and these must be sufficiently well disciplined so that they are not imposed upon children and so restrict openness and searching.

Since the values people hold play so basic a part in their behavior, teacher education must become more concerned with the exploration of personal attitudes and values. Emphasis needs to be given more to the kind of person a teacher is becoming than to the specific techniques of teaching. This means that students cannot sit listening passively to lectures about teaching or read books to pass tests. They must be involved in discovering meanings for themselves as they identify their own problems and raise questions about the teaching-learning process. Emphasis upon "why" rather than "how" would make "methods" a problem solving experience in which students could learn how to use themselves most effectively in creating an environment for learning.

TEACHING FOR OPENNESS AND CREATIVITY

The Development of Needs

At one time the cultural heritage comprised the sum total of curriculum content. Mastery of the traditional academic subject matter was seen as the goal of education and to be informed in the various disciplines into which man's knowledge has been organized was to be fully and finally educated. There are watchdogs of education today who urge the return to "solid subject matter learning," who would legislate what ought to be taught at every grade level, and who equate skills and factual information with substantial knowledge. They overlook the fact, long apparent to responsible educators, that such learning is little more than indoctrination and that what one does with skills and information is dependent on factors other than the degree of mastery. In short, education is more than the acquisition of facts, and skills are merely means to the end; the development of effective, thinking, creative people demands more than a pouring in of information.

Recognizing that the function of education is something more than transmitting the cultural heritage, many schools have directed their efforts to analyzing the needs of pupils and planning a curriculum which would meet those needs. The satisfaction of the immediate and personal needs of students by itself, however, is not enough. Education is not serving its purpose in the development of adequate personalities if its only concern is for the specific felt needs of children and young people, whose perspective may be limited by their immaturity and inexperience. Teaching for openness and creativity calls for the development in the student of an ability to recognize needs he never knew he had. It rejects the either-or proposition of subject matter versus adjustment, of academic training versus the fulfillment of children's immediate goals. It transcends immediate need gratification and creates new goals for learning.

Teachers create goals as they help children to understand the meaning of and see the need for new learnings. The six-year-old who has been introduced to the wonderful excitement of stories and who has come to see books as the source of the particular information which he desires *needs* to learn to read. Children who are given responsibilities for student organizations *need* to find out the most effective procedures for self-government. Students introduced to the probabilities of space travel *need* the knowledge and the projection of scientific investigation. Readiness for new learning is taught. As children are faced with new problems and encouraged to interpret data, as they are given opportunities to explore the unknown and find their own meanings, their need for learning is expanded. Creativity, then, is the product of a curriculum which opens experiences to children, creates new needs to know, and provides them with the skills which enable them to put curiosity into action.

Basic Tools and Skills Are Needed

No one creates in a vacuum; theories are not developed from ignorance. New ideas are built upon old ones, and if creativity is to be encouraged, students need the basic tools and skills which make exploration and discovery possible. Recognizing that the traditional academic skills and subject matter are means and are not the ends in themselves does not deny their importance, for without them the individual is powerless to create. Children need facts to think with, ideas on which to feed, knowledge from which to generate new and fresh solutions. The idea is not to teach the same facts to all children or to make learning a process of fact memorizing and fact reciting. Rather, it is to help every child learn to find the facts that are important to his study, to be able to make full use of the vast storehouses of information available in the library, in the laboratory, in the museum and gallery, and in the words, works and minds of others. Teaching must build a solid respect for information, must enable pupils to think critically and to evaluate data available to them, to back up their opinions and their judgments with research. No worship of facts for facts' sake will do, for we know facts will change and information increase, but creativity hinges on ideas and, to become creative, children need to know.

The acquisition of tools and techniques is an important part of the curriculum, but the value of these learnings for the development of creativity demands that the approach be one of exploration and experimentation. Techniques should open the way to new experience rather than restrict children's thinking and behaving. For example, children need to know the techniques of applying paint to paper, but there is a difference between teaching these techniques and teaching children what to paint. They need to know how to read, not what to read; how to experiment, not what to try. The tools for inquiry are essential, but the freedom to inquire must be available if creativity is the goal.

Teaching for Maximal Progress

The organization of teaching—planning, grouping, selection of materials, and use of authority—influences the progress children make in becoming more open to experience. We know that creativity is likely to be greater when involvement is high and that students who feel a personal commitment to learning tend to be more productive and more creative in their work. One method teachers use to encourage such personal involvement is student participation in planning. As pupils have opportunities to state their purposes for a unit of study, block out plans for jobs to be done and evaluate their progress, their sense of self-direction and responsibility is increased.

As long as the teacher plans the work and directs each activity, it is the teacher who creates—it is his work—and pupils learn only to conform to his direction. It is the real and active involvement in planning which encourages creativity and allows children to experiment with new and different approaches. But such involvement must be *real.* By allowing children to plan only about things which do not matter to them, we run the risk of teaching them that democratic processes do not work. Pupil-teacher planning that is staged, that requires children to mouth meaningless ritual or to guess what plans the teacher has already decided, can negate the importance of planning and restrict creative thinking. The areas in which children may be given honest responsibility for planning are often limited by the requirements of the curriculum, by school policies and schedules, and by the teacher's own responsibility for common learnings. We do not ask young children, for example, to plan the balance of their learning activities or older students to decide course content and class schedules. There are laws about compulsory attendance and educational requirements that must be met. Certain limitations are necessary and should be recognized. Yet within the established limits for student involvement in planning, freedom to plan and to make choices, even though they may prove to be wrong choices, must be granted.

Grouping can also contribute to maximum involvement and maximum progress. Children can be lost in large-class instruction, can be insulated, by the very size of the group, from any feeling of belonging. The teacher who values creativity plans the kind of grouping that allows each child to learn at his most rapid pace and to make his unique contribution to the class. The variations of such groups are unlimited. Skill learnings in arithmetic, reading, spelling, handwriting and the like may be best achieved when children who currently have the same needs or are working at the same level are brought together for instruction. Grouping in these areas needs to be flexible and groups may be reorganized as learning rates vary, or groups may be dissolved as particular skills are achieved. Work in social studies and science may call for other groupings based on common problems to be solved, shared interests, or the use of resource materials. There are times when committees may need to carry out jobs for the class as a whole, when teams need to write and edit, when small groups want to come together for a listening or an art experience, or when individuals may choose to work independently. The size and the membership of various groups are determined by the purpose to be accomplished, and it is important that grouping arrangements be kept fluid and flexible. It is the fixed, static classification, the labeled class assignments which close children to their experience. Openness is fostered best as boys and girls have opportunities for involvement in the many kinds of groups which can contribute to their progress.

Secondary schools can extend the advantages of flexible grouping arrangements as they provide for the individual selection of courses. Instead of assigning students to rigid track programs or requiring them to select a single structured sequence of courses to be followed exclusively, many high schools offer individual programs for each student. With appropriate guidance a student is then able to select particular courses in accordance with his levels of achievement and ability, his interests and his educational and vocational goals. Program revisions can be made without penalty to the student. The program planning which is possible when required courses are kept at a minimum and the range of electives is increased fosters the interest exploration and the self-direction necessary for optimum progress.

Organization of Materials

Organization of materials also affects the development of creativity. Exclusive use of the stereotyped basal reader, the graded spelling book and arithmetic text, the single textbook in science and social studies, restricts children's perceptions. To learn openness, boys and girls need to have available a wide range of instructional materials—an accessible library, references by different authors representing different points of view, books within their range of reading ability that invite use and extend individual interests. Books of all kinds—books that challenge, that teach, that are ready sources of information and new ideas—but not books alone. Children also need access to materials which represent something other than verbal abstraction. They need pictures, maps and globes, projections, films and television, models and graphic representations. They learn, too, by listening to records, recordings, radio, television —the whole range of audio aids. Finally, to be creative, children need materials from which to create; materials that invite doing. Schools should provide laboratories and workshops, corners and resource rooms where things can be manipulated, ideas tested, creative expression encouraged. Materials which can be contained in pupils' desks or on teachers' shelves are not enough. The classroom needs to be extended into other space and into the community to give pupils the challenge of vivid and meaningful materials for learning.

Attitudes Toward Subject Matter

How subject matter is viewed determines its usefulness. Children should be helped to see the content of mathematics and science, of geography and government and the other social sciences as ways man has found to meet situations and solve his problems. The knowledge man has accumulated is an important source of information, but we are living in a changing world with a changing way of life. The new situations and new problems we face today and which we cannot predict tomorrow call for new ways of seeing and dealing with the world. Subject matter is too often used as a way of teaching people to look backward, to recite past performances, instead of as a medium for preparing students for future developments. Content then becomes sterile, even negative, if it inhibits new leads and new solutions. Education must deal with subject matter, not as an end in itself, but as a means of helping children to achieve the intelligent imagination and creativity necessary to find adequate answers to the world's increasingly complex problems.

Subject matter must also be completely open to students. There is no information a person ought not to have. It is necessary, therefore, to provide ways to help a child face the facts about the world in which he lives. Teachers do this to a much greater degree in the areas of science and mathematics when the approach is one of discovery rather than of history. Here children have opportunities to observe, to experiment, to test and prove their findings. Newer teaching methods in arithmetic and in the laboratory sciences encourage pupils to discover what is real, to measure and record, and to base conclusions on objective data. The scientific method has long been respected as the way to learn in the laboratory, and teachers who teach its use are helping children to face reality in the world of physical science.

But not all data can be calculated or discovered in the test tube. All values cannot be proved objectively. All problems of human relations and institutions do not have immediate solutions or single right answers. Children need to be helped to find ways to explore the social sciences, to obtain accurate and realistic information about the world of people, of government and social change, of cultures and human values. Here schools have done less well. We teach facts of citizenship and produce citizens who do not vote. We teach the history of a democracy and do not face with children the problems of democracy today. We teach the dignity of man and overlook the number of Americans who live as second class citizens. We teach the theory of international understanding and co-operation and censor facts about competing ideologies.

Structure of Learning Activities

Censorship is not appropriate in the classroom. All information should be open to children as they seek answers to problems which are real to them. There may be no right answers, but the data available to children must be accurate and realistic. Open ended questions, free discussions, the use of many and varied sources of information, opportunities to question established theories, to think critically and to challenge accepted beliefs—these are some of the ways teachers can help students to use content to produce new ideas. No longer can the single textbook approach, the censored sources or the limited and limiting use of facts suffice.

The structure of learning activities must leave room for children to grow. The strictly planned day, the page-by-page assignment, the kind of schedules which require frequent change of activity, leave no room for thoughtful discussions, no time to pursue important questions. Children require structure. They need help in setting purposes; they need teacher guidance in defining plans and learning for meaning. But this does not mean the persistent nagging of teacher-assigned things to do. It does not mean the tight structure of every assignment or the "read the chapter and answer the questions" kind of approach. Structure that ties up learning in neat packages, that answers questions finally, that marks "finished" the learning of any unit of study, does not facilitate teaching for openness. Learning may be narrowed or cut off entirely by the nature and number of requirements.

Instead, teachers who encourage creativity provide opportunities for the extension of learnings through broadly conceived and loosely structured activities. They open subject matter for children (as opposed to covering it) and encourage thinking beyond the facts as they use projective approaches, unsolved problems, and open ended questions. To ask children to trace the history of communication is one thing; to explore with them how communication affects culture is quite another. Listing the industries of Alaska is a paper-and-pencil exercise, but thinking is invited when the facts are presented—"Whaling was once a very important industry in Alaska. A change in man's social needs caused a decline in this industry." Children are challenged to go beyond—"What happens to people who are thus put out of a job? Should the government help these people?" It is the unsolved problem rather than the factual question and answer that encourages freedom of thought and children's respect for their own mental processes. It can help them to change concepts in the light of new evidence and to build a sense of personal responsibility for increasing knowledge and solving problems.

Opening Up New Experiences

More loosely structured activities also provide opportunities for children to make decisions. The attitudes we build toward learning are much influenced by open structures which help children to find self-direction for their own learning. With more opportunities for choice, we might have less compliance, less conforming, less dependence on teacher direction, less asking "what should I do now?" and more active involvement, more individual responsibility for learning for tomorrow. It is not easier teaching, but it is more purposeful learning that open structure invites.

The great current need for people who can generate new, fresh solutions demands that schools give attention to the development of inquiring minds. New experiences beyond routine subject matter and reading and writing exercises need to be opened for children. We want children to be critically perceptive of all of their environment, using the various senses other than seeing and hearing alone. They need to know the full range of sensory reactions—how things taste and smell and feel. Our almost exclusive orientation to the visual and auditory closes to children the rich experiences available when opportunities are provided to discover and appreciate new flavors and odors, new textures and touch. Children learn with all of their senses; such learning needs to be opened.

Children also learn as they encounter cultures different from their own. Too many schools are limited by the cultural confines of their own communities, and the learnings they provide for children reflect this restriction. Instead, we must provide experiences which introduce children to customs and traditions, religions and institutions different from their own. Part of such introduction can be vicarious learning as long as it is based in reality and not in the stereotyped or superficial folkways which characterize too many typical social studies units. But it is more than information that is needed; more than a factual study of other people and their ways of life that is required. New learnings in this area must include emotional as well as intellectual experiencing. Learning about people involves an empathy, a feeling with them, an acceptance of differences, and an appreciation of variability in values and behavior. This can best be achieved as children have opportunities for personal contact and interaction with other groups, as they visit at firsthand other communities, churches, schools and cultural centers.

Finally, creativity can be fostered as communication is opened up for children. The strong emphasis which the school places on language demands that teachers understand how children differ in language development and what environmental factors stimulate or limit its growth. Language learning is unique for each individual, and the influences of the family, the socioeconomic level and the subculture need to be taken into account as we test and teach and make judgments about children. The teacher, too, must be acutely aware of the language he uses and its influence on pupil behavior—how requests are made, directions given, criticism or acceptance implied by tone of voice or turn of phrase. To make language a more meaningful medium of communication, children must have many opportunities to talk with both adults and other children, to engage in discussions to clarify meanings, and to work through the misunderstandings which semantics and usage may create.

But language—the abstraction of verbal symbols—is not the only avenue of communication, and here again the school improves learning as it makes new media available. Children are encouraged to be creative as they are helped to experiment with other ways of expressing their own unique ideas. For some it may be painting or drawing, for others music or dance; it may be sculpturing or model building, pantomime or mathematical expression—each medium can convey personal meaning. Communication implies a two-way process, a reception as well as an expression of ideas, and response cannot be overlooked. To understand the meaning of creative work, to feel what the artist was feeling, to see the world through his senses, builds the child's awareness of the rich variety of communication media and invites their use.

Encouraging Experimental Attitudes

The release of creativity in the classroom does not occur by chance. It requires a careful restructuring of learning activities to encourage and support experimental attitudes. Experiences must be planned to extend children's ideas, to develop their skills of divergent thinking, and to stimulate the fluency of idea production. Brainstorming, "out in the blue" thinking, speculating "what would happen if" (if we had no language, if pills replaced food, if no one paid taxes, if—and children are quick to supply the conditions), are gimmicks, yes, but techniques, too, that help some children to break through the barrier of rigid question-and-answer thinking. The variations of such techniques are endless, limited only by the teacher's own creativity; for example, confronting children with pictures—"You tell the story"; with toys—"Make it better to play with"; with symbols—"You finish the picture"; with sentence tags—"You complete the idea"; with a safety pin or other everyday object—"Find how many ways this can be used"; with limericks—"You supply the punch line"; with unsolved problems and common tools that must be used in uncommon ways. These are games, wonderful fun for children, but they are opportunities, too, for teachers to identify and to encourage divergent, creative thinking and problem solving. Too often teachers have restricted children's curiosity and their play with ideas and have condemned the fantasies and the daydreams that may keep wondering alive.

A natural extension and development of children's fun with ideas is the attitude of trying and improvising, and this, too, must be fostered. It has been said that the genius of America is that it is a "nation of contrivers." This attitude of trying, contriving, improvising, should be encouraged and expanded in every direction. So many school activities are not creative in nature. Rote learning, factual recall, premature closure, pencil and paper tests—these and other modes of teaching need to be re-examined for their effect on openness.

The arts—music, painting, drama, dance—have long been considered areas for expression of self. Techniques are taught, but only when children see their need. There is room for individuality, for each child's unique creation out of his own experiencing and becoming. The arts are a vital part of a school program geared to teaching creativity, but creativity does not stop here. Too often we relegate the creative process to the art room, equating it only with self-expression. We overlook its usefulness in other subject areas. The creative process operates also in relation to the physical environment, and the whole range of science teaching can foster its growth. It is not encouraged by tracing the history of science or repeating workbook experiments or textbook assignments, although all of these may be necessary for the acquisition of basic skills and understandings. Rather, it is developed as students have opportunities to do their own investigating, to sense problems, to concentrate on possible solutions, to develop insights to be tested and elaborated. Science teaching must go beyond identification and classification if it is to produce the inventors and innovators our technological society requires.

Unsolved problems and questions of human values challenge creative thinking in the social sciences. Here, perhaps more than in any other area, openness and originality need to be emphasized. Children must be helped to learn how to learn about themselves and others, their cultures, their needs, their institutions, their efforts to build a better way of life. Learning the facts is not enough; "why" and "how" must be added to "what"; not right answers but best answers must be encouraged. The problems are real, and teaching efforts need to be directed to helping pupils understand those problems in all of their reality and to search for new and better solutions. Teaching of English or of the separate language arts can be expanded to a broader view of all of communication. Language is a living, changing process; it is not contained in formal grammar or spelling and handwriting exercises. Learning its use and its power can contribute to children's verbal fluency and originality, to their sensing ambiguities, to elaborating and building on ideas. Arithmetic, too, can be more than facts and aphorisms. Although one of the most sequential of all learnings, it can extend children's thinking to different number bases, to new approaches to problem solving, to a variety of solutions, to concepts, instead of facts, and to insights instead of rote learning.

ORGANIZATION OF THE SCHOOL FOR OPENNESS AND CREATIVITY

Teaching for creativity requires creative teaching. It calls for a facilitating environment and a restructuring of learning activities. It is not easy teaching, but makes new demands of every teacher and every resource. The price is high, but the development of adequate personalities who are creative and open to experience is the function of the school and the price must be met.

Schools are invariably organized with emphasis on either *the person* as a learner or on *the program* which must be slavishly followed. Some research that analyzed the roles of extension leaders indicated that leaders were either oriented predominantly toward the person or toward the program. Educational leaders, with their subsequent school organization, operate schools according to this basic orientation. For creativity, school organization must be focused on the learner because it is he who cradles within himself the creative potential. The program of the school must be "tailor-made" so as to release this potential. Kelley says this is not likely when the child as the learner must meet the "preconceived standards, grade levels, and all of the other paraphernalia of the adult-centered school."

Mechanical Factors Affect Openness and Creativity

The buildings, their type of construction, location and size are highly influential factors for openness which affect creativeness. Oftentimes schools, built for posterity, have been so substantial that future modification was impractical if not impossible. Flexible, movable, adjustable walls may add different dimensions to new ways of organizing classroom settings for creative learnings. This will facilitate all types of group work, but at the same time it should provide a place for the student "to get away from it all." This urgent need was reflected in a statement recently heard by a high school teacher when a student blurted out, "I am worn out with groups—I want to get somewhere to think and work on my own." Quiet "alone spots" are premiums in the school of today (and even in the community) where one can solo his work and thoughts, giving his own unique organization to experience.

School settings should make it possible for students to have what Maslow calls "peak" experiences. He further states that all of the peak experiences are (among other characteristics) integrative, combining observation, insight and feeling, and they are life-validating, that is, they make life worthwhile. The school plant and curriculum should be so organized as to facilitate creative experiences in children and youth, and the experiences should not be peripheral education, but should be the primary focus.

The School Can Be Extended for Creativeness

The schedule can be flexible, thus providing opportunity for children and youth to expand beyond the "two by four" teaching methods (within the two covers of the book and four walls of the classroom). Flexible scheduling makes it possible to extend the classroom so that the open environment becomes a living laboratory. In these new settings there are varied opportunities for extended learnings and creative leadership.

For example, an adventuresome elementary principal planned a three-day overnight outing for his sixth grade students with the purpose of extending the classroom to the out-of-doors. Their academic learnings took on new meaning as functional arithmetic was needed for time schedules, amounts of food and water; science came to life through creative discoveries as students were surrounded by and absorbed in nature study and the science of living things. This elementary school principal who had known these boys and girls from the first day of the first grade remarked, "One of the most significant things that happened was the leadership that emerged in this new environment. James had never shown any capacity as a leader, but he proved to be a natural on the nature trail. He was most adequate in this new situation and was respected in the new leadership role because of his knowledge of living science. Similarly a shy, timid girl emerged as a natural organizer and leader of the clean-up detail."

Modifications of the routine school pattern and extension of the school day have provided time and facilities for clubs and other interest groups of students who were intrinsically motivated. Time, facilities and encouragement should be provided students who wish to work together. Students who are attracted by mutual interest, students who are stimulating and challenging to each other, as well as the highly motivated, should be taken into account in the organization of the school day. However, on occasion, the interest and subsequent pursuit of a particular student may be of a solitary nature, and the school should take this into account. School leaders with flexible and open types of school organization, plus positive relationships with teachers and students, can be instrumental in facilitating creativeness. Marie Rasey summed it up when she said, "The creator creates and is himself created." [1]

[1] Marie I. Rasey. "Creativity and Its Psychological Implications." *Educational Leadership* 13: 288; February 1956.

CHAPTER 11

THE FEELING OF IDENTIFICATION

FROM KELLEY

Man is a social being built in relationship to others.

The fully functioning person thinks well of others and therefore sees his stake in others.

The life good to live depends on the quality of the people around the individual. His world needs to be populated by people whom he can view as facilitating.

The life good to live is a cooperative one. When the person is part of something (consulted and involved), then he becomes responsible.

FROM COMBS

The feeling of oneness with one's fellows produces in the truly adequate person a high degree of responsible, trustworthy behavior.

The truly adequate personality has the capacity for identification with his fellows. The feeling of identification seems to produce a deep sensitivity to the feelings and attitudes of others.

One learns to identify with others, depending upon the nature of his contacts with the important people in his life.

FROM ROGERS

When we are able to free the individual from his defensiveness, so that he is open to the wide range of his own needs, as well as the wide range of environmental and social demands, his reactions may be trusted to be positive, forward-looking, constructive . . . one of his deepest needs is for affiliation and communication with others.

When an individual is fully himself, he cannot help but be realistically socialized—sensitive to other individuals with whom he is in relationship.

FROM MASLOW

The need for love characterizes every human being that is born. No psychological health is possible unless the "inner nature" of the person is fundamentally accepted, loved and respected by others.

No ideally good relation to another human being, especially a child, is possible without "being-love"—especially it is necessary for teaching, along with the Taoistic, trusting attitude it implies.

THE IDEAS

There is agreement among our four invited authors that fully functioning people have a feeling of oneness with their fellow men and a conviction that all human beings are involved in man's destiny. They seem to be acutely aware that what happens to other people has an effect on what happens to them. This does not imply conformity or sameness, since adequate people have little fear of being their unique selves. Nor does it mean a "hail fellow well met" attitude. It means, rather, a sincere feeling of identification with other human beings and a strong desire to be useful, to contribute, to be responsible and to serve humankind. While some fully functioning people spend much of their time alone, their work nevertheless expresses a real concern for others.

Combs, Kelley, Maslow and Rogers are very much in agreement concerning the idea that adequate persons are responsible and trustworthy and that survival of our democratic society depends on an increasing number of responsible and trustworthy persons who have the capacity for identification with their fellow men. They recognize that we live in a tremendously interdependent and cooperative society which requires members who think well of each other, who trust each other and who see their stake in others.

The four authors perceive human beings as basically cooperative, constructive, forward-looking, trustworthy and responsible. They reject the pessimistic views of the nature of man which have plagued us for centuries. They find little justification for beliefs which imply that it is human nature for man to be belligerent, lazy and selfish. It is only the maladjusted and inadequate people who find it necessary to engage in such destructive behavior and to pit themselves against their fellow men. Fully functioning people trust others and are themselves trustworthy.

IMPLICATIONS FOR EDUCATION

These concepts have far reaching implications for educational thought and practice. Accepting children as responsible and trustworthy human beings from the very beginning of each new class is by no means a universal assumption. We are just beginning to realize what is really involved if we attempt to practice in the classroom the implications of these concepts.

First and foremost, schools must foster identification and help children to gain a realistic feeling of belonging. To do this a child needs to be surrounded by people whom he can view as facilitating, with whom he can develop satisfying relationships. Identification is learned from experience with others and the school should provide experiences which make this learning possible. Teachers must be experienced as friendly representatives of society. Classrooms themselves must be "good" societies on a small scale. The school must emphasize sharing and helping in an atmosphere of mutual trust where everyone can experience a feeling of oneness. When children are actively involved in the teaching-learning process and feel that they have a part in the functioning of the school, they become responsible—they become trustworthy. As Kelley suggests, children are not likely to sabotage something they consider to be their own.

Cooperation

The feeling of identification is most likely to be found in schools which foster cooperative rather than competitive experiences. Identification is learned from experiences which bring people together rather than set them apart. Hence, identification is more likely to be learned from cooperative rather than competitive relationships. Competitive experiences here refer primarily to competition among individuals such as competition for marks, prizes and the like. Such competition is essentially a destructive force in the development of a person's feeling of identification. Competition fosters movement against or away from other people and, in general, a mistrust of one's fellows. Cooperation, on the other hand, encourages trust and movement toward other people and the affiliation and communication with others necessary for identification.

This is not to imply that all competitive experiences are destructive. Competition between groups in a friendly atmosphere may very well foster cooperative behavior within groups. If such experiences in cooperation increase an individual's feeling of identification, then they can be of value. However, if cooperation within a group is achieved at the expense of hostility toward a much larger segment of mankind, even competition between groups needs to be questioned. For example, it is debatable if cooperative experiences on athletic teams in our highly competitive sports era are worth the cost. When "win at any cost" attitudes prevail, there is certainly little chance of participants' developing an increased feeling of identification outside their own membership. Believing that a feeling of identification is important for the development of fully functioning people, we need, therefore, to take a closer look at competition between groups as well as individuals and to determine whether we can afford the continued encouragement of such practices.

While there is competition in many facets of our society, it does not follow that we need to provide more of it in our schools. The mere fact of the existence of a practice in the larger society does not warrant its unquestioned inclusion in the curriculum. There is a serious question concerning the advisability of imposing competition on children in a classroom. A close look at the classroom will reveal that it is quite different from those normal societal situations where competition prevails. Men and women have many choices concerning the age and sex of associates, size of group, physical surroundings and area of specialization in which they compete with others. Even then, they are more likely to cooperate than compete. Much of the time they are not forced to compete with the same individuals with whom they cooperate. School children, on the other hand, do not have such choices. They are usually placed in one room with one teacher for at least one year, surrounded by people of the same age, half of whom are the opposite sex, and are expected to work and play in the same general academic and activity areas. Competition under these circumstances is not at all like that of adults. Furthermore, if competition is imposed on all the children in a typical elementary school classroom, a child is placed in the difficult position of competing and cooperating with the same classmates. Such an atmosphere stands little chance of fostering identification.

Not only do we need to know where competition serves a useful purpose and where it does not, but we need to know its limitations. There are many half-truths about the value of competition which do not become whole-truths when competition is increased. Little do we realize the high cost we pay in human discouragement as a result of the many losers and few winners in competitive classrooms.

We cannot afford this loss if we hope to maintain and enhance our democratic way of life. Combs [1] states three misconceptions concerning competition which are representative of our many false beliefs in this vital area and suggests facts based on what we know about human behavior and the society in which we live:

Myth: We live in a competitive society.
Fact: We live in the most cooperative, interdependent society the world has ever known.

Myth: Competition is a powerful motivating force.
Fact: Only those compete who think they have a chance of winning. The rest ignore the competition.

Myth: Competition is a useful device for controlling and improving quality.
Fact: Competition is inefficient and outmoded as a means for quality production.

Rather than attempt to make competition, which seems to work for a few, work for all and attempt to convince all people that sportsmanship and fair play are the highest of all virtues, let us, instead, consider limiting competition to games where winners and losers can relate as dignified

[1] Arthur W. Combs. "The Myth of Competition." *Childhood Education* 33: 364-69; February 1957.

and worthy human beings with no loss or gain of status. Let us avoid the use of competition as a panacea. Instead, let us encourage the broader use of cooperation from which much greater degrees of identification are likely to result.

Perhaps we should emphasize again that cooperation does not mean blind obedience or conformity, but rather an active, responsible type of behavior in which there is little fear of saying "no," being different or making mistakes. There is a difference between being cooperative and being obedient; between being responsible and following directions; and between being trustworthy and being neat, nice and courteous. The essential difference lies in the distinction between *active* behavior and *passive* behavior.

Identification and Activity

The feeling of identification is a consequence of interaction. It grows out of experiences in human interrelationships. Such relationships are hindered in classrooms where activity is frowned upon and passivity rewarded. To foster identification we need more schools and more classrooms with a climate which encourages active-constructive behavior.

Almost without exception teachers and administrators today say that they prefer people who are active and constructive in their behavior. An informal expression of opinion concerning the ideal student, obtained by one of the members of the Yearbook Committee during the past 10 years, tends to verify this.

He found, for example, that teachers and administrators *say* they prefer "active-constructive" people. Upon further analysis, however, it became apparent that the basic preference of teachers as they actually work with the children in classrooms was "constructiveness." Administrators, too, preferred constructiveness in teachers. Thus, constructiveness was prized more than activity. This sounds fine at first glance, but the meaning these teachers and administrators assigned to constructiveness was more like *good, obedient* and *courteous!* Even though teachers expressed an intellectual preference for active-constructive children in the classroom, they really wanted passive children. Active-constructive children apparently make too many mistakes for teachers who give top priority to "goodness." Thus, in practice, many teachers and administrators encourage passive rather than active behavior. This is not conducive to the development of fully functioning people, to the kind of interaction required for developing strong feelings of identification.

A similar paradox exists in regard to discipline. Teachers prefer both well behaved and well adjusted children. But the things teachers need to do to produce adequate people, such as freeing and trusting, are directly contrary to what is usually thought necessary for discipline, such as control and coercion. Unfortunately, many teachers have not yet found the courage to relax their control. As a consequence many settle for well behaved children, a condition that can be quickly and certainly produced, rather than well adjusted ones, who require greater freedom and longer time to develop.

Teachers who have an understanding of responsible and trustworthy behavior, as exemplified in fully functioning people, would make different choices. They would choose active rather than passive students, knowing that it is only out of active interaction with the world that the self can grow and develop. Destructive behavior would be viewed by such teachers as a mistake or as a result of misconceptions, both of which can provide the stimulation for valuable learning experiences. Out of active participation and active cooperation with no fear of "bad" behavior comes responsible, trustworthy behavior. In other words, in order to encourage a large percentage of active-constructive learners, teachers must find the courage to accept upheaval. They must learn to live with some chaos without being threatened. If they want active and creative people, they must be prepared for some confusion and problems. This seems to be difficult for teachers who set "good" behavior as the primary and absolute goal for children. Perhaps this is one of the first changes needed in the attitudes of teachers in order for the school to contribute significantly to the development of fully functioning people.

Elimination of Segregation

Another destructive force in the fostering of identification is segregation. When children are segregated by race, religion, sex, intellectual ability, socioeconomic status, or even age, they are deprived of the opportunity of learning to identify with all of mankind. When children learn through experiencing segregation that large segments of mankind are inferior or superior as human beings, it is difficult for them to acquire a feeling of oneness with their fellow men. It is important that teachers provide children with opportunities for interaction with people who are different, in an atmosphere where difference is valued rather than feared. Children can then learn to relate to a wider segment of mankind and to increase their faith in people who appear different from themselves.

We need to take a close look at the structure of classrooms today and to assess realistically our segregation practices. While segregation because of race and skin color is a disgrace internationally and certainly a serious threat to the fostering of identification, it is by no means the only way in which we practice segregation. Many children spend their entire school day year after year with people of the same religion, sex and socioeconomic status. They are thus cut off from the experiences with people who are different. In addition, many of these same children grow up in the narrow culture of a suburb or a tenement area. We need to ask the question, "Can we afford such restricted experiences in our struggle for a truly working democracy as well as for world survival?" Education in the future will have to come to grips with this problem.

While other practices of segregation are more subtle and often overlooked, they are nevertheless threats to effective identification. One example is the time honored practice of placing children of approximately the same age in each grade of our almost universal graded system. Children no longer have the opportunities they once had in our "country" schools to relate effectively with children of different ages. The revived interest in the ungraded school and classroom may result in a wider range in our classrooms of the future. The day may come when we will structure each classroom in an elementary school like an old-fashioned "country" school and thus assure children of experiences with many different age groups. Whether we eventually choose to make such changes must remain to be seen. At this point we can at least question the advisability of forcing children to spend as many hours per day with the same age group as they do at the present time.

Another example of subtle segregation is the practice of placing children with similar I.Q. scores in the same group. Ability grouping, as it is usually called, is experiencing once again a wave of popularity. From reading groups in first grade to classes for gifted students in the high school, some students are segregated according to ability and achievement. We shall not stop here to argue the merits of such grouping for facilitating learning. There is the possibility, however, that ability grouping may limit a child's experience in learning to identify with many types of people. To the extent that an assignment to an ability group pegs a child as to ability and status, it tends to reinforce feelings of either inferiority or superiority, neither of which is conducive to the development of fully functioning people.

In an even more indirect way, there is the possibility that ability grouping encourages and reinforces the very practices which make it difficult for children to become more active, responsible and trustworthy. At a time when teachers need to develop more understanding and respect for uniqueness and individual differences, homogeneous grouping tends to convince them that all the children in a given class are pretty much alike. Since all the children in a homogeneous group are often assumed to have approximately the same ability, it makes sense, for example, to teach them the same subject matter at the same time and in the same way, to give each child the same set of examinations, and to give marks based on the bell-shaped curve. A low mark merely means that a child is not working to capacity and that he must be misbehaving, wasting his time or just loafing. Ability grouping thus tends to sanction mass teaching and the competitive marking system and prevents teachers from learning more about individualized instruction and self-evaluation. Individual learning and evaluation help children to find the courage to become their fully functioning selves.

CONCEPTS OF THE ADEQUATE PERSON CORROBORATED IN CURRENT PRACTICES

Practices which provide students with the opportunity to be involved as active participants tend to foster identification and contribute to the development of responsible and trustworthy people. Practices which help students to feel that their ideas and actions really count and that they truly belong make possible feelings of identification and the development of more fully functioning people.

The following three practices are illustrative of those in a few schools today which the concepts in this yearbook corroborate: (a) self-government; (b) planning, subsequent implementation and self-evaluation; and (c) encouragement.

Self-Government

Student governments or student councils provide one of the richest opportunities for the development of a feeling of identification and experience in being active, responsible and trustworthy. If the school is very small, every student can participate in every meeting as every member of a family can participate in a family council. A. S. Neill [2] gives a vivid description of self-government in his coeducational private school, Summerhill, with an enrollment of 45 students. Usually, however, with larger schools such grass roots participation must take place in homerooms or other classroom groups and a representative student council is required for student government of the total school.

While a student council is a necessary and important part of student government and a rich experience for those who participate, the most valuable experiences in over-all participation take place at the homeroom or classroom level. Here, all students can participate as equals, with every person, including the teacher, entitled to one vote. The chairmanship can rotate so that every child has this experience. In the classroom, matters concerning everyday relationships can be discussed. Rules and regulations, if necessary, can be formulated. Regular meetings rather than emergency meetings can be planned so that participants experience living out the consequences of their decisions whether the decisions were

[2] Alexander S. Neill. *Summerhill; A Radical Approach to Child Rearing.* New York: Hart Publishing Co., 1960. 392 p.

mistakes or not. When people are aware that they are involved in making decisions which really matter and that they are trusted to vote intelligently, they become more and more active, cooperative and responsible.

It is important to point out here that identification is learned from participation in *real* experiences. Valuable as student governments can be in giving students feelings of belonging and identification, such learnings can easily be destroyed by fearful teachers and administrators who attempt subtly, or not so subtly, to manipulate and control decisions or resort too often to the veto. Under such circumstances, students may come to the conclusion that their student government is not a real thing but a game. If it is a game, who shall blame the students if they treat it so?

Many faculties also have effective self-governments. Small faculties usually make important decisions as a total group, whereas large faculties rely heavily on a faculty council consisting of representatives from teaching and administration. Although the structure is important, the vital key to successful self-government is how participants relate to one another. Members must feel that they can participate both as equal human beings and as their unique selves. It is crucial that there be a total faculty atmosphere of mutual trust in which members can really trust their representatives on a faculty council. Administrators need to trust teacher groups to make decisions. Faculty involvement in making important decisions not only helps teachers to feel more important and more responsible but also makes education itself appear more worthwhile. Faculty involvement consistently seems to enrich the quality of interpersonal relationships which in turn seems to improve the effectiveness of self-government.

Planning, Implementation, Evaluation

Teacher-pupil planning is similar to student government, but it is confined primarily to the teaching-learning process in the classroom and is often more individualized. Obviously this does not refer to the teacher manipulated planning in which the teacher waits for his own ideas to come from the students. It is important that teacher-pupil planning be sincere and that it take place among persons of mutual dignity and integrity. Within the limitations set by state laws and school rules, students need to feel that their ideas will count or teacher-pupil planning becomes a sham. Any attempt by the teacher to guide with a capital "G" or coerce, however nicely or sweetly, is almost sure to sabotage teacher-pupil planning. Students are keen observers and are experts at spotting pseudo democracy.

In much the same manner, administrator-teacher planning must be a truly creative and cooperative effort in which each person is important and in which an individual's ideas really make a difference. Administrator-teacher planning merely for the sake of "rubber-stamping," while making a pretense at democratic planning, is a farce. Teachers are usually interested in serving on planning committees but, if, for example, limits of decisions are not clarified or if decisions in question are already decided by budget, teachers resent, and rightfully so, being involved. Only involvement in planning in which participants have a part in decisions, in which their judgment adds to the quality of decisions, and in which they see the decision put to use results in increased feelings of identification.

Perhaps the most important aspect of the total process of teacher-pupil planning and the teaching-learning process is self-evaluation. Self-evaluation both completes and begins the cycle of learning—planning, work and evaluation. Whether it is an individual or a group project, evaluation gives a student a feeling that he is involved and, of course, leads to better and better planning and work.

Many teachers have learned that one of the great harms we do to children is to take away from them opportunity to participate in evaluative procedures. Failure to involve a person in evaluation robs him of much of the excitement of learning. Responsibility for learning can only be learned by *being given* responsibility—not by having all, or even part of it, taken away. In classrooms where children are learning responsibility effectively, teachers attempt never to do for a child what he can do for himself.

In a similar way, parents as well as teachers are becoming more effective in their parent-child-teacher-school relationships. Many teachers invite children to take part in parent-child-teacher conferences and thus involve the child as a responsible participant. Parents are learning, also, not to do for a child what he can do for himself. Unless it is literally a matter of life or death, parents are learning not to rob children of the valuable experience of establishing their own relationships with teachers and schools. If homework or discipline problems arise between a child and his teacher, for example, such parents encourage the child to evaluate, plan and work out his own solutions. Children learn responsibility by being provided with opportunities to assume it. When a child knows that he is assuming some worthwhile responsibilities and thus feels responsible, he develops a strong feeling of belongingness and identification.

Adequate persons, we have seen, are responsible and trustworthy. Such patterns of behavior, however, are not learned through being treated as irresponsible or untrustworthy. Responsibility can only be learned from involvement, from being given a chance to try one's wings. Giving children responsibilities, of course, runs the risk that they may make mistakes. These mistakes, furthermore, may even be annoying, embarrassing or, worse still, expensive to adults, so that there is a great temptation to withhold responsibility. This can often be rationalized by assuring ourselves that we are not really robbing the child of an opportunity to learn an important lesson—"We are only waiting until he is older and more mature." Unfortunately, protecting children from making mistakes only prolongs their dependence and makes the assumption of responsibility even more difficult. If through our own irrational fear of mistakes we rob children of their opportunities to learn responsibility, we have no one to blame but ourselves if later they behave irresponsibly or feel no identification with values we hold dear.

Encouragement

Nothing is more encouraging to a student than the feeling that adults really trust him. Such encouragement helps to create the feeling that one is a trustworthy person, and fosters basic feelings of self-respect, on the one hand, and identification with one's fellows, on the other. Some teachers trust every child from the very beginning of their relationship and students are able to sense it. Such teachers accept a child fully as he is, regardless of his behavior or his intelligence, and concentrate on what he can do rather than what he cannot do. This is a most powerful means of inviting trust from students and attaining mutual trust. This does not mean that a teacher should be a doormat or a naïve fool, but it does mean the teacher must have infinite patience while suspicious students wait to see if the trust is genuine. The result is worth the effort, however. We certainly cannot hope to develop more trustworthy people if we do not surround them with people who trust them.

Freedom is equally encouraging. A child is quick to perceive the subtle difference between an ultimatum and a choice, even when only between two things. When one has a choice, he is free to say "no" as well as "yes." The freedom to say "no" without loss of status prevails in few of our classrooms today. Such freedom seems to be on the increase, however, as more and more teachers are learning the value of freedom and acceptance. When children can comfortably say "no" to a teacher, one can guess that there is a relationship of mutual respect as human beings. This is a must before students can accept freedom without fear. Only in a free atmosphere, with mutual trust for each other, can students learn to be active, responsible and trustworthy.

As mentioned earlier in this chapter, the imposition of competition (especially the marking system), segregation, and the rewarding of passive behavior are practices to be questioned. These practices foster passiveness, irresponsibility and mistrust, even hate and fear. They are destructive forces working against the development of a feeling of identification.

Practices which rely on methods of discouragement rather than encouragement are to be questioned also. Methods of discouragement, for the most part, are based on fear, coercion, bribes, force, pressure, punishment and, in general, personal imposition of teacher authority. Perhaps the most discouraging of all is autocracy hidden behind niceness, kindness, patience and even "understanding." Erich Fromm [3] has referred to this as "anonymous authority." This anonymous type of control can be very misleading. On the surface it usually appears that discipline and learning are improved. What really happens, though, is that the superior-inferior relationship basic to autocracy is subtly reinforced and the subordinates (students) have even less desire to be active and responsible. Students may be more obedient and conforming but not more fully functioning. Such an atmosphere is not encouraging and does not develop an increased feeling of mutual trust or identification.

Almost all methods of discouragement are based on misconceptions concerning the nature of man, such as the belief that man is basically lazy and bad. Unfortunately, many teachers today still believe that students will not learn anything unless they are forced to do so and that one must let the students know who is boss or there will be no work or order. These assumptions make it extremely difficult for many teachers to trust students. There are still teachers who believe that "familiarity breeds contempt" and are, literally, afraid to be friendly with students. These almost universal methods of discouragement are certainly to be questioned if we hope to develop responsible and trustworthy people with a strong feeling of identification.

NEW PRACTICES SUGGESTED BY THESE CONCEPTS OF THE FULLY FUNCTIONING PERSON

It is difficult to suggest practices which are entirely new since there have been teachers and administrators at all levels of education who have practiced one or more of these concepts from time to time in the history of education in the United States. We are reminded of teachers like Caroline Pratt [4] and Hughes Mearns [5] who trusted children enough to give them tremendous freedom. They found that children assumed responsibility to work under these conditions. Teachers, in many of our

[3] Erich Fromm. *Escape from Freedom.* Toronto: Oxford University Press, 1941. 305 p.

[4] Caroline Pratt. *I Learn from Children; An Adventure in Progressive Education.* New York: Simon and Schuster, 1948. 204 p.

[5] Hughes Mearns. *Creative Power; The Education of Youth in the Creative Arts.* Revised edition. New York: Dover Publications, 1959. 272 p.

experimental laboratory schools, involve students as active participants and trust children by giving them many choices such as embodied in the principle of self-selection introduced 30 years ago by Willard Olson.[6] The trust, freedom and acceptance in Marie Rasey's [7] college class, described in *This Is Teaching*, and in Nathaniel Cantor's [8] graduate class, described in *The Teaching←→Learning Process*, illustrate well the practice of many of these concepts.

There have been and are many presidents, superintendents, supervisors and principals who have practiced these concepts in administration and supervision. Suffice it to say, however, that it is not easy to practice these concepts in large, unwieldy systems organized vertically from top to bottom where competition for higher status and salary overshadows any desire for cooperation. Our best examples are usually found in small schools or small units of large systems. One admires Goddard College for stating in its catalog that students are *not* marked. The freedom described in *Summerhill* [9] seems to prevail throughout the entire school organization. Unfortunately, relatively few educational systems have developed to the point at which student marking systems and teacher rating plans have been eliminated.

Horizontal Versus Vertical Organization

Generally speaking, we must find a way to organize schools and classrooms horizontally rather than vertically. That is to say, classroom and school atmospheres need to be created in which human beings relate to each other on a horizontal plane rather than a vertical scale. In a horizontal organizational structure, people learn to be useful as unique and different individuals and yet relate as equal human beings. In a vertical organizational structure, difference is used to determine status and people relate as superior and inferior human beings. A horizontal organizational structure seems more likely to encourage active, responsible and trustworthy behavior. Since almost all participants in a vertical organizational structure are subordinates, such an atmosphere actually promotes passive and irresponsible behavior. We need to learn to create an atmosphere of freedom without license—in which people are free to be themselves and

[6] Willard Olson. *Child Development*. Second edition. Boston: D. C. Heath and Co., 1960. 497 p.

[7] Marie Rasey. *This Is Teaching*. New York: Harper & Brothers, 1950. 217 p.

[8] Nathaniel Cantor. *The Teaching←→Learning Process*. New York: Dryden Press, 1953. 350 p.

[9] Alexander S. Neill, *op. cit.*

in which they have a feeling of identification with others who are free to be their unique selves.

It is vital for us to recognize that the traditional methods no longer work. Even though we are still in a period of transition from autocratic to democratic relationships, there is no turning back. For any one person there is no gradual transition from the old to the new. The break has to be clean. Pessimistic views concerning the nature of man and methods of discouragement have to be discarded. One has to enter *wholeheartedly* into a cooperative adventure with those involved. Mistakes will be made and new problems, often more complicated than before, will emerge. We must learn to view these new problem situations not as catastrophes, but rather as valuable learning experiences which would not have been possible if the mistakes had not been made in the first place.

To be more specific, administrators and supervisors need to provide teachers with more freedom to work. Staff members, too, need to feel identification and involvement. All members of the staff need to feel that they are acceptable as they are, that they are trusted and that they can be themselves. Channels of communication need to be open. Staff members should be involved, not just placed on committees. Regular faculty meetings in which members are active participants are often sufficient. People will feel involved if, when given responsibility, they are trusted and given freedom to be responsible. Cooperation should be encouraged, but not as a way of competing for top rating. Each teacher should be encouraged to evaluate himself and his teaching and to become more fully functioning in his own unique way.

In the classroom, teachers need to provide students with freedom to work. Anything which chips away at a student's freedom to learn should be eliminated. Teacher-pupil and individual planning with many choices should replace typical assignments. Self-evaluation should replace teacher imposed evaluation. Teachers must learn the "art of encouragement" as they trust and invite students to accept freedom and responsibility to work.

The important thing is not the specific method used but rather the way people relate and feel toward one another in the classroom. If the teacher, through sincere trust and acceptance of each student as he is, can develop a relationship of mutual trust and respect for the student as a human being, specific methods are of little consequence. This is not to say that one teaching method is not more effective than another in specific classroom learning situations, but rather that, for the purpose of creating a feeling of identification and of encouraging students to become more responsible, it is how people relate which is crucial. For example, one could argue that the discussion method is far superior to the lecture method, but students can be manipulated as inferiors, even though in an indirect way, in a discussion situation as well as in a lecture situation. In the same manner, a teacher can lecture as well as conduct a discussion without imposition of personal authority. While his unique role may be talking and the students' role listening, they can still relate as equals. It is the relationship which encourages students to become active, responsible and trustworthy, rather than the specific method of teaching.

Involving the Teen-Age Group

Perhaps an even greater challenge than the improvement of human relationships in the classroom is improvement of the over-all relationship between teen-agers and adults in our society. It takes an ingenious parent today, for example, to find ways to involve teen-agers as truly responsible people without recourse to coercion, power and argument. In fact, the opinion expressed by some experts that adults are at war with teen-agers depicts only too well our failure to come to grips with this problem. The reference to the idle young adult group from 16 to 21 years of age as the displaced persons of the United States is a serious indictment of our whole society.

While the community and the church can do much to involve young teen-agers as responsible human beings, the school and the home still play the major role. Teachers and parents need to create more ways of increasing the feeling of identification young teen-agers have in our society. Many of our youth have learned only too well that they do not belong in our society. First and foremost, warfare existing between adults and teen-agers must come to a halt. If adults want peaceful relations with teen-agers, then adults must take steps toward establishing a truce. They need to begin by accepting young people as they are. Communication must be reopened, but this cannot even begin so long as adults regard teen-agers as unworthy of respect or as fair game for humiliation and belittling. Most of us probably talk too much. Even grownups do not listen to people who treat them as unimportant, inferior beings.

If teachers and parents desire trustworthy youngsters, they will have to go all the way in trusting their teen-agers. People learn to perceive themselves as trustworthy by *experiencing* being trusted. If adults desire responsible youngsters, they will have to be more ingenious in involving teen-agers as active participants, knowing that people who are involved learn responsibility and become more responsible. Some parents have found a family council a realistic and helpful means of involving children as active participants in the family. Obviously, parents would have to accept children as trustworthy to begin with or they would not have any faith in a family council. Although family councils vary considerably, the basic ideas of rotating the chairmanship, of each member's having an equal vote, and of regular meetings seem especially important. Agreement concerning planning and the sharing of responsible tasks essential to effective functioning of the family is usually determined in the family council. Emergency meetings are frowned upon because it is felt that members should have a set period of time to experience and evaluate the consequences of their decisions and their involvement in assuming responsibilities. While a family council is only one of many ways of involving children, it does serve to illustrate how parents can give children more experience in active, responsible and trustworthy behavior.

Helping Youth Feel Identified with Society

Involving the young adult group from 16 to 21 years of age and helping them to perceive themselves as important and useful human beings in our society is a particularly difficult task. Meeting this challenge will take all the ingenuity and energy we can muster. It will require a total community approach involving schools, homes, churches, business, industry and every other responsible segment of our communities. At the outset, we must come to grips with the problem of economic exploitation of our young adults. It is equally urgent that we find ways for more young adults to satisfy their normal intellectual, physical and social needs.

For the young adults who continue their schooling in high school and college, the problem is somewhat alleviated. This is particularly true if they have no economic worries. A few students manage to develop a feeling of importance and identification as a result of outstanding academic work or participation in extracurricular activities such as athletics, but the opportunities are extremely limited in most high schools and colleges. Both teachers and administrators need to create new ways of assisting students to develop a greater feeling of identification. More needs to be done *with* students rather than *to* students. On the assumption that all courses in a given high school or college are worthwhile, students should be given many choices. If, in addition, teachers provide students with many choices in the classroom, students will be involved at least to this extent and thus become more active and responsible.

Based on the assumption that post-high school education is the most hopeful way at present to provide young adults with a sense of importance and a feeling of identification, it follows that the opportunity should be available for all our youth to continue their education full-time. Thirteenth and fourteenth year programs, junior colleges, technical institutes and business schools, as well as colleges and universities, should be readily available for interested youth. The assumption that a large percentage of our young adults cannot profit from higher education and that, therefore, admissions standards should be very restrictive is certainly open to question when one considers the contribution higher education can make to the feeling of identification of all youth who sincerely desire it. From this point of view, it would be hoped that more institutions of higher learning would move toward a full-time year-round program designed to serve a wide range and maximum number of students.

Every effort should be made to eliminate economic barriers to higher education. Any extension of free-tuition education is a sound investment. The relatively low wages paid to students who need to work their way through college is certainly to be questioned. The increase in both public and private loan funds for college students, however, is very encouraging. Many students are beginning to have a relatively free choice between mortgaging their future and attempting to work and pay-as-you-go. As we begin to see education as a social investment as well as an economic investment and show our faith in young adults by investing generously in their future, they in turn may see themselves as more important members of the human race and as more responsible risks for the future.

Unfortunately for the young adults who drop out of high school or never continue education beyond high school graduation, the problem of identification is much more difficult. With many of our unskilled adult workers unemployed, there is little chance for a young man to find employment. It is almost economically impossible for him to marry and lead a normal family life. A young woman often has better opportunities for employment or marriage or both. Even at that, it is not always easy for a young woman, or for most women for that matter, to feel important, to develop a strong feeling of identification in our so-called "man's world." We still need to be more accepting of women as equal human beings, as well as more accepting of children, adolescents and young adults as equal human beings. Furthermore, we could be much more creative in helping women to feel more important as mothers and housewives. There certainly is not a more responsible and trustworthy role in our society than that of rearing our children and youth. A young mother should have a strong feeling of identification with humankind.

We must meet these challenges if the young people of today are to become active, responsible and trustworthy citizens of tomorrow. We must resist losing faith in our youth and cracking down on their freedom. Instead, it is necessary to trust them, support them, encourage them to venture, and accept them as they are. We cannot afford to have anything short of fully functioning youth as well as adults. Only when both sexes, all ages, all races, and people from all walks of life have a stronger feeling of identification with all of humankind will we be well on our way to helping people become their fully functioning selves.

CHAPTER 12

THE ADEQUATE PERSON IS WELL INFORMED

FROM COMBS

The truly adequate person must be well informed. One must certainly have a field of perceptions, rich and extensive enough to provide understanding of the events in which he is enmeshed and available when he needs them.

Rich and extensive perceptual fields are a product of the kinds of opportunities an individual has been exposed to. . . . Mere exposure to an event is no guarantee that the event will be perceived by the individual or be available on later occasions.

An adequate person seems to have many more such personal meanings.

More than confrontation with events is necessary to insure inclusion of perceptions in the field and their availability on later occasions. This availability seems dependent upon at least two factors: (a) the individual's discovery of personal meaning and (b) the satisfaction of need.

FROM KELLEY

We choose that which the self feeds upon. The direction of the growth of the self depends upon those choices. We cannot see that which we have no experience to see. The psychological self feeds on ideas, which come from other people. Without the stuff of growth, the self becomes less adequate, and the whole person loses its ability to do, to venture, to create. The fully functioning personality thinks well of himself.

FROM ROGERS

The hypothetical person who is fully open to his experience would have access to all of the available data in the situation, on which to base his behavior; the social demand, his own complex and possibly conflicting needs, his memories of similar situations, his perception of the uniqueness of this situation, etc. All of the available data would be used, and it would be presented in accurate rather than distorted form.

FROM MASLOW

To make growth and self-actualization possible, it is necessary to understand that capacities, organs and organ systems press to function and express themselves and to be used and exercised, and that such use is satisfying, and disuse irritating.

Capacities clamor to be used, and cease their clamor only when they are well used. That is, capacities are also needs. Not only is it fun to use our capacities, but it is also necessary.

What we call "knowledge" (which is usually highly abstract and verbal and sharply defined) often serves to blind us to those portions of reality not covered by the abstraction. That is, it makes us more able to see some things, but less able to see other things. Science and education, being too exclusively abstract, verbal and bookish, do not have enough place for raw, concrete, esthetic experience, especially of the subjective happenings inside oneself.

THE IDEAS

The four invited papers present us with three major concepts of tremendous significance to education. We might state them as follows:

1. Learning is a function of the exploration and discovery of personal meanings.
2. Adequate persons are well informed.
3. What produces greater adequacy also facilitates learning.

LEARNING: THE DISCOVERY OF PERSONAL MEANING

Combs gives more emphasis to the informed character of the adequate person than do the other writers. He points out the increasing necessity for abstract and technical knowledge in order to act successfully in the modern world. This knowledge, however, must be of a very personal kind. It is not enough to possess simply a store of information. The need for extensive and available information will require *both* exposure to ideas and opportunity to explore and discover personal meaning. Learning is a process of discovering personal meaning; it is more than the acquisition of facts.

In another ASCD publication, Combs [1] has pointed out the importance of this very personal view of learning. There is a wide difference, he says, between knowing and behaving. Learning, if it is to be effective, must produce some change in the behavior of the learner. To accomplish this there must be more than the mere accumulation of facts; there also must be a sufficient discovery of personal meaning of these facts so that the individual will act on his information when the appropriate time and place occur.

[1] Arthur W. Combs. "Personality Theory and Its Implications for Curriculum Development." In: *Learning More About Learning*. Washington, D.C.: Association for Supervision and Curriculum Development, a department of the National Education Association, 1960. p. 5-20.

Learning, in the eyes of our invited authors, is a process of increasing the scope of available personal meanings, increasing sophistication in ways of perceiving so that new experiences are seen for what they are and incorporated into the perceptual field. This view is strikingly similar to Dewey's doctrine of reconstruction of experience. New experiences are not simply accumulated, added on, appended, attached; they are integrated into one's total experience to result in a new structure. What is added by our four authors is the recognition of the part played by perception and the emphasis placed upon perception at the immediate moment in the life and behavior of the individual. The job of the school is to work with present perceptions, with feelings, attitudes and ideas of learners so that they grow in the direction of greater adequacy.

Learning and the Self

Our authors imply that learning is affected by a positive view of self, by openness to experience, by identification with others, by the student's goals and values and the process of becoming in which he is engaged. They speak, too, of personal feelings, beliefs, attitudes and of student's *meanings* about facts. These are not the factors influencing learning which most of us learned in our college days. We are not accustomed to looking at the problem of learning in such terms. Yet, if our invited authors are correct, these factors have inescapable effects upon the learning that goes on in our classrooms and hence upon our success as teachers. We may ignore them if we wish, but we do so at our peril. The factors which affect learning go right on affecting learning, whether we pay attention to them or not. To ignore them is simply to make our own success or failure an accident rather than a controlled and predictable event.

This view implies that learning is individual and personal, that things are learned only in the degree to which the learner discovers the unique meaning of things to his particular self.

This has far reaching implications for an educational system formed to deal with all the children of all the people. It raises interesting questions about mass methods of teaching, about rigid organization, about attempts to teach the "average" child. How does one produce individual learning in a mass enterprise?

What do these concepts mean for our time honored beliefs about the value of "being objective"? These authors tell us that learning is deeply personal, involving matters of feeling, attitude, belief and personal conviction. Has education really to do with such matters? Are facts not enough for learning? These will be troubling questions, indeed, for some teachers.

When we understand that learning means involvement of self and not mere acquisition of facts, we recognize that there will be a wide variability in the meanings each person holds. This means that students must have many more opportunities for selection of experiences. Yet in many places we are not set up so. Rigid structures and required courses seem to inhibit the extension of the well informed person's range of personal meanings.

ADEQUACY: A FUNCTION OF BEING INFORMED

These papers suggest that the fully functioning personality is well informed about himself. He is aware of and accepts his feelings, and trusts them as guides for behavior. In addition, Combs writes, the perceptions of the fully functioning person must also include keen awareness of the "events in which he is enmeshed." Considering the complex network of relationships to people, places and institutions in which each person is enmeshed, it appears that the individual needs breadth of information about social institutions, technical processes and the nature of the physical world he inhabits. The rich perceptual field described in these papers includes understandings of relationships of size, space and quantity; it encompasses the knowledge of principles related to matter and energy; the perceptual field also includes knowledge of means of getting more information and ways of synthesizing and relating bits of information to formulate answers to problems.

Because he has a rich perceptual field, the adequate person is able to act intelligently in our complex world. No insecure self concept stands in the way of his acting honestly upon his perceptions. This means that the well informed person becomes not only the "cultured person" in terms of having mastered essentials of the culture; he is, rather, the "cultivating person," the adequate person who is functioning to his fullest potential.

The business of transmitting information, the accumulated culture, from one generation to the next has always been a basic function of education. It is the thing we know best how to do. Helping people learn is the job society has given us and we have done it well. But we need to do better yet. We cannot stand still. A wider, broader world calls for more and more that needs to be taught.

The emphasis upon development of a well informed person, who has a wide and deep range of personal meanings about the world as well as himself, raises many questions about the kind of information needed. What is good to know? To function effectively in the modern world, one needs an increasing store of meanings about the nature of his physical and social world. Traditionally, the academic knowledge of the scholar or white collar worker was valued above skills and knowledge of the machinist or foundryman or farmer.

The definitions provided us by our four authors, however, do not restrict adequacy or self-actualization to the academically sophisticated. If self-realization is to be truly a goal of education, we shall have to broaden our understanding of what it means to be well informed. This in turn will call for a broader concept of the adequate curriculum and the inclusion of much now considered outside the scope of public education.

INTERACTION OF ADEQUACY AND LEARNING

The development of personal meanings for a rich store of information is a purpose of the schools. Both knowledge of abstract, verbal terms, which express concepts about the world, and knowledge of self and feelings are included in the information the adequate person has available. Each person selects, organizes and interprets the sensations he receives in terms of his beliefs, values and needs. One of the major determinants of perception is his self concept. The process of perception involves differentiation and selection from the environment which the learner "sees" at the moment. When we recognize that the self concept is learned, the role of the school in this learning becomes increasingly significant. Schools not only teach, they contribute also to the creation of the learner. What produces adequacy assists and encourages learning as well.

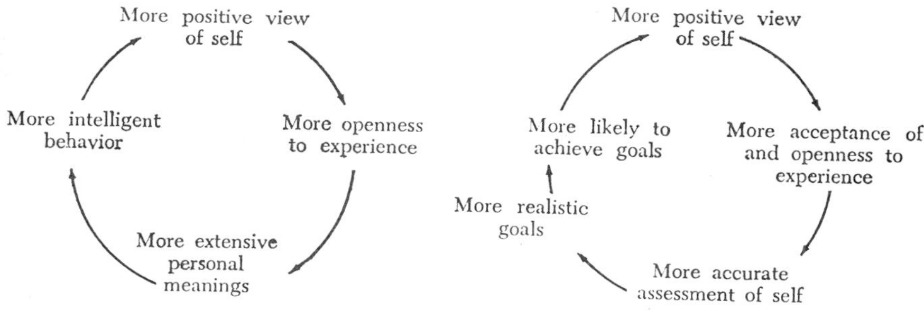

More intelligent behavior results through the development of rich, extensive and deeply personal meanings. These personal meanings about the world and people are derived as the individual becomes more open to experience. Openness to experience is dependent upon feelings of adequacy, on the one hand, and contributes to greater adequacy, on the other. (See figure above.) It is both a product of adequacy and a key to greater adequacy.

Rich, extensive and available personal meanings are both the products and producer of the adequate personality. Adequate persons are well informed, and rich information contributes to greater adequacy. It is the time honored business of the schools to help people become informed. Education serves to modify an individual's perceptions as it provides more and varied opportunities to perceive. As the educational process reduces threat and helps the individual develop a positive view of self, it makes possible more extensive personal meanings which become the basis for more intelligent behavior. An understanding of the nature of adequacy can help the school realize its traditional function more surely, and simultaneously will help produce more adequate people.

Adequacy and learning are not opposite goals. Achievement of adequacy facilitates learning. The characteristics necessary for the production of adequate persons are also the characteristics which produce efficient learners. The adequate person is able to act intelligently because he is informed. At the same time, no insecure self concept stands in the way of his acting honestly upon his perceptions. Education can only be effective to the extent that it develops people with self concepts that result in intellectual exploration, not concepts of self that continually intrude and get in the way.

A rich, available perceptual field is only one of the several characteristics selected to describe the fully functioning person. These characteristics are interactive, functioning to strengthen each other. A positive view of self, openness to experience, identification with others, and integrity contribute to the development of extensive personal meanings. The interaction of these factors in large part determines what is learned and how well. They set the stage for the process. To produce more efficient learning, teachers will need to learn more about children's perceptions of themselves and of the world.

Teaching for Adequacy Does Not Demand "Softness"

Although a person learns he is able from the use of his capacities in successful experiences, the complete absence of frustration is dangerous. To be strong, a person must acquire frustration-tolerance. The child with a good basis of safety, love and respect-need-gratification is able to profit from nicely graded frustrations and to become stronger thereby. The adequate person learns about his strength and limits by overcoming difficulties, by meeting challenge. He finds enjoyment in a great struggle. It has been said that a characteristic of genius is that it enjoys getting into difficulties for the sheer joy of getting out again.

Learning involves, therefore, an individual predisposed to learning by being open to experience, to perception of new things or ideas, and the transformation of previous ways of looking at the world into a new perceptual field. Schools play their part not only by putting new experiences in the way of the perceiver; they function importantly in their influence upon the individual's developing receptivity or perceptiveness or openness to experience—or just plain readiness. The individual is "ready" who has a positive self concept and who is therefore free to go adventuring in intellectual realms of gold. No unsatisfied needs for status with one's peers, for affection or for independence stand between the learner and experience either as an obstacle or as a clouded glass through which new experiences are seen but darkly. On the other hand, the individual who is insecure, who is so worried about his self that he is always seeking to protect and preserve it, is not free to deal with new experience at its face value.

A most important factor in fostering development of the well informed person is the well informed teacher. He must be able to identify broad concepts, recognize children's readiness for them and provide experiences which will make it possible for children to gain personal understanding of these concepts. Above all, the teacher creates a climate which reassures each student that he is learning and encourages each student to stretch in acquiring meaningful information. Teachers become more informed when supervisory practices encourage them to develop new personal meanings, to gain more information, to become more curious, and to become more aware of the meanings they hold about themselves, about people and about the universe.

The teacher who explores freely to discover meaning will stimulate students toward intellectual pursuits. The teacher cannot wear blinders himself and urge students meaningfully to look all about them. While the breadth of knowledge (perceptual field) that belongs to the teacher is one of the age-old ideals, the teacher cannot be a pedant with "loads of learned lumber in his head," unable to make use of his knowledge. He must demonstrate that his perceptual field is available to him in his teaching and in his personal, social, political and economic life.

PRACTICES CORROBORATED BY SELF-ACTUALIZATION

In the pages to follow we have attempted to illustrate some practices which seem to be supported by the self-actualization concepts our four authors have presented. Such a presentation can in no sense be definitive or inclusive. Good teachers everywhere have found their own ways of contributing to such ends in their own unique fashion. The ideas we have discussed here, therefore, are but samples of practices that have come to our attention.

The four papers suggest the adequate person is well informed about himself and his world. Information about his abilities, beliefs and feelings helps the learner set realistic goals; thus he achieves success and reinforces the feeling of adequacy. This feeling in turn makes it possible for him to move toward more new experiences and thus to gain more knowledge. The learner must see himself in the process of learning.

A successful experience in a reading lesson led seven-year-old Bruce to say, "I read so well today I didn't know it was me. I'll bet I can do good tomorrow, too." Bruce is learning about himself, coming to trust himself as one who can learn. How has he built this concept? He has been given materials with which he could succeed. He has been given time. In his school he was not stamped "failure" when he didn't learn to read in the first grade. There were opportunities to learn about animals and machines through pictures, books, films and field trips. His teacher *believed* he wanted to learn, and expressed the idea that he was constantly learning. On the previous day, for example, Bruce spent a great deal of time watching a snail move about the aquarium. After talking with him and guiding his observation, the teacher said to the class, "Bruce has learned much about snails this morning. We can learn from him." As Bruce told of his observations, he was building a concept of himself as a learner—one who could get information in many diverse ways.

The student in a highly departmentalized high school, with several teachers and subjects, can be helped to see relationships and set realistic goals. The following anecdote serves to illustrate:

I had Edward in tenth grade science class and I also observed him during physical education period. He was a member of the varsity basketball team and, when there was opportunity, I saw him practice "free throws" by himself. I saw him do this on several occasions.

Today I asked Edward why he was so interested in "free throws" and whether he was practicing for a contest. He answered, "No, the coach told us that the important thing was not winning the game, but the real question was did I play my best for me?"

"So you are concerned with what you can do for Edward, eh?" I asked.

"Yes, that is the reason I have been practicing free throws by myself, just to see how I can improve."

"Have you improved any?"

"Yes, I have," he answered. "At first I could make only three out of ten; through practice I can now make an average of seven out of ten."

"That's fine, Ed."

I then asked him if he could see the relationship between improving himself in "free throws" with the ball and improving himself in science. He was pensive for about a minute and then said, "I should learn science because I'm interested in it and I guess I shouldn't try to beat the other kids by trying for the best grade, but just do the best I can—yes, like the coach said —to do the best for me."

Students need many opportunities for critical or analytical thinking, to see relationships and to set realistic goals for themselves.

As teachers record children's behavior they compile anecdotes which may be used to help children know themselves. Sparky had been the terror of the first three grades. His teacher told him she wanted to help and would jot down the times he received special attention. Perhaps such a record would help them determine the kind of help he needed. With a noncommittal grunt Sparky raced out of the room.

At the end of the week the record was long. Sparky had fought, kicked, thrown a book at a child, and yelled during music. Then the teacher read examples such as, "Sparky brought two turtles today and he told interesting facts about them"; "At recess Sparky stopped to help two younger children find their ball"; and "He made good contribution in planning ways to learn about magnets." Sparky was instantly alert and asked, "Didja write that about me? Didja really write that good about me?" The teacher was helping Sparky learn about himself. Most of us would probably be shocked if we could see a record of the kinds of responses we make to students in the course of a day. Studies on this question usually show that teachers make many more critical, mistake-pointing-out, deflating kinds of comments than they do positive, self-enhancing statements—this in spite of our common understanding of the importance of reward and encouragement in the learning process.

Use of Audiovisual Aids

Taped or televised recordings of student discussions and classroom activities can be useful in helping children to know themselves. Children are often amazed when they hear the sound of their own voices and see themselves in action for the first time. They listen with new perception to their own speech and ideas and can analyze the effect of their contributions to a discussion. They see themselves in the process of learning, can evaluate their successes and their needs, and find tangible evidence of the progress they are making. In the process, the observing teacher may gain valuable clues as to what ideas and feelings the children have about themselves and their world. For example, Kathy's listening and learning about herself led her to say, "I think I got my ideas in today without being so bossy. I know I like to talk, but some of them were good ideas—and I didn't interrupt anybody." Again, John revealed something of himself when he commented, "Some of us didn't get into it. I know I didn't say anything. After all, who wants his mistakes recorded?"

The teacher who listens may also react to her teaching behavior. Such was the case as one teacher reviewed with a small group the playback of a discussion. Her question, "How come we so often have new ideas and the talk comes faster after I turn off the recorder? Do you think some of you might be afraid of this machine?" One child's answer was quick, "No, but I think it bothers *you*. You see the recorder turning and all of that empty tape going by and you ask us another question before we have time to think about the first one. We need some time to get our ideas out and you're watching so we won't waste the tape."

Television and tapes may also be used by teachers to gain information about themselves. New insights are possible as teachers see themselves and the roles they play with children—controlling, directing, encouraging, facilitating learning. The outside view of one's self is revealing, and a fresh sense of awareness is sometimes indicated by such comments as, "I really talked too much—I was pushing so hard to get them to see what the author meant"; "I was comfortable in that situation—I seem to have relaxed and the children, too"; "Martha needs more time—the group was rushing her there and I didn't notice." Such information about self has very real personal meaning and may provide the basis for private evaluation or for a shared "talking-through" with supervisor or principal.

Teacher training institutions are finding kinescopes of student teaching valuable aids in helping student teachers perceive themselves in the professional role. In one experimental program the student teacher is given the kinescope to use as he wishes. He may view it alone or share it with the supervising teacher or university supervisor. We need to explore new ways of helping teachers become informed about themselves. However, there is a danger that such tape and film records will create a situation which will imply that teachers should adopt a stereotyped teaching role. We need to find ways to use these media to deepen and extend important learnings and to help students evaluate their effectiveness as they learn to work with children.

Further research is needed to determine children's perceptions. We know very little about how things look through children's eyes. We need to develop techniques to identify factors which extend or limit the personal meanings children gain in school and out of school. If personal meanings are the heart of learning, preservice and in-service programs will need to help teachers become more aware of children's perceptions. It should not be supposed that personal meanings apply only to the individual's own person. The principle holds as well for learning objective facts.

Personal Meaning of Subject Matter

The school curriculum may broaden the perceptual field of children as it provides opportunities for them to discover personal meanings in academic learning. In arithmetic, where teacher presentation and pupil practice have been generally accepted methods of instruction, children can be helped to draw generalizations and to develop their own understanding of relationships. Even mathematical laws, when discovered by children, can have personal meanings which memorization and objective proof cannot provide. This was illustrated by a group of eight-year-olds who discovered and tested the commutative law. The children were using number line and counters to explore groups of equal size. Suddenly Paul's eyes lit up, "Look," he exclaimed, "the answer's always the same. Three times four are twelve and four times three are twelve and two times six and six times two are the same and so are two times five and five times two. It's always the same. When you turn the groups around, the answer's the same."

Paul's discovery was accepted by many of the class, and children proceeded to test and demonstrate this new finding. But a few of the youngsters expressed a healthy doubt as to the absolute nature of Paul's statement; it might not work with large numbers and they were sure there must be some exceptions. These children worked—long after the rest of the class turned to other tasks—checking, trying, testing the application of the rule. Finally, they were ready to report to the group, again with the real satisfaction of personal discovery, that Paul's law was tested and found true. Children do discover meanings as they are given opportunities to explore subject matter, meanings which have significance for personal learning.

A re-examination of our organization of time may point to ways of providing time for children to immerse themselves deeply in the subject matter as did Paul's group above. We will need to plan the school day so there are large blocks of time when the child may work without interruption. As one child said in the daily evaluation period, "It's fun to dive and dig into material so you can come to your own conclusions." Flexibility in schedules should provide opportunities for such study for several days, or even weeks. The individual may be released from daily assignments given the rest of the group so he may continue his pursuit.

The emphasis upon acquiring personal meaning for information suggests the teacher will become increasingly concerned with individual instruction, yet will provide group experiences in which children may come to discover common meanings, values and attitudes. More frequently, the teacher will play a clarifying role and serve children in a resource capacity. He will listen carefully to what children have to say and respond within context, thus helping the child to build upon and extend meanings. In a warm and supporting manner the teacher will find ways to help each pupil evaluate his work specifically enough to guide his next effort. The teacher assists the child in building intellectual power by helping him develop an ever-increasing number of alternatives and assuring him that the teacher is willing to give assistance, if necessary.

Physical Facilities Contribute to Meanings

The school of the future must be designed so that facilities are open for boys and girls to build rich perceptual fields. Resource rooms should be provided where children may go to explore new meanings, for example, in science, art, mathematics and music. Here children of different ages would work side by side or together in finding personal meanings through experiences with many materials. Resource teachers would be available in the rooms, at least part of the time, and seminar teachers could work with children who express special interests in going beyond the classroom activities. The library would include a wide variety of reading materials, films, filmstrips and teaching machines for use by individuals or small groups. A student could check out a tape or recording and hear it through earphones in a library or a special listening room. Students would have access to carrels or individual study spaces in the library and classrooms. Science rooms would provide storage space for individual projects. Buildings will be planned to provide for the individual study suggested by the ideas of these four authors.

Teachers, Too, Learn Through Personal Meaning

Although the teacher is plagued by static "I-have-arrived" course, grade, degree and certification practices, there remains within the person a desire to become a better teacher—a better informed teacher in areas that are important to him. Effective in-service programs must be geared to the learner, i.e., the educator, whether teacher or administrator. Too often in-service programs, which are supposed to keep the educator informed, become programs in which things are *done to* the teacher instead of *with* the teacher.

Teachers want to be well informed; they desire information if they can see that it "makes sense," if it is not imposed. Such was the case in a certain high school when a need developed that created a setting for some valuable in-service work.

A group of high school teachers sought information when they expressed concern about the grammatical errors their students made in speaking and writing. The English teacher replied to the complaints of teachers of other subjects, "I can't see why . . . because they teach them the parts of speech as well as other grammar, from the time they reach the fourth grade and from then on through high school. As for my students in eleventh grade English, they can diagram any sentence from the most simple to the most complex."

The teachers of subjects other than English agreed there was lack of "carry-over," that is, that students made grammatical errors in their writing and speaking.

At the next faculty meeting this group of teachers expressed their concern to the total group, and there were echoes from the group similar to those made previously. After some discussion each teacher saw that he had a responsibility to help students in his particular field or subject to speak and write more effectively. Information was gained from research findings, by seeking help from English professors in a nearby university, and by working with their high school supervisors. In time the English teachers, as well as the teachers of other subjects, saw ways of dealing with the problem other than by diagramming sentences (which had not been too successful). Instead of diagramming sentences each student was helped to recognize his own "grammar demons," which were selected by the student from the meaningful writing and speaking he was doing each day in each subject.

The result was improvement on the part of the students in ability to write and speak more effectively and with fewer errors. The most significant outcome was the recognition on the part of this high school faculty that students' behavior can be changed or modified if the method used is personal. In addition, the English teachers stopped their use of diagramming sentences, a practice which research had proved ineffectual years before this concerted effort for improvement took place.

In another curricular area, mathematics, we also see the need for being well informed. The National Council of Teachers of Mathematics indicated for years that students were high in computational skills, but weak in their ability to reason. Industrial leaders who depend upon work in their research laboratories have also told us that students who were employed by them have knowledge of arithmetic computational skills, but lack knowledge of the underlying principles of mathematics and the ability to reason. They expressed the need for additional "know-how." A group of public school teachers and several mathematics professors worked together and developed a plan for getting at the underlying mathematical concepts which were needed so much more than a focus on rote computational skills. As soon as this material became available, mathematics teachers clamored for it. They attended in-service study groups for the purpose of learning this new approach and how to use it in helping their students. The teachers became better informed, felt more adequate, and renewed their enthusiasm for their work in dealing with modern mathematical concepts. This in-service program did not have to be imposed. For years the teachers had been dissatisfied and there was a real eagerness (readiness) to become better informed. These teachers realized that previous competency in the area of mathematics was not sufficient either for teacher or student.

Educators should work more closely with colleagues in the social sciences, sciences and humanities to identify the large concepts in each field which should be developed in elementary and secondary schools. For example, a group of teachers has been working with an economist to understand principles of economics which can be understood by children. As the economist works with children and teachers, he recognizes readiness and the need for firsthand experience so that children may gain personal meanings for concepts related to the production and consumption of goods and services.

PRACTICES THESE IDEAS QUESTION

Not only the discovery and transmittal of knowledge but the uses to which knowledge is put must be a concern to society. It is desirable to examine school practices which facilitate or impede the appropriate use of knowledge. Examples of knowledge "taught" and "learned" which have made little difference in the behavior of the learners are numerous. Among the first investigations to compare knowledge and behavior were those made by Hartshorne and May [2] in their studies of deceit. These studies indicated that knowledge of proper rules of conduct did not assure adherence to those rules. A more recent example may be found in the Jacob study [3] of the change in attitudes among college students as a result of completing courses in the liberal arts. Significant relationships could not be established between college courses completed and changes in student attitude. It seems clear that teaching which deals exclusively with the recognition (identification and definition) and recall of facts has little influence on behavior.

Teaching which will influence behavior will utilize student initiative, purpose, exploration and, often, firsthand experience. Learning growing out of personal involvement and commitment is likely to make a difference in behavior. School tasks designed to extend knowledge and understanding will provide opportunity for students to compare facts, to select facts which are relevant, to predict results on the basis of selected facts (look at "what-if" aspects) and to otherwise generalize on the basis of pertinent information. The use of questions that require only identification, definition or recall is of limited value.

[2] H. Hartshorne and M. A. May. *Studies in the Nature of Character.* New York: Macmillan Co., 1928. Vol. 1, 720 p.; Vol. 2, 559 p.; Vol. 3, 503 p.

[3] P. E. Jacob. *Changing Values in College; An Exploratory Study of the Impact of College Teaching.* New York: Harper & Brothers, 1957. 174 p.

Use of the common assignment selected and justified by the teacher or other leader also has limited value for developing the kind of knowing that is likely to make a difference in behaving. Further, unless listener interest and other readiness are well developed, a lecture is of very little help insofar as influencing behavior is concerned. The preparation and delivery of a logical exposition contribute significantly to the learning of the person preparing it. For the listener it provides hints, clues, points for take off and some encouragement, but for the idea to gain significant meaning, the listener must build his own logic, put together his own exposition by building on, tying in, rearranging, extending and associating his own concepts.

A college sophomore said, "It is so different here. I feel I should never ask a question. Oh, I know I could, but the professor has his lecture so organized and I get the feeling I shouldn't interrupt." Thus curiosity is dulled. In a very real sense learning must grow out of the individual's own *striving* for understandings.

These implications are pertinent for the teacher in the elementary school and in the high school, for the college professor, and for supervisors and administrators in their dealings with the teaching staff. Unfortunately, on the one hand, much teaching by television, "large group" teaching and some machine teaching must often rely on haphazard pupil readiness and upon low pupil interest, involvement and commitment. Usually pupil purposes must also be ignored. On the other hand, these teaching devices must usually rely upon pupil mental activity that is limited to recognizing and following meanings built by someone else.

The use of television lessons raises some serious questions which conflict with the theory of learning as discovery of personal meaning. Television lessons are usually prepared as lectures or demonstrations. The lessons are paced for the "average." There may be questions to stimulate pupil exploration, but next day the class must be ready to meet the preplanned, taped lesson, regardless of interesting problems which arose in the follow-up session and which should be explored before moving to the next topic. There are knotty problems to be solved here. How can we use these promising new devices most effectively? We cannot permit enthusiasm for technical marvels to destroy the personal experience on which real learning depends, lest we find we have "thrown out the baby with the bath water." On the other hand, we must not drag our feet at confrontation with what is new and different. There is assuredly a place for television in education and we need to find and use it as rapidly as possible.

The child who experiences learning through solving his problems is building a rich perceptual field. Many media should be used. Television, films, tapes and other aids can provide the vicarious experience children need when it is not possible to have firsthand experience. Do all children in a group need to see a particular film or television lesson? Does the material suit these learners at this time? These questions must be answered by the teacher. We need always to keep in mind, however, that the device or method is not the important factor—the learning process is.

The trend toward more and more departmentalization we are currently experiencing often inhibits the integration of learning and development of personal meanings. When children must move to another room or another teacher on a preplanned schedule, they must interrupt the flow of ideas. Time is lost in movement, and orientation to a new area of study requires still more pupil time. Teachers who meet 150 students each day find it difficult to be aware of the uniqueness of learners. When teachers deal with large groups or teach the same subject to successive classes, there is a tendency to present information according to a prestructured, logical organization. But people do not learn things in such neat, logical patterns. The appreciation of the logical sweep of knowledge can only occur after the acquisition of facts, and this is often a most haphazard, illogical sort of sequence. Furthermore, the individual pupil may not become involved with the process of seeking information for himself if he feels protected from personal responsibility in a large group.

We have moved so far toward such departmentalization, particularly in our high schools, that there is a very real danger that what we do for convenience may actually be antithetical to real learning. If learning is truly individual, a matter of personal meanings, this fact may be ignored in teaching, but the principle cannot be suspended. We may close our eyes to its operation if we wish, but we cannot avoid the consequences. Even the ostrich knows he is not going any place while he sticks his head in the sand.

There is need to examine all our practices—even those that seem at first glance to be most forward looking and unquestioned—with an eye to what happens from the child's view of the matter. Individualized reading programs, for example, may offer children opportunity to read much more widely, but there is a danger that children may read only for plot and teachers may be mainly concerned with reading skills rather than with the meanings children are gaining. In discussing books, children must be free to express their interpretations.

Each reader brings his own background to the story; each will identify with a character of his choice. In reading *Call Me Charley,* by J. Jackson, for example, one nine-year-old identified with Tom, the boy who tried to befriend the young Negro, Charley, who came to an all-white school. Expecting all the children to identify with Charley, the teacher rejected this pupil's comments when she said, "But Tom wasn't a very good friend of Charley's when he behaved this way." Thus she disapproved of a position which showed far more perception of the conflicts involved. It may be this child understood that the character, Tom, behaved only as he could, with the understanding he had. The discussion moved ahead, but one pupil had another experience which seemed to say, "You shouldn't think for yourself—you should try to say what the teacher wants." Such experiences prevent children from gaining personal meaning.

The school of the future will be increasingly concerned with the development of adequate persons, recognizing that one of the characteristics of the adequate person is his extensive, rich and available store of meaningful information. This abundant knowledge will have been derived through individual purpose and exploration in which the student involvement will make it easy to move from knowing to behaving. It will be concerned, not only with providing subject matter, but with what this means in the personal world of the learner. It will take full advantage of our new understanding of the interrelationship of adequacy and learning. Through the production of more adequate persons, it will advance learning; better informed people will be more likely to achieve self-actualization.

CHAPTER 13

CONVICTIONS, BELIEFS AND VALUES

FROM KELLEY

The fully functioning person develops and holds human values . . . the better the life, the better the values. He knows no other way except in keeping with his values.

The fully functioning person sees the value of mistakes—has little need to be always right.

The fully functioning person learns not to see others as threats, but as assets.

FROM COMBS

The existence of a value system which prizes openness (valuing new experience) contributes to acceptance of and openness to experience.

Arranged in order of increasing meaning, we speak, for example, of looking, seeing, knowing; of understanding, belief, conviction. The deeper, more personally significant the perception, moreover, the more likely it is to affect behavior. Adequate people seem to have many more such personal meanings and, as a consequence, much more of their knowing affects behavior.

Adequate persons usually possess a deep sense of duty or responsibility and are likely to be democratic in the fullest sense of the word.

FROM ROGERS

This process of healthy living involves the courage to be. It means launching oneself fully into the stream of life with confidence in the self as a trustworthy instrument for encountering life.

FROM MASLOW

We need a validated, usable system of human values that we can believe in and devote ourselves to (be willing to die for), because they are true rather than because we are exhorted to "believe and have faith."

It is necessary, in order for children to grow well, that adults have enough trust in them and in the natural processes of growth . . . to let them *grow* and help them in a Taoistic rather than an authoritarian way.

THE IDEAS

Combs, Kelley, Maslow and Rogers seem to be in agreement that fully functioning people have sincere beliefs and values with a high degree of clarity and have the courage of their convictions. These beliefs and values are not just intellectual or abstract ideas but, rather, deep and consistent convictions which affect actions. Adequate people seem to attach many more personal meanings to their perceiving and learning, and thus much more of their knowing and feeling affects their behavior.

The four authors stress that a fully functioning person knows no other life except in keeping with his values and that he has the courage to be himself. They emphasize that an adequate person has a system of human values to which he is sincerely devoted and for which, if necessary, he is willing to die. Such a value system, furthermore, contributes to its own continuing achievement because it prizes openness to experience which, in turn, develops more and better human values, beliefs and convictions.

The four authors perceive a fully functioning person, also, as one who has the courage to be imperfect. Adequate people seem to see the value of mistakes. They perceive mistakes as one of the better means of creating opportunities for new learning experiences. They have little fear of being wrong as well as little need to be always right. Because of this attitude toward mistakes, they have little worry or fear. As a consequence they are much freer to be themselves and to develop a personal system of values.

Self-actualizing people are no namby-pambies. They have strong and clear-cut value systems, so much so that, when necessary, they can take a position contrary to externally imposed concepts. They are persons of conviction and belief and their values play an active part in their daily lives.

IMPLICATIONS FOR EDUCATION

These concepts have far-reaching implications for educational thought and practice. We are beginning to see learning as a problem of a total personality. We are beginning to understand that, unless behavior has changed, one has not really learned. It is becoming more and more clear that the key to effective behavioral change is an individual's personal discovery of meaning. It is values, beliefs and personal meanings which affect behavior most markedly. People without beliefs, values and convictions cannot be counted upon in a society whose very survival depends on active, responsible and trustworthy people. For example, studies show that American soldiers imprisoned during the Korean War who succumbed to brainwashing were mainly men without firm beliefs and convictions. Consequently, because they did not stand for something in themselves, they were easy marks for brainwashing by people whose beliefs were so strong as to be practically a religion. Beliefs and convictions are crucial to a people who would survive in an ideological struggle.

Knowing and Behaving

It is imperative that we take a closer look at the distinction between knowing and behaving. For many generations education has done an excellent job of *imparting* information. Students, for the most part, have done pretty well on verbal examinations. It does not follow, however, that this "knowing" has significantly affected behavior. An alarmingly small percentage of what an individual knows intellectually seems to get under his skin and truly to make a difference in how he thinks, feels and acts. Combs [1] states the problem very succinctly: "Our greatest failures are those connected with the problem of helping people to behave differently as a result of the information we have provided them."

We are coming to understand that much of this failure is due to lack of personal discovery of meaning. For example, many a student teacher fails to change the way he behaves in a classroom as a result of his work in educational psychology. A simple idea, such as ignoring misbehavior, can be discussed and demonstrated in a college classroom. Prospective student teachers may be able to state the principle, but there will be little difference in their work as teachers unless they can concurrently experiment with the idea as they relate to children they care about. Students need opportunities to discover the personal value and usefulness of the concept. Without such personal meaning there is little hope that classroom learning will go beyond the final examination.

Adequate persons are, among other factors, the product of strong values. The implication seems to be clear, then, that educators must be interested in and concerned with values. Unfortunately, this is not the case in many schools and classrooms today. The emphasis is too often on the narrowly scientific and the impersonally objective. As we have pointed out in a preceding chapter, children often get the idea in school that how they feel and what they think is not very important compared to scientific and objective facts. Without fully realizing it, we have sometimes taught children that personal meanings have no place in the classroom. Many children perceive school as a place where one is forced to do things which have little pertinence to life as he experiences it. Education must be concerned with the values, beliefs, convictions and doubts of students. These realities as perceived by an individual are just as important, if not more so, as the so-called objective facts. This does not mean that factual materials are not useful in making sound value judgments or in formulating constructive social policies, but rather, that an overemphasis on the

[1] Arthur W. Combs. "Personality Theory and Its Implications for Curriculum Development." In: *Learning More About Learning*. Washington, D.C.: Association for Supervision and Curriculum Development, a department of the National Education Association, 1959. p. 5-20.

scientific and the objective impedes self-fulfillment. Facts have no value in themselves alone. It is only as facts find their way into human organization of convictions, beliefs, frames of reference and attitudes that they come to fruition in intelligent behavior.

Teachers and Values

In like manner, schools must be concerned with teachers and their values. Teachers need to be encouraged to be themselves and to be free to communicate their humanity. Unfortunately, too many teachers believe that professional behavior requires them to lose their humanness. Within the broad limits of good taste both students and teachers should be free to explore and test values without restraint or fear of criticism. Teachers must stand for something if for no other reason than to give children something to push against. Values, beliefs and convictions must be admitted to the classroom situation. They must be respected and cherished if students are to develop their own beliefs and values. Ethics, morality, human feeling and emotion need to be part of the curriculum if the school intends that teachers and classrooms will affect student behavior significantly.

Teacher education can and must play an important role in producing teachers with values and convictions both in preservice as well as in-service education. The college classroom should be a place where students can test values and develop the courage of their convictions. Students need to be surrounded by college teachers who stand for something themselves, while respecting the ideas and beliefs of students. College teachers should encourage students to develop their own unique values and their way of practicing them, rather than the "right" values and the "right" methods. It is particularly important that student teachers work with cooperating and supervising teachers who have strong convictions and who are not threatened by other people with differing values and convictions.

Learning Values Takes Time and Effort

In providing opportunities for students to develop values and convictions, we often fail to realize the length of time and the amount of difficulty involved. Even though we know better, it is often assumed that values can be manipulated and changed as simply and easily as intellectual concepts. The ease with which students memorize material and accumulate knowledge is misleading indeed. Not only does change in an individual's system of values and, as a consequence, change in behavior come slowly, but the more personal and basic the values, the slower and more difficult the process of change. Somehow, we must find more time in the school day for the teaching of values with more freedom for personal discovery, whether it be directly through experience or indirectly through discussion, role playing, reading, viewing or listening.

A Democratic Climate and Learning of Values

In general, this means that we must find ways of creating school and classroom atmospheres which facilitate the process of exploration and discovery of personal meaning—where there can be a freeing, expanding and changing of perception. Students need to have many choices; when they discover something of interest, they need to have plenty of time to work at it. Self-selection in an environment rich in materials, where students sense that how they feel and what they think are important, can be extremely effective in helping students to become more fully functioning. Through acceptance and trust, particularly, teachers play a strategic role in this learning process.

Realistically speaking, this means at the outset that we proceed to eliminate the barriers against this process of exploration and experimentation for students. One of the biggest over-all barriers is the autocracy which still reigns in many of our schools and classrooms. We give lip service to democracy and *know* somewhat about it, but few administrators or teachers have found the courage to dispense with autocracy, to *change their behavior* and take the plunge into creating democratic atmospheres. Most of the barriers against exploration are part and parcel of autocratic atmospheres.

Teachers need to find the courage to face realistically their allegiance to values which are basically autocratic and to disown them once and for all if we hope to be free to develop democratic ones. When we attempt to mix autocratic and democratic values, we find that our efforts in either direction become sabotaged. Basic autocratic values are *not* compatible with basic democratic values and never will be. People behave in terms of what they believe is important. Teachers do, too. Each of us needs to look to his own values, beliefs and convictions and ask, "What do I *really* think is important?"

Semantically speaking, the words *democratic* and *autocratic* do not always communicate clear meanings. Unfortunately, they have become highly charged words often bordering on "name-calling." Since the terms are used many times in this chapter, perhaps it would be well before proceeding further to attempt to spell out what democracy stands for as opposed to autocracy. In general, words like facilitating, freeing, encouraging and accepting are associated with democracy, while restricting, coercing and discouraging are associated with autocracy. More specifically, a few dichotomies will illustrate more subtle differences. For example, democracy, in the way we are using the term, stresses equal rather than superior-inferior relationships; trust rather than fear; encouragement rather than force; freedom without license rather than obedience; cooperation rather than competition; challenge rather than threat; recognition rather than praise; self-discipline rather than punishment; and satisfaction rather than reward.

The attitude toward difference often differentiates democracy from autocracy also. Fully functioning people seem to value difference. They are comfortable around people who are different. Democratic teachers accept and welcome students who are different. Students are encouraged to cooperate as unique individuals and yet relate as equal human beings. They are given freedom to select work which is challenging, yet work with which they can cope. There is a minimum of the fear, worry and threat which shut people off from the very experiences which provide growth and change.

Faulty Assumptions

Another related, but somewhat different, barrier to the freeing, expanding and changing of perceptions is the array of faulty assumptions which hamper many people today. Schools not only have to cope with misbehavior of students resulting from faulty values, but they have to be concerned with the validity of the basic assumptions students learn in classrooms and in the schools in general. Psychologists and psychiatrists involved in psychotherapy are very much aware of the effect of fallacies on behavior. Teachers need to take a closer look at the basic assumptions which guide much of their behavior in the classroom. A look at these assumptions will often prove to be quite a sobering experience.

Let us take a look at a brief summary of a few unrealistic assumptions and irrational ideas as suggested by some psychotherapists. Ellis,[2] for example, in discussing rational psychotherapy, included the following irrational ideas: (a) the idea that it is a dire necessity for an adult human being to be loved or approved by everyone for everything he does; (b) the idea that one should be thoroughly competent, adequate and achieving in all possible respects; (c) the idea that one should be dependent on others and needs someone stronger than oneself on whom to rely; (d) the idea that the past is all-important and that because something once strongly affected one's life, it should have the same effect indefinitely; and (e) the idea that it is exceptionally difficult to find the right solution to many human problems, and that if the precise and right solution is not found, the results will be catastrophic. Such fallacies are widely held in our society. Since values are taught whether teachers

[2] A. Ellis. "Rational Psychotherapy and Individual Psychology." *Journal of Individual Psychology* 13: 38-44; 1957.

are aware of it or not, one wonders how many of these ideas are taught directly or indirectly in our schools.

Dreikurs,[3] an Adlerian psychotherapist, questions the following popular beliefs and social values and suggests that they are not compatible with democratic values: (a) the desire for self-elevation, (b) the idea of perfectionism, (c) idea of masculinity and femininity, (d) fear of mistakes, (e) personal success, and (f) the idea that reason and objectivity are always preferable to emotion and subjectivity. Dreikurs suggests instead that we value unique usefulness, cooperation, and relationship as equals rather than self-elevation or personal success; that we stress humanness rather than masculinity or femininity as such; that we value the courage to be imperfect rather than perfectionism and the ensuing fear of mistakes; that we value and trust emotions and subjectivity as complementary modes of reason and objectivity. To say the least, this is a provocative list of faulty social values, any one of which would provide food for thought for the teaching of values in our schools today.

Erich Fromm[4] has contributed significantly to the understanding of our major moral problems in a way closely related to our discussion of values. He suggests three problem areas: (a) authoritarianism, (b) exploitation and (c) inequality. He questions seriously our valuing anonymous authority rather than the overt authority of the nineteenth century. He considers both types as irrational and harmful and suggests valuing rational authority which is based solely on competence and knowledge if and when authority is useful. It is his belief that practically everybody exploits himself through his worship of *things* and suggests that it is time that we put *man* back in the saddle. In other words, things are the supreme values of many people rather than the ideas of man and his potentiality to become. Many students perceive school learning as an acquisition of marks and degrees rather than a useful tool in becoming more human—more fully functioning. Fromm is convinced that equality today, which has replaced much of the cruel inequality of the past, has often come to mean sameness and conformity. He suggests that we should value instead creativity and difference, overcome the split between affect and intellect, and find the courage to be our unique selves.

While this only represents points of view from rational, Adlerian, and neo-Freudian psychotherapy, they are somewhat representative of newer frontiers in psychology and psychiatry. Rogers has suggested that the values of fully functioning people are highly similar to those of persons

[3] R. Dreikurs. "Psychotherapy as Correction of Faulty Social Values." *Journal of Individual Psychology* 13: 150-58; 1957.

[4] Erich Fromm. "The Moral Responsibility of Modern Man." *Merrill-Palmer Quarterly*. Fall 1958.

who have successfully experienced psychotherapy. Educators can ill afford to overlook what psychotherapists consider essential learnings. If the learning of basic human values, including the rejection of faulty values, is so vital that therapy cannot proceed without it, perhaps education cannot progress without such learning either. Counseling or psychotherapy is a process of learning, too, and what is basically true of learning in one setting is generally applicable in another. If teachers hope to encourage the development of more fully functioning people, it would appear that psychotherapy has much to contribute toward the teaching of values. Much of what Carl Rogers has written concerning client-centered counseling, for example, has equal applicability to the construction of effective learning situations in the classroom.

Let us discuss in more detail one of the suggested faulty values—self-elevation. Is this really a faulty value? Is not self-elevation, a popular value in our so-called competitive society, taught in practically every home and school? To be a success in our classrooms, do we not motivate students to "win out" by getting high marks? As long as there are competitive classrooms, students will be learning that to be successful one must elevate himself above others and will perceive a classroom as a place where human beings relate on a vertical scale with only the few at the top "winning out" and the rest failing. Self-elevation is not a condition to be sought for its own sake. On the other hand, if the school and classroom atmosphere is cooperative and students relate on a horizontal scale as unique as well as equal human beings, one can be successful by being useful. It is not the accomplishment of elevation above others that is praiseworthy, but the accomplishment of a worthy goal. Self-elevation will not be highly valued in such an atmosphere. Failure will no longer mean moving down the scale and losing status, and thus will not be feared.

Here is a challenge for teachers and administrators. The implications for education are manifold. If we value self-elevation and accompanying ambition in our typical classroom today, how many children can become fully functioning? An optimistic guess would be very few. Are such values faulty? If so, do we need to change the values or do we need to change the classroom atmospheres? We probably need to re-examine both. One thing is quite certain: If we value a democratic classroom atmosphere, we had better get started finding out how to create one with particular emphasis on how *we teachers behave*. We need to ask what values characterize self-actualizing persons. Following that, we need look to ourselves to see how well we hold these values. After that, we may hope to produce the values more effectively in students. This is likely to prove uncomfortable, but may also be highly rewarding.

The Value of Work

One of the most confusing areas in the teaching and learning of values centers around the perceptions teachers as well as students have of work in the classroom. Do teachers value work? Do children value getting into work or getting out of work? Maslow reports that fully functioning people seem to see little difference between work and play. Their work is more like play. If education is going to be devoted to the ever-increasing development of adequate people, it would appear from almost any assessment of student attitudes toward work that this area will need considerable attention.

Knowing the negative attitude that many students develop toward schoolwork, as well as what they learn from parents with negative attitudes toward work, it could be concluded that work is not highly valued in classrooms, schools or communities. It is recognized as a necessary activity but one to get out of more often than one to get into. In many situations, though, it seems that students do not perceive schoolwork as being something important or valuable. It is often something to get over with for the sake of satisfactory marks and graduation requirements.

Teachers certainly stress the importance of work and appear to value it highly. There is some question, however, as to whether teachers truly value work. While stressing the importance of work, they often perceive it as a necessary evil. The suggestion, "Hurry and finish your work, children, so you can go out and play," is far too familiar. Work and play often become dichotomized. Of course, if work is pure backbreaking drudgery, we should learn how to finish it in the shortest possible time in order to be free for more worthwhile pursuits. Should schoolwork, however, fall in this category? If schoolwork is done primarily for marks or for the teacher, there is real danger that it will become drudgery. Certainly it will seldom be perceived as play.

Teachers are in a strategic position to improve the value and dignity of work. The creation of a truly democratic classroom atmosphere is the basic prerequisite. Teachers can help children to learn that play and work are on the same continuum—that work can be as satisfying as play. Children need to find out that work and learning go hand in hand and, as a consequence, that learning is satisfying also. In short, teachers can help children learn to value work.

There is a common belief that work is fatiguing while play is refreshing. The fact, however, seems to be that what is fatiguing or refreshing is more related to length of time at the task and the attitude toward it. If schoolwork were more highly valued by both teachers and students, many of our traditional practices would make little sense. Teachers and students would seldom feel the need for long weekends and long vacation periods for the purpose of recuperation. Afternoons in our elementary school classrooms, for example, would no longer need to be devoted to "easier" subjects and classroom games. While it could very well be that our compulsory school day is too long and that work during the afternoon hours is inefficient, teachers at least would not feel compelled to devote the morning hours to the more difficult and distasteful work and to get it over with as soon as possible. If work were highly valued and students were given considerable choice, the typical distinctions between difficult work and easy work and between work and play would be at a minimum. One of the major implications for education based on such a perception of the value of work could be the need for a re-examination and redesigning of the daily, weekly and annual time schedules of our public schools.

Valuing Difference and Change

Other human beings seem to be valued highly by fully functioning people. The integrity and the differences of others are highly respected by adequate people. Not only do fully functioning people trust themselves as trustworthy instruments for encountering life, but they trust that others will grow and find their place without being forced or coerced. If teachers were to give top priority to the valuing of others, more children, regardless of their progress in school or their behavior, would be accepted as worthy human beings. There would be no place for punishing and coercing.

Perhaps the one over-all implication for education drawn from the discussion of fully functioning people by our four authors is that education must value change. As people are ever-moving and ever-becoming, education needs to move into the future with them. We need to de-emphasize tradition and the past and devote more energy to the present and the future. Schools should be places where students can grow and change as total personalities. Most of the suggestions in the preceding paragraphs call for change—for the valuing of change. Educators can no longer afford to deplore and resist change. Too many teachers are still insisting that things must be done the "right" way. In such an atmosphere, goodness becomes synonymous with conformity. Messiness, noise, confusion and mistakes, out of which may come originality, creativity and genius, are suppressed in favor of neatness, quiet, order and "being right," out of which can come conservatism, cowardice, rigidity and smugness.

We have spoken of the importance of teachers who value change. It is even more important in supervisors and administrators. If administrators desire courageous and creative teachers who are forward moving and open to experience, they must welcome, value and encourage change. Experimentation must be facilitated and even, sometimes, protected. Differences in teachers must be appreciated and encouraged, not just tolerated. To do this, supervisors, administrators and teachers will, themselves, need to overcome their fear of making mistakes. Change will only occur in an atmosphere where change is valued, difference is warmly appreciated and mistakes, which are the inevitable concomitant of trying, are accepted as a normal part of the price of growing. Each person can only behave in terms of what seems to him important. To induce values in others, then, administrators and supervisors need to be sure that they really hold the values they say they do and that this message is getting through to those they supervise.

CURRENT PRACTICES THESE CONCEPTS CORROBORATE

Education does make a significant difference in the system of values, sincere beliefs and basic convictions of many individuals. School and classroom atmospheres, in varying degrees, do have influence on how students think, feel and behave. The concepts expressed by our four authors support many of the practices of good teachers everywhere.

These concepts certainly corroborate the pioneering practices of courageous teachers who sincerely attempt to establish democratic atmospheres in their classrooms. To create a classroom atmosphere with a minimum of fear, threat and worry is no easy task. Many teachers wonder whether it is worth the effort. Yet, our four authors clearly imply that democratic rather than autocratic atmospheres are basic to the teaching and learning of those values which are held by fully functioning people. Even though creating a democratic atmosphere is an ever-continuing process and there is no magic formula, a few teachers in a relatively small number of schools have the courage to work at it and are making progress.

The following are practices which these concepts corroborate: (a) cooperative classroom atmospheres, (b) trusting classroom atmospheres, (c) friendly classroom atmospheres, (d) challenging classroom atmospheres, (e) student self-discipline and (f) student self-evaluation.

A cooperative atmosphere, as opposed to a competitive atmosphere, is highly conducive to the teaching and learning of values, beliefs and convictions which are compatible with our way of life. For teachers who value cooperation highly, there is no compromise with competitive attitudes and methods. This does not rule out individual endeavors or imply that all work and learning are group work. It merely means that one learns to value cooperation by experiencing it and at the same time learns the difference between competition which is fun and competition which is destructive to our way of life. Education has made considerable progress in this direction in the past 25 years, particularly in the primary grades.

Many teachers have learned to create a trusting classroom atmosphere. Not only do such teachers trust students and the students trust teachers, but the students trust each other. Mutual trust is the highest form of mutual respect. Only in such an atmosphere can children be encouraged to reveal their feelings and values—the first step to doing something about them. When children are afraid to reveal themselves, exploration and discovery are handicapped. They cannot commit themselves and develop the convictions, beliefs and attitudes which are essential for a sense of purpose and direction. Classrooms today are certainly friendlier places in which to work and learn than at any time in the history of public school education. This is a step forward. Such an atmosphere is highly conducive to the freeing, expanding and changing of perceptions which, in turn, affect values and convictions. Teachers in such classrooms have learned how to be friendly representatives of society rather than just being paternal and nice. A friendly relationship is a must if a teacher hopes to have a democratic classroom atmosphere. We learn so much more from our friends.

An ever-increasing number of teachers are learning how to create a challenging classroom atmosphere rather than a threatening one. Such teachers have learned that so-called lazy students are *not* basically lazy, but rather that they *act* lazy for a purpose. Laziness is a product of boredom, not of motivation. With this belief, teachers no longer have to feel helpless as they do when they assume that man is basically lazy. It no longer makes sense to believe that lazy students will not work and learn unless forced. Instead, students can be encouraged to change their behavior or their purpose or both.

More and more teachers are discovering the subtle difference between self-discipline based on freedom without license and self-imposed obedience to authority based on fear of punishment, even though the punishment may be fair and humane. The decrease in corporal punishment in our schools is certainly a step forward; but, unfortunately, other forms of punishment—low marks, the taking away of privileges, and verbal lashings—are still with us. Teachers who help students learn self-discipline, through experiencing in a friendly atmosphere the natural consequences of their behavior, have no need to impose personal authority and resort to punishment. Such teachers are in a favorable position to encourage the expanding and changing of values, beliefs and convictions.

Self-actualizing persons are people able to see themselves clearly and frankly. This calls for self-evaluation. While the punishing aspects of the externally imposed marking system are recognized and disliked by many teachers, the rewarding aspects still receive considerable support. Teachers who believe in self-evaluation have no use for the marking system whether it be for punishment or reward. They believe that intrinsic satisfaction from self-evaluation, whether it be success and progress or failure and new directions, will be the ultimate in encouragement. Self-evaluation is particularly necessary to deeply personal learnings involving values, beliefs and convictions.

CURRENT PRACTICES THESE CONCEPTS QUESTION

Practices which are diametrically opposed to the practices discussed in the previous section are certainly to be questioned, for example: (a) competitive classroom atmospheres, (b) classrooms where there is blind trust or no trust at all, (c) classrooms where teachers remain aloof from students, (d) threatening classroom atmospheres, (e) classrooms where discipline is based on obedience to authority and (f) classrooms where motivation, discipline and evaluation are rooted in the universal marking system. It would be questionable, indeed, if values, beliefs and convictions learned in such classrooms would be conducive to the development of fully functioning people. In fact, it would be questionable if students in such atmospheres would expand or change their values, beliefs or convictions to any significant degree.

Observing that our way of life requires laws, many teachers assume that a law abiding society is synonymous with a controlling one. As a consequence, they teach the importance of conformity and obedience to authority. They overlook the fact that most of us do not obey laws because we are afraid to break them; we obey because we know it facilitates getting what we want. Our society is not based upon a reliance on authority, except when individuals threaten the rest of us. The foundation of our way of life is fundamentally cooperative. "I drive on the right side of the road, not because I am afraid the police will catch me on the left. I drive on the right because I recognize the sense in doing so in order that we all get more surely where we want to go." The emphasis upon authority is misplaced; it is the people and their enlightenment, not authority, that makes a society livable instead of a jungle.

The assumption that all children in a classroom must learn obedience to authority in order to adjust to demanding superiors in our society is shortsighted indeed. It is doubtful whether a very large percentage of the girls are doomed to face a demanding "boss." Most boys will have a choice of vocations as well as some choice of employers. Even the armed forces, once the epitome of authoritarianism in action, now plead for men who can think for themselves even as the lowliest of privates. As with competition, there is an array of faulty beliefs and values related to the assumption that an authoritarian atmosphere is best for children.

Practices which discourage friendliness and rely on the assumption that it interferes with learning and creates discipline problems need to be re-examined. A friendly atmosphere that welcomes play forms the very foundation for an atmosphere of freedom and responsibility to work. Practices which take the fun out of school are certainly to be questioned. Hard work goes hand in hand with or follows hard play. The assumption, however, that one must toil or work hard as a youngster in order to be an efficient and effective worker as an adult needs to be questioned. It could very well be that people who lacked many opportunities to play as children are the very ones who have a compulsive desire to play useless games rather than engage in useful work as an adult.

Assumptions concerning the value of homework need to be re-examined. Teachers who value and trust students have no need to *impose* typical homework assignments. Such teachers assume that people have the power within themselves to grow and to become. Stimulation, suggestions and challenges are more than sufficient to encourage work and learning outside the classroom, providing students see the point in learning. Nobody works hard at meaningless tasks. Belief in homework assignments and implied conformity, as well as subsequent recitation and competition for marks, are to be questioned if we hope to develop more self-propelled and fully functioning people.

In general, any classroom atmosphere which places value on working for marks and working for the teacher needs to be questioned. Such classroom climates seldom encourage children to help each other. It is often dishonest to cooperate and disobedient to be different in such an atmosphere.

NEW PRACTICES THESE CONCEPTS SUGGEST

At the outset, teachers must find ways of behaving which add up to the creation of democratic classroom atmospheres. This does not mean that no mistakes will be made, but it does mean that, through continuing self-evaluation and group evaluation, we will discover our irrational ideas and faulty assumptions and proceed to change our perceptions, beliefs and values as well as our overt behavior. This is a big task and we are only in the beginning stages. But we must get on with it if we hope to affect significantly the development of fully functioning people.

Maslow suggests in his provocative book, *Motivation and Personality,* that, if we hope to understand man, we must perceive him as being on another continuum from that of animals. As a thinking human being capable of creating purposes for behavior and of projecting himself into the future, he just does not behave like an animal unless forced to live an animal-like existence. In attempting to understand fully functioning people with strong beliefs, values and convictions, then, we need to question seriously our assumptions and beliefs based on the study of inadequate people who appear to behave more like animals and study, instead, fully functioning people and the atmospheres in which they grow.

In a similar way, a democratic classroom atmosphere needs to be perceived as being on an entirely different continuum from that of an autocratic atmosphere. Teachers need to see that one does not move toward the creation of a democratic atmosphere by creating a benevolent autocratic one, even if it is effective in accomplishing some goals. If we believe that a democratic classroom atmosphere is conducive to the development of fully functioning people and that an autocratic atmosphere is not, then we must see clearly that we cannot cling to values which are basically autocratic. This is a conviction few of us have learned as we have struggled with our middle-of-the-road positions for years hoping beyond hope that patience, niceness and even understanding would rid us of the ineffective results of autocratic atmospheres. It is time that we left the autocratic continuum once and for all and put our energy into finding a place on the democratic continuum.

The lesson yet to be learned by most teachers is how to relate as equal human beings and, at the same time, to continue to relate as unique and different individuals. As Erich Fromm has suggested, most of our efforts toward equality in the twentieth century have resulted ultimately in more conformity and sameness. We must find ways to relate as equal human beings without destroying uniqueness. It can be done, but there are only a few guideposts as of this time. We need courageous teachers willing to blaze a trail based on their convictions concerning trust and faith in human beings, freedom, acceptance, cooperation and creativity; willing to learn how to create a classroom atmosphere in which there is order and work by involving students in planning and evaluation and by being *firm with their own behavior* rather than being firm with students' behavior through imposition of authority, force, coercion, punishment and rewards. As Combs has suggested, "Teaching is a relationship, but there can be no relationship with a nonentity." It would speed up progress in this direction if more teachers who find such courage could communicate their experiences as A. S. Neill has done in his description of *freedom without license* in his recent book, *Summerhill.*[5]

Fully functioning people are people with strong values, beliefs and convictions. So are fully functioning teachers. Children learn their values from the important people in their experiences. To help them grow toward greater self-actualization in the next generation, we need to look at the values we hold in this one. As teachers struggle toward self-realization, they contribute to progress for all of us.

[5] A. S. Neill. *Summerhill; A Radical Approach to Child Rearing.* New York: Hart Publishing Co., 1960. 392 p.

CHAPTER 14

DIGNITY, INTEGRITY AND AUTONOMY

FROM MASLOW

We have, each one of us, an essential nature which is intrinsic, given, "natural" and, usually, very resistant to change . . . . Every person is, in part, "his own project" and makes himself.

In them (self-actualizing people) the conative, the cognitive, the affective and the motor are less separated from each other . . . . His spontaneous reactions are as capable, efficient and right as if they had been thought out in advance.

At the level of self-actualizing, many dichotomies become resolved, opposites are seen to be unities and the whole dichotomous way of thinking is recognized to be immature.

No ideally good relation to another human being, especially a child, is possible without "being-love." Especially is it necessary for teaching, along with the Taoistic, trusting attitude that it implies.

FROM COMBS

People learn who they are and what they are from the ways in which they have been treated by those who surround them in the process of their growing up.

Because they feel essentially sure about themselves, self-actualizing persons can feel a higher degree of respect for their own individuality and uniqueness and as a consequence are less disturbed or upset by criticism. They can remain stable in the midst of stress and strain. They can utilize themselves as trustworthy, reliable instruments for accomplishing their purposes.

The feeling of oneness with one's fellows produces in the truly adequate person a high degree of responsible, trustworthy behavior . . . a deep sensitivity to the feelings and attitudes of others . . . trust in others.

An essentially positive view of self permits adequate people to be effective nonconformists when necessary.

FROM KELLEY

The fully functioning personality thinks well of others; he therefore sees his stake in others. . . . He comes to see other people as opportunities, not for exploitation, but for the building of self. . . . He sees himself as an ongoing part of a world in movement—in process of becoming.

The better the life, the better the values accumulated. The one who sees human beings as essential to his own enhancement develops values related to the welfare of people.

He knows no other way to live except in keeping with his values. He has no need to continuously shift behavior, depending upon the kind of people nearest him.

We are tempted to call this courage and integrity. This is another way of saying that one has what it takes to live as life really exists and to do it all in one piece.

SOME COMMON IDEAS

All four writers build upon inherent assumptions: (a) that each person is worthy of respect; (b) that each grows continuously from birth to death, at all times merging the past and future into the *now;* (c) that each is a product of an inner core, developed and modified by experience; (d) that interaction with people is the strongest environmental determinant in the self concept; (e) that when the environment is basically unthreatening, the individual's own behavior toward elements in the environment is basically open, self-and-others-trusting, interactive, sympathetic and constructive; and (f) that in this environment dignity and integrity emerge as characteristics of people.

All imply that self-understanding and acceptance are reflections of understanding and acceptance by "important people" in the environment, and lead the individual to accept, to face up to, and to move toward, rather than away from, life. Implicit in all the papers is tremendous faith that the fully functioning person is a maturely responsible person, is uninhibited by rigidity or falseness, identifies broadly and deeply, is free-flowing in his contacts with life, and experiences in highly, sometimes sharply perceptive, integrative and creative ways. Great dignity and integrity of person and trust in one's own being are marks of these individuals.

This unrestrained, unforced, confident bearing seems to reflect an internal synthesis of favorable feelings the individual has about himself—feelings of competency and self-trust. The adequate person seems to approach any situation openly, becoming part of it, exploring and assessing it, sensitive for familiar and new meanings in order to embrace them in his conceptual and perceptual fields; that is, he moves into the situation feeling competent to deal with it. This concept of himself as a trustworthy instrument to carry out his purposes gives him an increasing autonomy and self-unity which shows itself in a consistency of feeling and action that is all of a piece, indicating that the possessor is basically an integrated being, that within him forces are operating harmoniously.

This person, because of the basic integrity of his being, is able to deal effectively with disharmony, dichotomies and unsolved problems, being able to resolve, tolerate and, when necessary, take nonconforming attitudes and actions. He reaches out to be of use to other people, expanding himself to identify broadly with others, sometimes on a world-wide basis.

He has peak moments of sharp, insightful experience in which he moves midway between a "spiritual world" and the known world. In these moments perceptions deepen, dichotomies and disunities disappear, and he is one with the universe. These moments give zest to living, making life meaningful and rich.

IMPLICATIONS FOR EDUCATION

An appreciation of the idea that dignity and integrity are learned characteristics holds implications which are central to the philosophical basis of the school and which permeate the entire operation of the school.

Implications for the Philosophical Basis

The school that is interested in the development of adequacy in people is necessarily committed to cherishing and nurturing the best in every human being who enrolls in it. This is in complete harmony with the expressed values held dear in the United States and engendered by our people in many parts of the world. We believe in the right of every person to reach his best fulfillment and that the institutions of government are instruments to make this possible. We have based our form of government on the belief that people, utilizing their best potentialities to face up to problems, are completely capable of exercising their own government, that is, of making decisions which are in the best interests of the total population. The school, then, which takes seriously its commitment to the fullest development of its people, must facilitate this process.

The Philosophy in Action

The discovery of self as a person of dignity and integrity is learned as a consequence of one's experience with those about him. Learning to trust one's own organism comes about as a result of experiencing success and through being treated as though one were important, reponsible and worthy of respect. When a school system sets out to establish as its primary goal the development of fully functioning people—people of dignity and integrity; people who are proud and forthright—the well-being and growth of every individual becomes important. Children learn from their teachers who they are and what they are, while teachers learn the same things from children and from the teacher's colleagues and supervisors. It is a difficult, if not impossible, task to teach what one does not feel is true in his own experience. It follows, then, that the first step in the production of persons of dignity and integrity must be a staff with members who feel this way about themselves.

Every member of the school staff becomes important in the production of such persons. Most important, the school administrator who sets the tone and direction must particularly grasp that how each member of the school system, from the lowliest to the highest paid worker, feels and thinks about himself, is a key factor in the way he functions—or fails to function. The administrator must come to see conception of self as the intrinsic core of growth and learning, affecting every child, every teacher, even himself. He begins to see his own role in the school system as one which helps others to function at their best; he sees this as the only way he can adequately discharge his obligation to give the community the best school system possible. His own philosophy about the nature of man, about how people learn and grow and, most of all, about *what* they learn about themselves and *what inspires* the learning then permeates his own field of operation: with the school board, the community, the central office staff, the field staff in the various schools, principals, teachers, nonprofessional workers, children and parents. Wherever adults come in contact with children, from the administrator himself to the workers hired on an hourly basis, he helps them to understand that human values rank highest, and that he places value on the achievement of each person primarily in relation to its effect upon the development of children.

Kelley points out how difficult it is for adults in our society to really respect the individuality of the young. The reason, he says, is that although we claim to be democratic, our ways of rearing children are thrust through with authoritarianism. This is especially true of our educational process because much of it draws from earlier preprofessional times. This means, of course, that we, too, acquire authoritarian ways. It means that all members of the school system will probably have had experience with lines of authority; some of them will have learned "the hard way" to distrust the spoken word and to watch shrewdly for indications in the direction of authority or cooperation. The "what does he want me to do?"—whether spoken or unspoken—will be there, and it is answered in deeds more convincingly than in words.

The Leader's Philosophy Is Far-Reaching

The leader's philosophy in action affects the lives of all children in the school system. The way he feels about people, and the manner in which he operates, is felt by the lowliest and most elevated person on the staff and the weakest and strongest child in the system. The leader who is characterized by self-trust, openness and trust in others will, by his very behavior, help others to learn self-trust, openness and trust in others. He will help them to acquire stature and integrity. He will solicit and weigh opinions and ideas, work cooperatively on school problems, hear all sides of difficult problems, take and show a genuine interest in fellow workers as persons as well as workers.

The approach to school problems used by Mr. Harwick, a school superintendent in a suburban area, illustrates some of the ways a self-and-other-trusting leader can act in situations affecting the entire school system. Calling the professional staff together, he said, "You have made known through the staff committee that you feel our schools need to examine the reading program to see if we are using the best possible means to help our children develop. What do you propose should be done?"

To the degree that the leader is self-trusting—that is, trusts that he can handle whatever comes as a result of this "open" setting—he can give responsibility to his staff without fear or hedging. This in turn creates in the staff a feeling of confidence in themselves. Furthermore, to the degree that the administrator is able to convey this "trusting" feeling to the staff, all of whom have backlogs of experiences and meanings, he will succeed in bringing the concerted and individual strengths of the staff to bear on the problem identified by them. Thus, two things are accomplished; a better job is done because more brains contribute to it and the faith of the staff in themselves is buttressed and encouraged. Mr. Harwick's self-confidence made possible listening to the staff. His trust in himself made it possible to trust the staff so he could afford to ask them what they want to do about it instead of telling them what they would *have* to do about it. As a consequence, the staff replied with a flow of suggestions like the following:

"I think we should test our children more often, so we teachers will not be working in the dark."

"We need help in re-examining the way we teach reading in the lower grades. When I get the children in the high school, it is too late to do much for them. Perhaps we should invite a specialist in reading to come and work with our whole school system for a month or two."

"That isn't long enough, unless we can have follow-up help for a year or two. This job isn't easy if we really do want to feel that every child has had a fair chance. There are some pretty difficult cases."

Mr. H.: "There are so many suggestions. How about a planning committee representing the various parts of the school system to work out a statement of needs and suggest some first steps?" (Agreement) "Will the professional staff committee consider this and let me have the names of the special committee on reading? Should there be any lay members on it?" (Discussion) "Well, if you feel uncertain about it, let's make the committee entirely professional, but I'd like to see it broadened at any point you feel comfortable to do so." (No attempt to violate others by forcing an uncomfortable situation on them, yet no apologies for his own position either.)

Teacher: "Mr. Harwick, I'd like to say something." (Everyone looked at speaker.) "There is one thing that is so plain it should not have to wait for committee work."

Mr. H.: "There is, Louise? What it is?"

Louise: "Well, it's our stock of library books. The teachers say that in some of our schools the books are old and worn out, and there aren't enough anyway. It's hard to find interesting materials for slow-reading boys in grades two and three, and it's hard to find even enough books to keep them flowing to the fast readers, especially in the upper grades."

Mr. H.: "Are you suggesting that we do something about this in the next budget?"

Louise: "Yes, or sooner than that." (Laughter)

Mr. H.: "Will you head up a committee to get reports from all schools on what they think is necessary and what they consider desirable? I'm not promising anything, but our school board is cooperative. We may have to find a way to let our parents know about this, too. After all, the public supports our schools."

It is evident that Louise's experiences had led her to approach this situation openly, seeing no threat to herself in it. If she saw a threat, the self-trust in her ability which she had also learned made it possible for her to enter the situation to speak up for the children—so she acted. As a result, she inspired the leader to trust her and found herself in a position of leadership in which she was able to help others to function cooperatively in the solution of a common problem. We can assume that Louise's ideas had been received well in previous experience, and that out of repeated successes she had learned to trust herself.

In the case of the superintendent, as leader, it is easy for him to establish an "open" setting. Since he is the legal as well as the professional leader, his responsibilities are great. He has a personal and a professional investment in outcomes. Not only is his professional reputation at stake, his family depends upon his income, his children are proud of him, and he feels that he must not "let them down." But, he, too, *has learned* his feelings and teaches others by his ways of behaving. Even in this simple everyday vignette, it is apparent that people are interacting on the basis of the feelings of integrity they have and, in turn, are affecting the feelings of self-trust and regard for others. The administrator's responsibilities do not set aside the principles of human relationships; they only increase the potency of their operation. They cannot be ignored or suspended, only put in operation positively or negatively, knowingly or unknowingly.

Adequate Administrators and Teachers Nurture Adequacy in Each Other

Adequate school administrators and teachers have qualities of dignity, integrity and autonomy and are able to create the "open" environments to nurture these characteristics in each other as well as in children and youth. An administrator should be chosen in part for his ability to release creativity in the adults who work with him, and for the ability to utilize the wisdom of others to help him reach judgments. Having genuine self-trust, he considers it a strength to wait for others, and does everything possible to act upon the best pooled judgments of his staff. He takes care not to allow the daily pressures to distract him from his goal, putting productive professional staff relationships first among the conditions necessary for a good school system.

Even the administrator originally chosen because he had a reputation as a good disciplinarian or needed to be "retired" from his job as football coach can learn to behave in these ways. These are not mystical matters, but things that can be learned by anyone. The first step is to discover they are important and worth seeking, for none of us spend much energy on what does not seem important to us. The number of adequate persons our schools produce can be increased by adminstrators who consider it important to surround children with persons of dignity and integrity. Such an administrator realizes the relationships of democratic processes to the development of free, honest people, and he takes care to make these processes a part of his own interaction with the staff and the children. He is aware that it is not the matter of administrator-staff contacts that is important, nor the particular tasks entrusted to staff members. It is, rather, the quality of trust, of faith, which penetrates these situations. An effective leader must really trust, not manipulate, people or decisions. He notes that mutual respect for dignity and integrity emerges where trust exists, and self-other appreciation runs deeply. Eventually, such behavior becomes habitual, a part of the "inner core" of his personality, and he is to a greater degree self-actualizing.

Supervisors and principals working in such settings "come alive." Their self-trust leads them to see themselves and to see the school and its opportunities in the larger context of society. Professional work is not a daily chore, stifling and rigid, but a service which is satisfying because it is at once self-fulfilling and creative.

Adequate Persons Often Emerge into Positions of Leadership

The dignity, integrity and trust of fully functioning persons in themselves inspire trust from others. Frequently, they are chosen for leadership roles because they can be trusted to take into account other people's ideas before making judgments. They can be counted on not to usurp authority, but to act with, for and through others. They make an effort to use fair processes and to reach fair judgments.

As people increase in adequacy, they seem to use their potentialities in a larger social context with less reference to self in selfish ways. Others are increasingly accepted as extensions of one's self, their well being considered as essential to one's own. "The one who sees human beings as essential to his own enhancement," says Kelley, "develops values related to the welfare of people." Combs implies that they may even envelop enemies in the circle of identification; that is, that they may perceive "enemies" openly, trying to understand them. The broader backlog of meanings which such persons have gleaned seems to enable them to develop values which lead them to put service to others above tangible rewards. They show interest, pity, compassion, warmth, humanity (Combs), and a nonhostile sense of humor (Maslow). Their inner lives are satisfying, and they do not seem to need the outward symbols of success that less adequate people require. They see others as extensions of the self, not as alien objects to be exploited.

Maslow,[1] in another book, says that such men and women are often in positions requiring sacrifice; they have "some mission in life, some task to fulfill, some problem outside of themselves which enlists their energies." Combs points out that they "work harmoniously with others in either a leader or follower role." In varying degrees, they are able to forego the immediate for long range goals and to see present events in a broader context. Some church and state leaders, teachers and other adults in the community are likely to be among these.

All Persons Need To Grow in Dignity and Integrity

While we find some people in almost every group who exemplify these self-regulating qualities to some extent, it is imperative that all people have continuous opportunities to grow toward a greater sense of self-acceptance, autonomy, dignity and integrity. Due to the authoritarian voices which surround children and youth as they grow up, many fall far short of the goal. In very few is the demand for self-expression so deeply imbedded in the core of the person that it seems to weather all obstacles and come to fruition. Yet the need is for each one, no matter how weak or how strong the capabilities, to have those experiences which will carry him beyond the consciousness of self into realization of self in the broader universe.

[1] A. H. Maslow. *In the Self.* New York: Harper & Brothers, n.d.

THESE CHARACTERISTICS CAN BE LEARNED

We are concerned in this chapter with the implications for education in helping persons develop into individuals of dignity, integrity and autonomy. We believe these attributes are, in large measure, concomitants of the environment which impinges positively upon the individual, reflecting especially the feelings about self as they emerge in relation with human beings. Situations where the conditions for social development are kept open and fluid are most favorable for the development of these characteristics.

Teachers who trust their own adequacy provide the settings in which teachers and children may also live in an atmosphere of self-trust. Teachers must be encouraged to live honestly and creatively with themselves and with children, studying them, making it possible for children to be themselves, listening to what they say, and observing what they do. The teachers' trust in themselves to take appropriate steps to help children acquire the sense of adequacy from which dignity and integrity flow must be encouraged.

Young children can learn to recognize that all persons behave both admirably and unadmirably at times. The teacher was helping Lee, a five-year-old, see that young Roy, who was under attack because he had spoiled their recent game, was not "bad," that he had not acted very well just then. After a while, something of the understanding of the integrity of humanness seemed to penetrate young Lee's mind, when suddenly he literally thrust himself toward the center of the circle, saying with deliberation, "I know what you mean. I like Mr. Castro, but I don't like what he does." The teacher inquired, "You mean you do like Roy, even if you don't like what he did today?" "Yes," said Lee, "that's how it is."

Here was an incident in which the teacher's readiness and ability to identify with Roy and to help children differentiate between the "inner core of humanness" and the changing, vacillating incidents of outward behavior helped a child better to understand both himself and others. Stimulating him to see a similarity to something he had struggled to clarify, his teacher enabled him in turn to bring clarification to the situation in the classroom. Such reaching out and reaching up "on tiptoe" increase the sense of dignity and integrity with which individuals meet future situations. Who knows where the widening circles of such influence come to rest? In this case it may be that the increased sense of dignity and integrity accrued not only to Lee, but extended to Roy and to other children who comprehended something of the nature of Lee's understanding. It might even have extended to the teacher, when in the still, small moments of self-evaluation she recounted and revalued the role she had played. "Sometimes," perhaps she says to herself, "they seem to learn more from mistakes than from the many right moves they make."

When an atmosphere of respect for dignity and integrity is created by an understanding teacher, children themselves can carry on the tradition. When children's own feelings of worth are fulfilled, they are free to fill the needs of others as well.

The following instance illustrates the personal dignity with which a child expressed her self-trust by ascribing dignity and extending warmth to another child, a newcomer in the group.

The principal brought a new child to the room. "I'd like to introduce Mary Wilk," she said. Mary was unkempt and her made-over ill fitting dress hung below her knees. The children stared at her. Mary looked uncomfortable.

Then Gladys, a very well dressed little girl, rose, came forward and said, "I'm the hostess, Mary. I'd be glad to have you sit at my table and I'll show you what to do. Do you know how to play Philadelphia Bat Ball?"

"No," said Mary, shyly.

"We'll teach you at recess time."

One would like to think that Mary could be responsive to this welcoming experience and, in due time, through trustful interaction with others, learn how to earn a place for herself by offering the same type of helpfulness to others in need of it. Children do not learn only from teachers. Warm, accepting, friendly, respecting atmospheres may compound their effects through the children themselves.

Here is another illustration:

The teacher of a sixth grade class was delayed, and the principal, passing by heard the children, accustomed to handling much of their own business, put the class president up for a hearing because he had pulled a knife on them a short time before. Alarmed, she stopped to listen. The fact that the knife was rubber didn't seem to soften the case in the eyes of the children.

"He had no business doing a thing like that."

"That's just like thugs—we're not that low."

Then the child in charge asked, "What do you think we should do?"

"Make him apologize."

"Take his office away from him. He isn't fit to be president when he can't control himself."

Charles' voice, half a sob, said, "I tried to get you to listen and you wouldn't. I didn't know what else to do."

"Ann."

A gentle voice was heard as Ann entered the situation. "I don't think it was all Charles' fault. We were wrong, too. If we had listened when he called the meeting to order, he wouldn't have done that. I think he should have another chance and we should act right, too."

A moment of silence. Then, "Yes," "I think Ann's right," and the chairman's voice, "All those that think the way Ann does, say 'yes.' "

Many voices responded. Then Charles said, "Thanks. I'll do my best. We'll have a meeting tomorrow morning."

The principal passed on down the hall, feeling that a climax had been reached and successfully passed, and that some children had stretched into the future in their understandings and their emotions. She knew, too, that once again children had demonstrated a fundamental sense of integrity, and that they could be trusted to go far in self-direction.

The Dignity and Integrity of the Profession

To produce an atmosphere in which dignity and integrity are encouraged, we need teachers who, themselves, are given opportunities to be people of such character. Children learn from their relationships, but you cannot have a relationship with "the little man who isn't there." Effective relationships exist only with people who are important to us; the rest we ignore or pass by. Teachers who are going to have *real* effects upon children, therefore, must themselves be somebody. We have not always valued teachers in our society. We have seen that people learn their self concepts through their experience with those around them, and this goes for teachers also. Much as we may occasionally forget it, teachers, too, are human beings. A society which takes a destructive attitude toward its teachers is treading on dangerous ground. Education has become important for survival itself. We can no longer with impunity undermine the morale of teachers. The day is gone when education was a luxury. Education has become a necessity, and we cannot afford to have it done badly.

We need teachers who stand for something, who themselves have the courage to be. We must have them, not because it is a nice idea, but because it is a vital necessity for producing the kinds of people we need to produce. To have such teachers we need, on the one hand, to eliminate the factors that impede and detract from their free operation as people and, on the other, to actively encourage and facilitate the development of professional integrity.

Among other things this means we must:

In the community . . .

Give teachers the freedom to be themselves, to be human

Stop demanding of them behavior standards out of line with the rest of the human race

Stop exploiting teachers for unreasonable tasks outside their professional duties

Above all, pay them enough to get the kind of people we need into the profession.

In schools . . .

Protect teachers from community pressures to teach for vested interests and encourage teachers in the freedom of the classroom to look at even the most unhappy events of our world

Treat teachers as people of dignity and integrity, trustworthy and responsible at every phase of our operation

Include and use teachers in decision making at every level of school operation

Encourage the professionalization of teaching

Encourage teachers to take a stand and protect and support them when such courageous action comes under attack.

Education Should Make Way for "Peak Experiences"

For the purpose of encouraging unity, education should give some place, says Maslow, to "peak experiences"—to raw, concrete, esthetic experiences, especially of subjective happenings inside oneself, "a central aspect of human life and of psychology." These experiences, Maslow continues, are integrative, combining observation, insight and feeling, and helping to validate life learnings. They should be treated, not as peripheral, but as central to education.

Thus, in school, the reading of a poem, the viewing of a thunderstorm or a rainbow, the warm, relaxed, friendly discussion of a common interest, the enjoyment of music or painting or dance, even the sharp struggle to express and understand differing viewpoints—all these are charged with meaning and can contribute to self-discovery and fulfillment. Students need time to browse, to paint, to muse, to dream, to think, to touch, to read, to love—to feel the quality of experience, its beauty and its ugliness. These things cannot be hurried—and today we are in a hurry. Our children must grow up fast. Childhood is no longer cherished as a period of life which is "its own excuse for being."

Experiences such as these are integrative, restorative. Enabling the person to rise above himself, above time and space, into an awareness of worth, of value, of wholeness, of unity with all others, they are sharply reality-creating. Such experiences bring insights which become touchstones for the future, gold mines of resources for reverie and recreation out of which self-realization is fostered. These experiences issue not out of scheduled preciseness or planned perfection; they are not ordered to happen. They derive gracefully out of effortlessness and timelessness, as escapes into a world known only to the one who experiences them. Such experiences give depth to perception, increasing understanding and the very stature of the individual. From these momentary ascendancies he returns refreshed, clear-seeing, guileless and courageous, reoriented with himself and his universe. It is this that, in our post-Sputnik fright, we are in danger of losing from our schools, if we ever had it.

SOME PRACTICES WHICH ENCOURAGE CONCEPTS OF DIGNITY AND WORTH

The Open Classroom

To explore and discover self most effectively, we need classrooms which do not place unrealistic limitations upon what may be explored. We need to create feelings that school is a helpful place where *anything* can be looked at, particularly those things of concern to young people. Schools must matter, but they cannot do so with censorship on what may be examined. Teachers and pupils must be free to look at what is *needed* to deal effectively with problems. This calls for open classrooms which encourage and help the exploration of the world, including unpopular causes, like communism; unhappy human relationships, like anger or divorce; human feelings and attitudes of whatever nature, like love, hate and kindness; even taboo subjects, like religion, crime or sex.

In an eighth grade, a small group was reporting to the class a story which pinpointed a family situation in which a daughter had rebelled against her father and run away. There followed an "open" discussion as to whether the daughter's action was justified. Quite soon the discussion evolved into a commentary limited to three children who supported each other in condemning the father. The teacher, noting this, said, "I hear only three voices. Doesn't anyone else have a viewpoint on this? Janet, haven't you read that book?"

"Yes," said Janet, "and I thought the daughter could have been more helpful to her father. I know he was wrong and was not fair to her, but he was her father and she owed him loyalty."

The discussion continued, now on the question of how much loyalty children owe parents and parents owe children. Finally, George burst forth impulsively, "He's just like my old man, mean and cranky. But he's my old man and most of the time I like him. You have to understand people like that." So, in an open classroom one child who had dealt with and resolved an ambivalence arrived at such maturity of insight that he was able to help others advance toward greater maturity.

Sometimes young people are on the spot to make use of the integrity they feel. An instance of this sort occurred at the twelfth grade level. Charles had been asked to run for president of the student council. He shrugged his shoulders and refused. The principal, hearing of this, sent for

Charles to encourage him to try. After hedging for some time, Charles said bluntly, "So you really want to know why I won't, Mr. Emmons? Well, it's because you can't do anything! The faculty runs it, and faculty members tell the kids what to do. I don't want a job like that. I want to think for myself and have the kids help me." Charles was elected. But suppose this feeling had never been brought out in the open? It could never, then, have been dealt with.

Another instance illustrates how a teacher helped an entire group of students who had learned to use subterfuge in dealing with their surroundings to recognize reality more clearly and deal with it more honestly.

In a summer school of six weeks, interest in a unit which was presumably "child-chosen" dragged heavily. Finally the teacher decided that something was wrong. Closing the door to visitors, she approached the children, saying that good living requires honesty and "working together," that she, as one member, was not happy because she did not feel that they were happy. Eventually a boy said, "Well, I can tell you I don't want to study the local community."

"But you didn't object to it when I asked you on Monday."

"I didn't know you well enough then."

The teacher then discovered that few of them really wanted to study it, but had thought it expedient to identify with the teacher in *what they thought she wanted.*

"But I don't care what we study," she said. "I told you that. This is a class which is not required to cover a particular thing. Now you must believe me and we must be honest with each other." Eventually they settled on aviation, and were on the way with new plans. Presumably each child now was a freer and a wiser person.

Giving Approval to the Honest, Sincere Expression of Others

Part of maturing is learning that the privilege of self-expression accompanies similar expression by others. Youth vacillates, as older persons do, in granting this privilege. Yet, when the situation is right, the more adequate person can be detected at work, and growth is sometimes obvious.

Child: "My church is best."

Another: "No, mine is."

First child: "Mine is."

Another: "Well, all churches are all right; it depends on which one your father and mother go to."

Child: "You mean the synagogue is all right?"

Child: "Sure. I guess it doesn't tell people to do wrong things, does it?"

It is an easy thing to squelch participation or communication when we become fearful of the outcomes of discussion or anxious to protect children from making mistakes. An open classroom must be willing to run some risks. It is a normal part of learning to flounder, run down cul-de-sacs and frequently get off the track. To discourage this is to interfere with learning and to rob children of opportunities to look. Without looking, there is no seeing or understanding.

Understanding Intentions and Protecting Participants

In the following instance, help in this direction is not spectacular, but quiet and thoughtful, and reflects empathy and self-unity. A boy who had been transferred from school to school for disciplinary reasons entered the class of a teacher who had been successful in inspiring self-trust in students who lacked it. Day after day Douglas sat, taking no part in what was going on. Occasionally the teacher quietly made it known to him that they would be glad to have his help in the various activities, but his social removal seemed impenetrable. School visitors—and there were many—criticized sharply, but the teacher threw a protective shield around Douglas. "Please—no pressure. I may be entirely wrong," she said, "but pressure has been used and it has failed. Waiting has not been used—for this short time he's mine, and I'm waiting."

Then the time drew near for an all day trip to the airport. Names were being listed and car groups organized. Softly into Douglas' ear the teacher whispered, "We'd love to have you go with us, Douglas. You could let us know about it tomorrow when you come to school."

There was scarcely a glimmer of acknowledgment—only a nervous shuffling of the feet. It was a complete surprise, when, very early next morning, before the other children came, Douglas appeared at the door carrying on a board an intricately made plaster of Paris model of the airport.

"Is it for us, Douglas?" asked Miss M.

"Yes," answered Douglas, shyly.

"Well, let's put it in a good spot where we can all see it."

As Douglas arranged his display, Miss M. stepped into the hall where Douglas' mother was waiting and weeping softly.

"He never went to bed," she said. "He worked at it all night long, and then couldn't wait to get here."

Miss M. knew that a crisis had been weathered. She knew, too, that there were many long slow steps to be taken and some regressions to be endured before Douglas' self-acceptance and self-trust would have the tensile strength to enable him to stand with dignity and integrity. In an atmosphere which protected him in his moment of need from difficult outside pressures and from the necessity of immediate action, Douglas could regroup his forces for another try. The door had opened; guidance would still be required, to be sure, but with firm and reassuring support.

Learning To Disagree Without Being Disagreeable

To maintain one's dignity in a dispute and to grant dignity to the other person are marks of increasing maturity and self-confidence. Paul and Bob, tenth graders, were in a situation which demanded this. The subject was the War Between the States; Bob was from Dixie and Paul from the North. The boys caught fire and the teacher and the other children obviously withdrew to the sidelines to watch the fray, some embarrassed, some amused and some frightened. It was too serious for intervention. Bob was defensive, and his defensiveness caused him to identify Paul with all the dishonor his heritage had made him feel. Paul was aggressive and self-righteous.

In the middle of the fray, Bob hurled, "Where do you have a man to match Lee? He's the greatest man the country has ever had—he should have been president!"

"Oh, I don't know," said Paul, "we had Lincoln and he *was* president, a great one. I guess he was the kindest man we've ever had. He could," faltering a bit, "he could even fight without getting mad." His futile hand gesture indicated his self-accusation. Embarrassed, he laughed; Bob gulped—and laughed—and the children relaxed. Later in the day, Bob and Paul were seen walking home together. When they returned, they asked if they could have a real debate about which man was greatest—Lee or Lincoln—and, to everyone's surprise, Bob wanted to speak for Lincoln and Paul for Lee. "We each know too much about our own man," they said, "and too little about the other. Besides, Lincoln and Lee liked each other." Both boys had learned respect for an opposing viewpoint; perhaps the other children had, too.

Developing Purposeful Direction with Others in Groups

In schools where dignity and integrity of children are a major concern of the staff, cooperative planning plays a big role. The staff carries much responsibility for the school. Taking into consideration the needs of the children and the larger society, they have the final decisions regarding areas to be studied, major activities of children, and many other things. But this authority has been given, insofar as possible, "by consent of the governed." Children have been taken into confidence, and they understand that in all large enterprises no individual or group can operate with complete independence.

Cooperative planning also plays a still small but deep role in those moments when the teacher and the child talk over "personal" matters of concern. When it is about progress, the child is helped to think out his own goals and plans. Some teachers, in order to encourage habits of distributing time well, have used a "contract" system in which agreements for work to be done are mutually reached. Yet once reached, there is no nagging by the teacher, no deterioration of personalities. With dignity each carries on his own life. Children work alone or in groups, helping and receiving, giving or getting help. Sometimes, when time has not been well planned, the expiration of the contract draws near without accomplishment, and the last few days are heavy with responsibility. At such times children chide themselves. The teacher listens, smiles, sometimes may even renegotiate a contract to lighten the load. In the next contract period, the chores are almost certain to be better distributed.

Autonomy, or self-management, is learned in an atmosphere where the adult helps to plan and expects results, but he allows the learner much freedom to learn how to budget time and when to work and when to play; he encourages self-conversation in which the student literally states his problem and tells himself what he ought to do, and then expects his own growth. The teacher in this setting is much more a friend than a pedagogue, much more a counselor than an advisor.

The true "group situation" (the interacting group—not the mere numerical group) provides a good climate for the development of dignity and certain kinds of autonomy, sometimes through negative as well as positive behavior. Group activities are group planned, however, with group, not teacher purposes. Each member does what he can do to set forward the group's purposes; the annoyer and the time-waster learn from the others that byplay, although attractive, is not to be tolerated when a group is working in a serious-minded way toward a coveted goal. As he learns to be an effective group member, however, he comes to place trust in his own integrity—in his ability to meet the purposes of the situation as they are, rather than to feel a need to distort the purposes to give himself a central role. Gradually, he makes gains in trusting himself and in using the self with dignity and autonomy to accomplish his goals, whether these are for work or for play. In fact, he becomes a more flexible, a more reality-centered, a more adequate person.

The teacher's strongest role in group activity should be as keeper of the climate or environment, helping to maintain its warmth, openness and richness. The lessons which children teach each other must not be too cruel, too hard-learned. Intruding only where he feels that his help is needed, withdrawing where it seems that his absence will contribute, making it known that, no matter what the shades of difference, he trusts the humanness of every child present, the teacher helps unobtrusively and often indirectly to set the stage for growth in self-acceptance, self-challenge, mutual trust and purposefulness. This is not a task for a weak teacher, but for one who has self-unity, dignity and self-autonomy. If he has these characteristics, his natural attitude toward children and toward conditions which will enhance their steady growth in positive self-perception may be trusted generally to be "right."

On school staffs, teachers with a high degree of self-acceptance can serve as facilitating persons to help others become more trusting. They actively improve interrelationships by such attitudes, for the integrity and dignity felt by a well integrated person reduce the threat felt by others.

SOME PRACTICES HARM DIGNITY AND INTEGRITY

We have already pointed out the degrading influence of authoritarianism, beginning imperceptibly in the young child's life, persisting, often increasing, at school. Punishment in the form of guilt and shame and reward in the form of acceptance and approval are also commonly used to coerce children into conformity. These and similar practices used in this way are genuine obstacles to the development of a high degree of adequacy. Among practices which should be examined are the following:

The increasing fetish of teaching subjects, particularly reading, at a given age or grade, despite the readiness of the child, seriously violating the autonomy of large numbers of children.

Increasing intolerance of natural play, diverting it to entertain adults. In some places no play seems any longer to be judged "good" if it is not "organized." The emphasis upon athletics in many places has become synonymous only with team sports open to but a few. Though some value occurs from this for a few, there is no doubt that others are shamefully exploited and we have given little or no attention to the destructive effects of disillusion and despair for those who do not "make the team."

The current demand for the grind of hard work—under the ruse that children must work hard, "must beat themselves out." For what? For survival—in a world in which modern developments proclaim that workers will work only a few hours each day and will have many hours of leisure? Some children in elementary schools and thousands in secondary schools spend interminable hours doing meaningless and uninspiring schoolwork at home to the detriment of family life, recreation, even entertainment. "All work and no play," it is said, "makes Jack a dull boy" —and indeed this may prove true.

Arbitrary measures of promotion, based "on external standards too difficult for some, and too easily attainable by others." [2] Negating the child's genetic—and morally honorable—patterns of growth and learning. Placing too much faith in what we have acquired some skill in measuring, even if these areas do not matter much, and ignoring those all important aspects of the human being more difficult to measure.

[2] *Conference Proceedings.* White House Conference on Children and Youth. Washington, D.C.: Superintendent of Documents, Government Printing Office, 1960. 85 p.

Authoritarian methods of deciding rules and regulations. Evidence shows that children and youth can be trusted to make "good" decisions in areas where they have experience and knowledge or, if they make faulty ones and are allowed to follow through, they may be trusted to see the error and take steps to correct it. What more can any of us do? Is not school a place where one safely *learns* the ways of democracy?

Arbitrary methods of grouping and segregating students, using limited goals (the development of the best) and evaluation of limited scope (usually academic aptitude or achievement), or cultural differentiations in terms of race, color, religion or economic status, reducing the dignity of large numbers of children in two ways: (a) by segregating some and running the risk of making them less acceptable to the rest of the human race; (b) by implying that many are second rate commodities, not worthy of the best the school can do.

Treatment of children as subordinates whose goals, ideas and activities have no value to the adult world. This lack of involvement, Kelley points out, is the cause of continuing warfare between adults and children and, indeed, between administrators and teachers.

Report card grades. Can we not make more use of the "steady growth" concept of progress? Can we not encourage growth along every line of development, but especially in the self concept of dignity and worth? Should we not rate the school a failure which does not steadily increase the feeling of dignity and adequacy in each one of its children?

Imposition of values from above; little opportunity to decide what is important, to talk things out.

The formation of cliques and sororities which become rigidly structured, narrowing the perceptions of children and youth.

Unrealistic use of time. Peak experiences require periods of "unhurry," of musing, of outward laziness—to meditate, to feel, to think, to observe, to enjoy, to deepen one's sense of orientation. These are necessary for the development of self-knowledge, of autonomy. Why must we always hurry along? Today's students are scheduled and hurried—in school, in the homes and communities, everywhere. When can strength in one's very own self flower?

The teacher's feeling that he must *produce*. Many a potentially good school situation is clouded by the teacher's expectancies. Something less than human development is the cherished goal: perhaps a favorable showing on a city chart, perhaps a principal's pride in "his" school, perhaps the teacher's own drive for achievement. Expectancies become rigid. Reading scores may soar; ego scores, diminish. Children's souls shrivel and wilt and wait for escape to a freer and more nurturing atmosphere. Can we not use what we know about individual differences, translating them in terms of the abilities of teachers and the situational differences of community schools?

Acceleration—the act of speeding up, of approaching a goal faster. The danger is not so much in the speeding as in the fact that speed may become the goal. "Nine-year-oldness is not good; you must be ten." "Ten-year-oldness is not enough; rush to be eleven," and so on. And so there is great loss of time while speeding. "We will not pass this way again," said a poet in a moment of insight. The time to be, to do, to achieve what one is *now* ready for, is lost in the urge to speed. *And this time will not return.* Those feelings and understandings which were right to develop may now never come. The urge to speed may well prove the great reducer of human worth.

Failure—the strong sense that some *must* fail and that failure builds strength. Where does all our observation and research on children and youth take us? Who is helped by failure? Even the self-perceptions of those who do not fail are not enhanced by the failure of other human beings. And certainly there is nothing but detriment to the self-conception of those who are arbitrarily labeled as failures.

Role self and real self. An individual is sometimes forced into a role which is alien to his real self. When this happens, he finds it difficult to assess or expose the real self. A case in kind is the student who became the class clown, but who, upon entering another school, renounced this role and became a serious student. Could this be avoided if teachers saw their roles as facilitators to help such a child explore and develop his natural self-role, thereby increasing his sense of dignity and integrity?

Some Practices Which Enhance the Self Concept

Where human development in dignity and honesty is put first, and other goals subordinated to more realistic positions—

Where each child's spiritual integrity—his right to be—is recognized

Where his individuality is considered an asset rather than a liability

Where his genetic growth patterns are respected and used as a basis for teaching

Where he helps to purpose and to plan

Where he can act freely, knowing those around accept him as he is

Where he can make an error—or even do wrong, and not lose face thereby

Where he can grow each day and know that he is growing

Where he can hold his head up high and meet the others' gaze

Where he can make friends, enjoy other people, learn how to extend a hand to help

Where he can learn the warm flood of gratitude that comes from being regarded with warmth

Where he can venture into unknown worlds and stretch his wings to find new truths

Above all, where he can experience success in subject matter, human relationships and the discovery of self as a person of worth and dignity—

In such an atmosphere, strong selves will grow, facilitated and tempered by the give and take, the struggle and the tolerance, the failure and the success, knowing that dignity which comes from being well loved and well respected.

CHAPTER 15

THE PROCESS OF BECOMING

FROM MASLOW

This force (dynamic force of the inner nature) is one main aspect of the "will to health," the urge to grow, the pressure to self-actualization, the quest for one's identity.

We can no longer think of the person as "fully determined" when this phrase implies "determined only by forces external to the person." The person, insofar as he *is* a real person, is his own main determinant. Every person is, in part, "his own project" and makes himself.

The process of growth is the process of *becoming* a person. *Being* a person is different.

FROM COMBS

People discover their self concepts from the kinds of experiences they have had with life; not from telling, but from experience. Adequate people . . . trust themselves and their impulses . . . utilize themselves as trustworthy, reliable instruments for accomplishing their purposes . . . can afford to take chances . . . do not have to be afraid of what is new and different.

FROM KELLEY

Since life is ever moving and ever becoming, *the fully functioning person is cast in a creative role.* But more than simply accepting this role, he sees creation going on all around him. He sees that creation is not something which occurred long ago and is finished, but that it is now going on and that he is part of it.

He sees himself as an ongoing part of a world in movement . . . in process of becoming. This follows from the whole notion of self and others and the acceptance that they can feed off each other and hence can improve.

FROM ROGERS

The self and personality emerge *from* experience, rather than experience being translated to fit a preconceived self-structure. It means that one becomes a participant in and observer of the ongoing process of organismic experience, rather than being in control of it.

The individual moves toward more acceptantly being a process, a fluidity, a changing. He lives in a more existential fashion.

Such living in the moment, then, means an absence of rigidity, of tight organization, of the imposition of structure on experience. It means instead a maximum of adaptability, a discovery of structure *in* experience, a flowing, changing organization of self and personality.

> The person who is in the process of becoming is . . . a human being in flow, in process, rather than having achieved some state . . . sensitively open to all of his experience—sensitive to what is going on in his environment, sensitive to other individuals with whom he is in relationship, and sensitive perhaps most of all to the feelings, reactions and emergent meanings which he discovers in himself.

THE IDEAS

The concept of the adequate personality as one consciously involved in the process of becoming brings an optimistic faith. The person who understands he is changing realizes he is creating self through experience. He looks forward to new experience. He has trust in himself as a free functioning individual, an instrument rather than a victim of his experience. He finds deep satisfaction in the process of becoming as he lives each experience fully. One of the major tasks of education is to produce citizens who are not finally organized and immovably structured.

The person who is cognizant of this process of becoming accepts change as a universal phenomenon. He welcomes change in himself, in others and in his situation. It follows that education must assume its responsibility for encouraging individuals to anticipate and to be able to cope with changes as they occur.

The adequate person seeks and accepts all aspects of experience as important elements in the process of becoming. The nonverbal aspects of experience are important to him as well as the verbal. He integrates thinking, feeling, knowing and sensing.

The person who is aware of the process of becoming and accepts changes in himself accepts the emotional qualities of life. Maslow suggests that healthier people accept impulses instead of rigidly controlling them. One characteristic of the adequate personality is his enjoyment of nonsense, fantasy and laughter. The process of becoming involves feeling and sensing as well as knowing. The fact that such affective experience is an essential dimension of becoming raises serious questions about the almost exclusively objective orientation of our society and its expression in our schools.

Finding joy in his own self-development, the person who is moving toward adequacy is willing to permit other people to "be," that is, he can accept others in the stage he finds them. He trusts them to grow and to "become." Administrators, supervisors and teacher educators are challenged by this concept to develop relationships which facilitate the process of "becoming."

IMPLICATIONS FOR EDUCATION

The Challenges to Teaching

The authors' concept of man in process—an ever changing, moving, becoming individual—challenges many of the beliefs and complacencies upon which school practices have been based. The fact that adequacy is a product of becoming means it is a matter of continuing growth. It means that children are not victims of life, hopelessly limited. All have the capacity to achieve in a greater or less degree and all can change, given favorable conditions for learning. It raises interesting questions about static groupings and about teachers' resigned acceptance of the few children in every class who cannot learn. It challenges special education for the slow learner when the term "special" serves to label or classify or limit opportunities for learning. It further questions our belief in the stable, inherited nature of intelligence and our firm faith in the intelligence quotient as a determining factor for identifying, classifying, grouping and teaching children. The problem of educating the gifted is seen from a new perspective. Instead of trying to find and teach them, the new challenge to education is *to produce more of them.* A view of the individual as becoming brings a new and optimistic view of the potential in every child for growth and development.

Educators who see themselves as continually in process, as learners as well as teachers, find the joy of becoming as they dare to accept challenges, to experiment, to try new approaches and apply the research of related disciplines. We must be aware of the factors which provide freedom to seek new experience. A positive self concept, identification with others and openness to experience are factors discussed in other sections of this volume. They are factors which permit the individual to move expectantly and with zest into the process of becoming. Education cannot ignore perceptions which contribute to inadequate behavior and limit the individual's freedom to seek challenge: negative definitions of self, inability to identify broadly with others, failure to accept reality of experience. The process of growth is impeded as children back away from new experiences, as teachers settle down in comfortable ruts of method and technique, and as schools attempt to maintain the status quo in a changing world.

Established sequences of defined curricula, fixed patterns and programs, rigid grade standards, unchanging physical arrangements, and instructional methods which rely heavily on question-answer techniques and a single text are conditions which tend to prevent the development of individuals who can accept change. The conditions in the school must free the individual to grow. Circumscribed choices, restricted areas of study and prescribed experiences limit learning. Individuals are a product of their choices, and teaching must not be a "fencing in" approach which limits the choices children can make.

Signs of Creative Teaching

Too many of a child's experiences in too many school situations say to him that he is not enough. When the teacher directs, controls, motivates, questions and evaluates, demands the excuse and asks the reason for behavior, the child must feel that it is wrong to be what he is. When teachers permit children to be what they are and not just what teachers want them to become, openness to experience and a self-directed moving into learning are possible. In such classrooms the following evidences of creative teaching and learning may be observed:

Less teacher domination; more faith that children can find answers satisfying to them.

Less teacher talk; more listening to children, allowing them to use the teacher and the group as a sounding board when ideas are explored.

Less questioning for the right answer; more open-ended questions with room for difference and the exploration of many answers.

Less destructive criticism; more teacher help which directs the child's attention back to his own feelings for clarification and understanding.

Less emphasis on failure; more acceptance of mistakes—more feeling on the part of the child that when he makes a mistake it is done, accepted and that's it. As one child said, "She doesn't rub salt in."

Children's work is appreciated, but praise is not used to put words in the mouths of children.

Goals are clearly defined; structure is understood and accepted by the group.

Within appropriate limits, children are given responsibility and freedom to work. "For once a teacher told us we could do it ourselves and really meant it."

Children are free to express what they feel and seem secure in their knowledge that the teacher likes them as they are.

Ideas are explored; there is an honest respect for solid information, an attitude of "let's find out."

There is a balance of common tasks and individual responsibility for specific tasks which are unique and not shared.

The teacher communicates clearly to children that learning is self-learning. Faith is demonstrated that all children want to become and pupils show satisfaction as they become aware of their growth.

Evaluation is a shared process and includes more than academic achievement.

Motivation for learning is high and seems inner-directed; pupil activity seems to say, "I've got a job I want to do."

The Right To Be Wrong

The right to make choices, which is central to becoming, implies also the right to make mistakes. Learning conditions which do not permit mistakes limit the child's freedom and his willingness to make his own choices. The very process of becoming involves the challenge of new experiences, of trying the unknown, and necessarily must result in mistakes. When children, teachers and administrators accept errors as a natural part of the learning process, growth is facilitated. The need to be always right, whether imposed by exacting standards or the expression of negative self-perceptions, is always a limiting, threatening condition. Education has a major responsibility to help children explore new experience and new meaning without penalizing or punishing the mistakes which are integral to that process. Adequacy is, after all, the product of freedom.

To ensure security, limits must be established which will provide challenge and "graded frustrations." The challenge to education is not to remove all limits, but to provide a stable structure which enables children to define the situation, to understand relationships and to evaluate their own behavior. Children and adults need to touch base, to sense surely where safety lies, if they are to function freely. Limits which are commensurate with the child's level of development also serve as challenges against which children can test their strength. A complete absence of frustration is deadening. Through the graded frustrations of classroom control, children learn to deal with reality and develop a necessary tolerance for frustration. It is only as children learn to cope with the reality of the environment that they acquire the strength of adequacy and achieve the balance between spontaneity and control to which Maslow refers. Schools must eliminate the restrictions and regulations built in by some administrators, but there is a need for reasonable limits which can ensure a degree of security and provide challenge for continuing growth.

The Challenge of Broader Experience

Schools are challenged to provide a balance of opportunities for nonverbal experiences, for a greater variety of visual, tactile and auditory devices. Firsthand experiences should implement abstract study. Children need time to explore the meaning of sound and motion, taste and touch. There should be many opportunities to enjoy feelings, to savor new sensory experiences. School programs which emphasize exclusively abstract learning and skill development limit the development of sensing and feeling which are also a part of the process of becoming. Large instructional groups and passive learning through television may sometimes be useful for introducing concepts, but cannot provide the essential personal experiences necessary to explore such areas.

The Need for Adequate Teachers

To develop people who see themselves in the process of becoming, the schools must provide teachers who are themselves well on the way toward becoming adequate persons. Other sections of this volume describe adequate persons as "open," "warm," "loving," "accepting" (of themselves and others), "confident," "informed" and "secure." The teaching behavior of such teachers would be characterized as being more responsive and less controlling than is current teaching in our schools. Such teachers would show understanding and acceptance through performing relatively more of such responsive acts as clarifying, meeting pupil requests, serving as a resource, interpreting, encouraging, being solicitous, offering alternatives and giving specific support.

These teachers would provide the necessary life space for pupil individuality, foster uniqueness and encourage pupil choices commensurate with pupil maturity. Such teachers would structure in a more open fashion; turn the structure back to the pupil or group, offering alternatives; set standards which are group developed or generally accepted by society. When necessary, the teacher would evaluate pupil performance in content areas and correct behavior.

Learning experiences which help children enter confidently into the continuing process of becoming can be achieved only to the extent that the teacher is a real and vital part of the learning situation. His personality and his joy in becoming create an atmosphere that frees children to make choices and to accept challenge. The genius of good teaching is not merely the satisfaction of needs but the creation of needs which the child may not know he has. When children are given opportunities for fresh experiences and are stimulated to explore meanings and develop insights and mastery, they have new needs to know. Teaching, then, becomes a process of helping children to satisfy their immediate needs and to create future needs in an ascending, never-ending hierarchy. The value of field trips, personal discussions and a variety of experiences can be realized to the extent that they increase the need to know and so motivate new learning. Teachers also facilitate learning as they involve children in planning and evaluating. Much has been written about the problem solving approach, pupil-teacher planning, and self-evaluation. Teachers are challenged to use these methods and to try new ways of working with children.

Organization for More Effective Learning

In organizing pupils for instruction, flexibility is essential to foster the development of persons who see themselves in the process of becoming. What is the best organizational pattern to provide opportunities for individual choices, for personal communication, for dealing with feelings, for the development of personal responsibility?

Individuality and uniqueness can be nurtured by schools only when there is sufficient physical as well as psychological space. When hordes of pupils are brought together in some of our "economically efficient" schools, the sheer numbers require formalized, standardized, regimented control of actions to prevent chaos. While under the immediate circumstances the regimentation may be necessary, no one seems to think of the consequences of 12 or 13 school years of this kind of diet. Under these conditions how could a child learn that uniqueness and individuality are cherished? Where would he develop the attitudes and behavior patterns of responsible, free men? A person learns his own values and what to value in the world through the way he is treated by the people close to him. If wealthy America provides only crowded classrooms in crowded school buildings located on small crowded school sites, then it would indeed be miraculous if pupils coming through these schools held individuality sacred or cherished uniqueness.

If there are a large number of pupils in the instructional group, then the teacher will have to regiment the pupils. If there are a large number of instructional groups in a school, then the administration will have to regiment the groups. The freedom available to individuals will always vary directly with the number of persons per square foot of floor or land space available to them. This seems to be particularly true of active children.

The trend toward smaller instructional groups must be continued and the trend toward crowding larger numbers of students into inadequate school plants will have to be reversed. Larger classrooms and school sites are needed to increase the relative amount of space per pupil. Often an instructional group will need space beyond the regular classroom for consultation, committee work, or laboratory and construction activities. Urban and consolidated school districts must find solutions to the pressure of increasing numbers of pupils and crowded buildings. Communities must face realistically the problems of financing and supporting building programs, and school administrators must experiment with organization of space, time and personnel which will allow children to engage actively in the process of learning and becoming.

Challenge to Professional Growth

In-service and preservice education programs are challenged by the concept of the adequate person as one who knows the joy of becoming. Are teachers encouraged to question the implicit, to be creative, to change practices? Are they encouraged to seek and to exercise genuine academic freedom? Are they protected from threat and coercion and encouraged to explore all experiences and all meanings with their classes? Is there respect for the uniqueness of the individual or is the goal of teacher education programs to produce persons who think and act and teach alike?

Teachers are generally highly self-critical, seeking better ways of working with children. Training and supervisory programs should provide for success experiences and support teachers when they are experimenting. Criticism or praise limited to one aspect of the teaching situation may undermine concepts of adequacy and say to teachers that they are not enough. Such barriers can block a teacher's willingness and desire to grow toward greater professional adequacy. Serious morale problems result when teachers do not see themselves in process, when the striving to become is replaced by conformity to set policies and supervisory control and direction. Teacher education programs and methods of supervision can be improved if the focus is upon helping persons to become more adequate and to learn means of fostering adequacy in others.

Challenge to Communities

Society, too, has a responsibility to teachers. Support must be provided so that teachers can become and can function more fully. Restrictive codes and regulations must be lifted. More opportunities must be provided for leisure time. Work loads must be reasonable with time for professional planning and study, time for relating to children. Teachers are generally dedicated, becoming people, and their status in the community should reflect and support their sense of adequacy.

The faith we have in others' becoming can only be realized as it is a genuine expression and a reinforcement of personal trust that each of us is continually in the process of self-actualization and is finding joy in that process.

PRACTICES WHICH ENCOURAGE OR LIMIT THE DEVELOPMENT OF ADEQUACY

Good schools and good teachers are continuously seeking new ways and conditions to facilitate development of understanding and the process of becoming. The practices which will be described are mere samples of ways of helping children see themselves becoming through teacher relationships, teacher behavior, school organization, evaluation procedures, supervision and teacher education.

Personal Communication

Learning about one's self is and must be personal. Yet many school environments tend to be exclusively that of the total group. New ways must be found that will encourage personal communication. Some elementary teachers have organized their classroom space to provide a place for quiet reflection and thinking through of problems and for uninterrupted conferences. A screen, a corner of the room, an unused entrance way, a pair of comfortable chairs away from the hustle and bustle of group activities invite this kind of very personal talk of experiences. Teachers have also found that an organization of time is necessary if space, however inviting, is to be used. A schedule geared to a tight sequence of reading groups and arithmetic classes cannot provide the time necessary for meaningful communication. There must be flexibility of time arrangements and a willingness to depart from planned activities when talk of personal experience is important to a child. And finally, teachers have demonstrated that there must be an organization of children which will permit the interested personal contact of boys and girls with their teachers. Experimentation with large and small group activities, with the use of resource personnel, with team teaching arrangements and with methods of sharing the responsibility for large group activities promises to provide opportunities for really individualized one-to-one relationships of teachers with children.

But no arrangement, no juggling of time or space, can make personal communication meaningful, can contribute to children's understanding of their own becoming, unless it is based on a genuine accepting relationship. No child explores deeply the meaning of personal experience unless the teacher who encourages that exploration has communicated to him unconditional, positive regard and empathic understanding. This is especially true on the secondary level. Acceptance is a necessary condition for honest communication, and teachers who establish such relationships create a climate which helps students develop insights into themselves in process. The value of such individual conferences was suggested when a 10-year-old reported, "Private talks have helped me. I've actually seen myself growing. I have discovered my own weak points as well as strong ones, and I'm having fun with the idea. I almost can't stop, like a small child with a new toy."

It is not only in close personal relationships that children learn to see themselves as part of the ongoing growth process. Such understanding may also be developed in small group relationships. When a group feels relatively secure and friendly, there is much its members can learn from each other. Teachers who encourage children to talk about their experiences, their feelings, their working through of problems and frustrations, report that young people gain deeper insights from such exchange.

Understanding the process of becoming in others is sometimes a first step in understanding and accepting that process in oneself. The nine-year-old who said, "When we were talking about Martha's experience,

I kind of put myself in her place and saw why she felt the way she did," was evidencing this growth in empathy. Beginning understanding of the feelings of others was also indicated when a sixth grade boy wrote, "I grew from the discussion because I learned how girls feel—I think this helped me because I never was a girl and I never knew how they feel when they aren't chosen." That such understanding of others can be projected into self-insight is supported by the following statement of a 10-year-old: "The discussion today untangled a lot of snarled knots inside me. I'm glad we got a chance to let loose and express our feelings. It's easy for us to 'pass judgment' on someone else, but it's real progress when we can see what's wrong with ourselves. The discussion helped me because I see other children have the same problems I do."

This kind of talk occurs only when teachers have created situations which *deserve* it. It will not occur under threat or on demand, but requires a climate of trust and mutual respect. While self-reports are not always revealing of self concepts, an awareness of self in process may be increased through personal communication. Could not more classrooms become laboratories for such learning?

"Remembering what I was" and "understanding what I am" may also help children anticipate "what I may become" and so learn something of the continuing, ongoing nature of man's attempt to achieve a more adequate self. A fifth grader's projection of her understanding of growth to the problems of maturity is reflected in this bit of writing: "My mother has always been overprotective of me. She does care about me, I guess, but she doesn't want me to grow up. Maybe it's because when kids grow up that automatically puts a mother in the older category, and who wants to be considered 40 or 50! I wish there was some way to prepare parents for this growing up process and the losing of children." Or again, looking ahead was evident when a nine-year-old, in reporting his grandparents' visit, wrote: "Old people need love and attention more than kids. We run around a lot and have so many things to do. They sit and think about themselves a lot and wonder if they are still needed."

Contacts with Other Age Groups

Contacts with several age groups are a natural part of children's out-of-school experiences. Watching young children's neighborhood play and seeing them in family relationships help us to be aware of how they learn through experiences with people of all ages, of their need sometimes to be the oldest, sometimes the youngest. Socialization might well be improved if opportunities for contacts with other age groups could be extended into the school situation. The process of socialization can proceed more smoothly and with less destruction of the inner core of personality if younger children are learning "how things are done" partly from older children.

The great majority of our schools, in their attempt to improve the efficiency of skill and subject teaching, have tended to group children on the basis of strict chronological uniformity. The six-year-olds are with the six-year-olds, the tens with tens, the twelves with twelves. This rigid age uniformity limits opportunities for children to see themselves in the growth process and points out the need for other grouping arrangements. This is not to suggest a return to the one-room school, but rather a willingness to experiment with more flexible cross-grade and -age groupings. That such experimentation is practical in many public school situations is evident from the reports of staffs who are trying nongraded classes, primary units and other administrative organizations. Teachers in traditional graded situations are also experimenting with team teaching and scheduled activities which at times bring together children of different age groups. We need more research in this area. Freedom to experiment and try is as vital to the becoming of a school system as it is for the children it teaches.

Wise Use of Records

Children may be further helped to see themselves becoming through the wise use of records. Pupil logs, samples of work collected over a period of time, children's own continuing evaluations, as well as teacher-kept records, enable boys and girls to recognize their progress and to see themselves in process. Such records provide valuable assistance to the teacher as he seeks to understand children's behavior and as he prepares for conferences with either pupils or parents, but are of even greater value to the child as he is encouraged to understand himself. They help to make more objective his remembering "as I was" and more reality-oriented his feeling of "where I am." One group of sixth graders kept individual logs over a year's time, each day recording their reactions, opinions and feelings. The logs were personal and respected by their teacher as private journals not subject to his criticism or evaluation. In addition to serving as daily attempts to achieve a greater measure of self-understanding and occasionally providing a safe release for emotional outbursts, the children used their logs to evaluate their growth as the year proceeded. The following excerpts from their evaluations indicate an awareness of becoming:

> I am slowly gaining confidence in myself and am beginning to give my ideas more, while earlier I thought my ideas were so simple that everybody knew them. I am beginning to disagree with people more now because I know now that there isn't always a "right."
>
> This year has taught me to know myself better. I know now that other children are like me and that they have problems, too. I have learned to take

criticism. I used to cry every time someone touched me. I am not so touchy now that I know the kids are just helping.

I'm more relaxed when I do things.

When I evaluate now I can look into myself and reason out why I do things.

I'm now less prejudiced about things and people. . . . I know how to present my ideas without being bossy. . . . I don't put off work like I did before, don't run away. This year has helped me grow up in my thinking and ways.

I have learned to think through a question. . . . I've had a chance to take part in the day's plan and to say in my evaluation what I think about the day, what was good, what was bad, and what needs to be improved. My whole attitude toward school has changed.

Discussions with children about their changing attitudes and feelings can help them understand the process of change. Schools also need to provide space for storing samples of the student's writing, for example, and to maintain a continuous record through high school. The youngster's folder might well include brief summaries of individual study projects, field trips, reports, types of art experience he has enjoyed. Perhaps records need to be kept much more for the child and his use than for teachers and administrators. We have used the phrase "develop interest" for many years, but schools have usually failed to maintain any records or help the student evaluate his changing and deepening interests.

Free access to all information, test data, cumulative records, evaluations and inventories is necessary for realistic self-appraisal. Students should be encouraged to seek full knowledge about themselves, their abilities and achievements, and the progress they are making. Only to the extent that they are informed can students develop an awareness of the process of becoming. These principles seem equally valid at all levels of schooling from kindergarten through the graduate school in teacher preparation.

Climate

The things teachers do and the way in which they do them constitute the major school conditions facilitating development of the adequate personality. Every day of living with children provides many unplanned opportunities for helping boys and girls realize the process of becoming. A climate which encourages full acceptance of feelings, of anger or sorrow or joy, can help children understand the emotional qualities of living. Children need freedom to explore their feelings, to discover what it means to have fun, to be spontaneous, to feel cross, to experience sorrow. Teachers can help even young children value emotional experiences and so enable them to grow in psychological health. It is a principle of guidance that we cannot accept or cope with that of which we are not aware.

The teacher can give the child time to let his emotion play itself out. Legitimate outlets for anger may be provided in materials and activities so that negative feelings can be expressed without feelings of guilt. Children need time and a place to be alone when the stimulation of group activities seems to be threatening. Being alone should not be a punishment, but a right when it is needed. Teachers can also help children recognize signs of tension and plan acceptable ways to relieve that tension.

Creative Experience

The whole range of creative and expressive activities provides opportunities for children to explore esthetic experience: art, dramatic play, music, dance, free writing, role playing, creative dramatics, building, gardening. These activities and the products which children create help them to see themselves in action, at this moment, feeling what they do. They involve children deeply in the very process of becoming. Reflecting on such involvement, one child wrote, "Time stole out on tiptoes and we didn't look up to see it go. I was busy writing poetry when it left."

Directional Behavior

It is quite evident that in order to foster the development of the adequate person, teaching is needed which is accepting, understanding, responsive, and which provides a minimum of restriction and control. Yet perhaps the most striking characteristic of teaching today (in a wide sampling of schools) is the amount of heavy teacher direction and control present. In her report of a recent investigation of teaching, Hughes wrote:

> The most frequent and pervasive functions performed by the teachers were in the category of controlling. The teachers directed the children in what they should do and how they should do it; what they should answer and how they should answer. The extent to which children can explore ideas, reach out in their experience and on their own, is very limited under controls of the kind presently exercised. In approximately two-thirds of the 129 records, the control functions performed by the teachers exceeded 40 percent of all teaching acts.[1]

Supervision

Teachers in service should be treated in the same way that the teachers are expected to treat students. Becoming teachers are more likely to see evidence of becoming in students. Teachers should be helped to grow through accepting, understanding and assisting them in identifying problems which they feel need solution.

[1] Marie Hughes. *A Research Report: Development of a Means for the Assessment of the Quality of Teaching in Elementary Schools.* Salt Lake City: University of Utah Press, 1959.

The supervisor who is aware that teachers are in the process of becoming works in ways which help them develop a positive view of self. It is not uncommon for the supervisor to work in such a way that he, the supervisor, becomes the person who is reinforced and enhanced, even at the detriment and de-enhancement of the teacher. However, it is possible for the supervisor to support, encourage and enhance a teacher in areas that are important to the teacher, thereby aiding in the release of his potential. The supervisor gets his self-satisfaction as he sees others become more self-fulfilled. Paradoxically, the giver becomes the receiver.

School Organization

Continuity of school experience and organizational arrangements which increase flexibility are necessary to facilitate development of persons who see themselves in the process of becoming.

Nongraded. The nongraded elementary school represents one promising pattern of organization. Each child is permitted to proceed at his learning rate without the requirement that he achieve certain standards at specified time intervals. The nongraded school is more than a relabeling of classrooms; it demands careful staff planning to define goals and procedures. The trend toward substitution of numerous reading levels or other designations of achievement may result in more rigid goals than traditional grade levels. The emphasis in planning for school organization should be upon groupings which facilitate socialization and development of a concept of adequacy.

Vertical and Horizontal Articulation. Efforts to improve the vertical and horizontal articulation of school units also promise to strengthen the continuity of the educational process.[2] That kindergarten and nursery school program is most effective which helps to orient children to group living and to make an easy and natural step into the more academic world of the first grade. Indeed, the kindergarten is ideally an integral part of the primary department and requires pupils to make no formal transition as they proceed into the next years of the elementary school.

A basic theory in the introduction of the junior high school was that it would bridge the gap between elementary and secondary schools. However, such an objective is not easily or automatically achieved; in fact, its introduction, in some systems, has increased rather than eliminated gaps in continuity. To ensure a smooth transition from sixth to seventh grade requires the coordinated efforts of both elementary and junior high school principals and supervisors, a close working relation-

[2] Association for Supervision and Curriculum Development. *A Look at Continuity in the School Program.* 1958 Yearbook. Washington, D.C.: the Association, a department of the National Education Association, 1958. 306 p.

ship of the teachers involved, and a sharing of pupil personnel data. Similar arrangements are necessary if problems of articulation between junior and senior high schools are to be solved with neither repetition nor omission of academic and social experiences.

Perhaps the most serious gap exists for those students who proceed from high school into college. College entrance requirements have for too long been accepted as the determinants of many high school curricula, despite the large percentage of colleges which have no specific unit requirements for admission. The trend today in many secondary schools seems to be toward even more fixed schedules and course sequences. Extensions of the traditional 12 year program to include grades 13 and 14 in public junior colleges are limited but suggest one solution to the problem of maintaining a continuity of general education.

The difficulties of effective horizontal articulation, particularly at the secondary school level, are no less pressing in view of the increasing emphasis on the number of units required for graduation, the addition of more "solid" subjects, the demand for extended sequences in science and mathematics. Careful analysis is needed as more schools are substituting track programs, ability groupings and constant course requirements for the more flexible arrangements of core curriculum organization, general education courses, exploratory courses and broad offerings of electives. The pressure for departmentalization, homogeneous grouping and specialized instruction is today being felt in elementary schools as well. The total problem of articulating compartmentalized learnings at every school level is a challenge facing curriculum workers everywhere. Its solution requires a willingness to break with tradition, to consider the experimentation which discredited many of the very practices which are presently being revived, and to seek more creative approaches to school organization.

There is a clear need for more flexible grouping procedures across grade and age and ability lines if children are to learn to value the process as well as the achievements of learning and growing. Can the structure for school experience be found in the experience itself, rather than being necessarily imposed by the schedule on the particular subject of study? Can we find more flexible organizations of time and space and children in order that the structure of specific learning experiences may be adapted or changed as the experience requires? Can we devise more flexible teacher assignments for longer periods of time and in new patterns of team and group responsibilities? The solution of these and the many related problems of school organization will help to determine how well we will provide for the growth of adequate personalities who can understand and accept the integrated and continuous nature of the process of becoming and who can participate fully in that process.

Evaluation

Evaluation processes are significant factors in the development of the person who accepts and understands the process of becoming. The papers presented in this volume support the view that evaluation should be a continuous examination of immediate experience rather than a procedure used at the end of a unit of work or at a specified time. Efforts to focus on the processes of the classroom, to observe the teacher and learner in action, to sample work over a period of time, to record the relationships between the learning climate and the effect on children and between what the teacher says and does and how the children respond, are consistent with the concept of the individual as a growing, dynamic organism.

The idea that the individual is the instrument and not the subject of his becoming lends support to the efforts to shift the direction from evaluation by others to self-evaluation. The wise use of records which focus upon one's own work and feelings has been noted. To become involved in self-evaluation, the learner must be willing to look at his experience honestly and without defense. Through action research the individual defines criteria for evaluating his effectiveness, collects evidence and interprets its meaning. Self-evaluation also requires a trust in self; it is supported by the empathy and understanding of the teacher or of co-workers.

The conditions which help a person see himself in process may be established in pupil-teacher conferences, pupil-parent-teacher conferences, or supervisory contacts which encourage free, personal communication. Cooperative evaluation based upon mutual respect and acceptance may be a process of mutual learning as each participant has the opportunity to express his convictions and opinions and profit from the feedback.

While certain of the emerging theories of evaluation are consistent with the goal of greater self-realization, serious questions need to be raised regarding many of our *evaluation practices.* For example, do not many of the grades and ratings which we employ imply that learning is finally achieved rather than suggest the continuing nature of learning? How often do children interpret an "A" to mean this learning is accomplished? Do not grades and promotion tend to mark the conclusion of a particular study and to discourage the learner who is interested in extending the process of learning? How often does evaluation imply to students that they have completed and are finished with a particular course or subject?

The almost exclusive use of objective tests which present limited choices and require the selection of single right answers must also be questioned. If the exploration of ideas and the development of personal meanings are important to learning, evaluation practices should be consistent with these goals. Testing procedures need to be more open-ended to allow pupils to express their understanding and interpretation of information. Knowledge of facts alone is not enough, yet much school evaluation is based on the testing of factual information. While essay tests are hard to grade and records of observed behavior do not lend themselves well to standardization and statistical analysis, they may contribute more to the student's understanding of his progress in learning than does comparison with a norm.

Too many ratings of both pupil and teacher performance are imposed and are based on criteria which the individual rated does not understand or has never accepted. What effect does this have on the relationship which is teaching or is supervision? How does it help the individual to become a more fully functioning personality, accepting the process of becoming and finding joy and satisfaction in that process? These and similar questions need to be faced and adequate answers found if evaluation of pupils, teachers or program is to contribute to the production of self-actualizing, becoming persons.

Child-Study and Guidance

A major implication is suggested when the idea that the individual is not the victim of his experience is related to child-study and guidance practices. If teachers and other school personnel could be helped to appreciate this concept, more positive efforts might be exerted in children's behalf. The feeling that many children are the victims of their experiences—of broken homes, unfortunate family situations, class and caste differences—is sometimes a deterrent to school action. This is not to deny that the child is deeply affected by his environment, as is the adult, nor, on the other hand, is it to say that he is completely free and independent of environmental influences. Rather, we need to see the child as continually involved in the dynamics of experience, neither controlled by nor in control of his environment.

This would imply, first, that school personnel have a responsibility to know the environment in which children are operating. Do classrooms, for example, provide the kind of interpersonal relationships which will enable children to grow through active participation in the educative process? Are expectations realistic? Are limits reasonable and appropriate to individual stages of maturity and, within these limits, are children free and encouraged to try things on their own? Are pupil-teacher ratios such that teachers can know children as individuals, or do overcrowded classes force teachers to rely too heavily on conformity to rigid standards and large group instruction? Are the services of fully qualified resource personnel—school psychologists, visiting teachers, guidance specialists—readily available to teachers? And are teachers themselves secure in their own preparation and experience; are they adequate personalities?

We need also to be aware of children's out-of-school experiences and of the home and community environment in which they operate. We need to know home expectations and attitudes toward school, the models a child chooses for identification, the value systems and patterns of socially approved behavior of his neighborhood. We cannot afford to be ignorant of the social class and cultural conflicts which children of minority groups may experience or of the trend toward alikeness represented in many suburban areas. Our effort must be not only to know the reality of each child's environment, but, more important, to understand how he sees it, what his perception of it is. All may contribute to a deeper and more empathic understanding of individual children and of the environmental forces which affect their becoming.

An important correlative implication, however, must be drawn if such understanding is to help us to see children as a part of their experience and to facilitate their emergence from experience as more adequate personalities. That is, we cannot use our knowledge of children's environment simply to categorize their behavior or to fix our images of what they will become. Neither can we blame parents or class or community for what children are, nor resign as helpless in view of detrimental influences of the environment. The optimistic concept provided by our authors that children are in process and that changes in self and personality are effected as new experiences are lived can do much to negate feelings of discouragement and frustration in working with children who have problems. The importance of the immediate experience as it affects growth and produces change gives new meaning to each learning experience which we create for children. Nor can we teach just for social adjustment. The emphasis many schools place on normative standards of behavior and on getting along with others impedes our acceptance of the variabilities which result when children are permitted to become. We need to understand and to accept the implications of helping children as they develop through personal experience, recognizing that such development will increase the range of differences in behavior.

Finally, the faith we have in children's becoming must be extended to a conviction that co-workers in education—teachers, supervisors, administrators alike—are also in process and that they, too, must be permitted to be and to become more adequate, self-fulfilling personalities. This is the basis of the school's responsibility for adult education and for the improvement of in-service programs, which are adult education in the profession. It implies the need for us to be concerned with the process of retirement, for ensuring that older citizens, including teachers no longer in active service, have opportunities still to be involved, still to be fully functioning participants in the search for adequacy.

Continuing Education for Becoming

The concept of the individual who is in the process of becoming underlines the importance of continuing education. Stereotyped "culmination activities" at the end of a "unit" often contribute to the feeling there is nothing more to learn about the subject. The image of a college degree which says one has "finished" learning inhibits the development of being in process. Supervisory practices which make it appear that it is a sign of weakness to ask for help actually hinder teachers in understanding the process of becoming. Maslow stresses the idea of need gratification as the person moves toward becoming. As one need is satisfied, the individual becomes open to other needs; the more he knows, the more he wants to know. Thus, schools which open doors, which keep curiosity alive, which make it possible for persons to satisfy their own needs are laying the foundation for continuous learning. Teachers must push out the walls of the classroom and extend the time of the school day and school year, so that individuals do not feel that learning occurs only within the classroom at a certain time, under certain types of direction. When the school helps the individual continuously to experience satisfaction of needs through exploring, contemplating, manipulating and enjoying the world, it seems likely this process will continue throughout life.

This process of becoming is not easy, and the school should not try to create an atmosphere in which there is no struggle. Rather it should serve to give support in the struggle to use capacities and to satisfy needs. Maslow points out that the process of growth means that as one moves into the unfamiliar he will experience loss and pain in leaving the comfortable past. Teachers must be encouraging, supporting and permissive as children move forward. The teacher needs to be aware of the feelings of the preadolescent who samples behavior patterns of the next level and give him support when he returns to the safety of previous patterns before moving outward again. Administrators and supervisors need to provide an atmosphere in which teachers, too, may find support when they leave behind familiar methods and materials to try new ways of working. Each person who more clearly understands this process of becoming reaches out to other personalities in warmth and sympathy, saying, in effect, "I understand. This is difficult, but there is no other way toward becoming."

Although growth does bring struggle and pain, there are also moments of peak experiences which seem to bring unity within the person. In this moment he feels identity with others and with the world. He senses he is at his best; he feels free and natural. It is a moment of being, when the process of becoming has momentarily ceased. Maslow suggests that the adequate person experiences more of these peak experiences. Such experiences may come when people have opportunities for esthetic experiences, when there is time for contemplation, when there is sharing with others, when there is self-discovery, when there is recognition of uniqueness. The conditions that have been described in these chapters which provide for openness to experience, creativity, trust and positive view of self make possible moments of peak experience. Schools need to permit more enjoyment of emotional experience. Children need to learn to have fun, to be whimsical, to enjoy senses of touch, taste and smell as well as visual and auditory senses. Nonsense and fantasy are needed in schools today.

It would seem that the source of these peak experiences is within the individual. Exhilaration, feelings of freedom, a feeling of being free of the past and future are sometimes sought through narcotics or stimulants. The peak experience described by Maslow, however, does not separate the individual from the world; he is rather at one with the world and more responsible in it. This latter concept presents a significant challenge to education: to help persons have more peak experiences which are derived from the process of self-discovery so there is no need for seeking such synthetic experience through chemicals which leave a harmful residue.

The development of adequate persons who see themselves in the process of becoming seems to hold significant promise for the future. The person who sees this process is open to change and trusts his impulses and values as guides for behavior in new circumstances. Such persons are probably most likely to adapt and survive as the environment changes. Such persons will be able to create ways to meet new conditions. We cannot predict the world of 2015 when today's kindergarteners will be dealing with a very different world of ideas, people and processes. We cannot know which bits of present information will be needed in that world. We can be very certain, however, that providing schools which facilitate the development of persons with adequate, fully functioning personalities is the best way to contribute some degree of stability to an uncertain future. The person who has a positive view of self, who is open to experience, who is creative, who is trustworthy and responsible, who has values, who is well informed, and who is aware that he is in the process of becoming is the person most able to survive and deal with the future. What is more, he will do a better job for the rest of us.

ASCD BOARD OF DIRECTORS

(As of November 1, 1961)

Executive Committee, 1961-62

President, WILLIAM VAN TIL, Prof. and Chair., Dept. of Sec. Ed., New York University, New York, N.Y.

President-Elect, CHESTER BABCOCK, Asst. Supt., St. Dept. of Pub. Instr., Olympia, Wash.

Vice-President, ARTHUR W. FOSHAY, Exec. Off., Horace Mann-Lincoln Inst. of Sch. Experimentation, Tchrs. Coll., Columbia Univ., New York, N.Y.

C. GLEN HASS, Prof. of Ed. and Dir., Lab. Sch., Univ. of Florida, Gainesville, Fla.

MARCELLA R. LAWLER, Prof. of Ed., Tchrs. Coll., Columbia Univ., New York, N.Y.

ARTHUR J. LEWIS, Asst. Supt., Minneapolis Pub. Schs., Minneapolis, Minn.

LILLIAN C. PAUKNER, Dir. of Curric., Milwaukee Pub. Schs., Milwaukee, Wis.

Members Elected at Large

HARRY BARD, Baltimore Jr. Coll., Md. (1964); ALTHEA BEERY, Pub. Schs., Cincinnati, Ohio (1964); MILDRED BIDDICK, Pub. Schs., Denver, Colo. (1963); FRANCES BLAKE, Pub. Schs., St. Louis Park, Minn. (1965); WILLIAM H. BRISTOW, Pub. Schs., New York City (1962); MARGARET CHENOWETH, Pub. Schs., Janesville, Wis. (1962); GEORGE DENEMARK, Univ. of Wis.-Milwaukee (1963); ALEXANDER FRAZIER, Ohio St. Univ., Columbus (1965); GENEVA R. HANNA, Univ. of Texas, Austin (1965); C. GLEN HASS, Univ. of Fla., Gainesville (1964); HOWARDINE G. HOFFMAN, Los Angeles Co. Schs., Los Angeles, Calif. (1964); AGNES D. KANTZ, Pub. Schs., Midland, Texas (1962); DORRIS M. LEE, Portland St. Coll., Oreg. (1965); ARTHUR J. LEWIS, Pub. Schs., Minneapolis, Minn. (1963); GERTRUDE LEWIS, Office of Ed., Wash., D.C. (1963); A. HARRY PASSOW, Tchrs. Coll., Columbia Univ., New York City (1963); GALEN SAYLOR, Univ. of Nebr., Lincoln (1962); HELEN H. SORNSON, Ball St. Tchrs. Coll., Muncie, Ind. (1962); RODNEY TILLMAN, George Peabody Coll. for Tchrs., Nashville, Tenn. (1965); FRED T. WILHELMS, San Francisco St. Coll., Calif. (1964).

State Representatives to the Board

Alabama—L. G. WALKER, Co. Supv., Marion; J. T. WILLIAMS, Pub. Schs., Gadsden. *Arizona*—MILO BELCHA, Univ. of Ariz., Tucson; JAMES J. JELINEK, Ariz. St. Univ., Tempe. *Arkansas*—HAZEL DABNEY, Pub. Schs., Pine Bluff; LILLIAN FAULK, Pub. Schs., Hulbert. *California*—URSULA HOGAN, Pub. Schs., Sacramento; EDITH MERRITT, San Francisco St. Coll.; MARY MITCHELL, Pub.

Schs., Palm Springs; Sybil Richardson, San Fernando Valley St. Coll., Northridge; George P. Rusteika, Alameda Co. Schs., Castro Valley. *Florida*—Marian W. Black, Fla. St. Univ., Tallahasse; E. L. Bowers, Pub. Schs., Pensacola; Sam H. Moorer, St. Dept. of Educ., Tallahassee; Glenn Thomas, Henry S. West Lab. Sch., Coral Gables. *Georgia*—Johnnye V. Cox, Univ. of Ga., Athens; Frances R. Hicks, St. Coll. for Women, Milledgeville; Durell Ruffin, So. Assn. Coll. & Sec. Schs., Atlanta. *Hawaii*—Lotty Canaday, Dept. of Pub. Instr., Honolulu; Ruth J. Morrell, Pub. Schs., Honolulu. *Idaho*—James L. Black, Pub. Schs., Nampa; William G. Ward, Pub. Schs., Idaho Falls. *Illinois*—Fred Barnes, Univ. of Ill., Urbana; Frances Fosse, Pub. Schs., Rockford; Anne Gustafson, Pub. Schs., Rockford; Cecilia Lauby, Ill. St. Normal Univ., Normal; Mildred Menard, Co. Pub. Schs., Kankakee. *Indiana*—Maurice J. Eash, Ball St. Tchrs. Coll., Muncie; LaVelle Fortenberry, Ind. Univ., Gary Center, Gary; William P. Moser, New Albany-Floyd Co. Cons. Sch. Corp., New Albany. *Iowa*—Mildred Middleton, Pub. Schs., Cedar Rapids; Merle Wilson, Pub. Schs., Des Moines. *Kansas*—Gladys Kaump, Pub. Schs., Dodge City; Sylvia Nelson, Pub. Schs., Topeka. *Kentucky*—Roy Eversole, Pub. Schs., Hazard; Ruby G. Northcutt, Pub. Schs., Ashland; Roy B. Smith, Pub. Schs., Owensboro. *Louisiana*—Theda M. Ewing, Iberia Parish Schs., New Iberia; John D. Greene, East Baton Rouge Parish Sch. Bd., Baton Rouge. *Maryland*—Vernon E. Anderson, Univ. of Md., College Park; Mildred Hoyle, Prince Georges Co. Schs., Upper Marlboro; Carey Lacey, Pub. Schs., Chestertown. *Michigan*—Ruth Bacon, Pub. Schs., Port Huron; Delmo Della-Dora, Wayne Co. Bd. of Educ., Detroit; Robert S. Fox, Univ. of Mich., Ann Arbor; Robert Kingsley, Pub. Schs., Midland; Leroy Selmeier, Pub. Schs., Grosse Pointe. *Minnesota*—Eino Kiskinen, Pub. Schs., Excelsior; Bernard Larson, Pub. Schs., Bloomington; Agnes McCarthy, Pub. Schs., Faribault. *Missouri*—Raymond A. Roberts, St. Dept. of Educ., Jefferson City; Hugh W. Speer, Univ. of Kansas City. *Montana*—Milford Franks, Montana St. Coll., Bozeman. *Nebraska*—Robert Ackerman, Pub. Schs., Omaha; Max G. McAuley, Pub. Schs., Omaha. *Nevada*—Monty Boland, Clark Co. Sch. Dist., Las Vegas; Nellie F. Burger, Clark Co. Sch. Dist., Las Vegas. *New Jersey*—Emil Massa, Pub. Schs., Teaneck; Harold Shafer, Pub. Schs., Ridgewood; George Sharp, Pub. Schs., Montclair; Robert Ward, Pub. Schs., Annandale. *New York*—Mark Atkinson, Harborfields Central Sch. Dist., Greenlawn; Gerald Cleveland, Pub. Schs., Syracuse; Grace Gates, Pub. Schs., Clarence; Bernard W. Kinsella, Pub. Schs., Rochester; Joseph Leese, N.Y. St. Coll. for Tchrs., Albany; Charles M. Shapp, Pub. Schs., New York City. *North Carolina*—O. L. Davis, Jr., Univ. of N.C., Chapel Hill; Martha Johnston, Pub. Schs., Charlotte; Madeline Tripp, St. Dept. of Pub. Instr., Raleigh. *Ohio*—Mary L. Beverly, Pub. Schs., Akron; Phila Humphreys, St. Dept. of Educ., Columbus; Ruby Kaphart, Allen Co. Schs., Lima; Russell A. Milliken, Ohio Univ., Athens; Lorrene L. Ort, Bowling Green St. Univ., Bowling Green. *Oklahoma*—Helen M. Jones, Okla. St. Univ., Stillwater; Cleo Melton, Pub. Schs., Ponca City. *Oregon*—William O. Engebretsen, Pub. Schs., Portland; Margaret L. Hiatt, Pub. Schs., Monmouth; Harold

V. McAbee, East Oreg. Coll., La Grande; Evelyn Piper, Pub. Schs., Eugene. *Pennsylvania*—Irving T. Chatterton, Bradford Co. Schs., Towanda; Gerald M. Newton, Pub. Schs., Beaver; Albert I. Oliver, Jr., Univ. of Penn., Philadelphia. *Puerto Rico*—Irma Vincenty De Lopez, Pub. Schs., Santurce; Cecilia Olmeda, Univ. of Puerto Rico, Rio Piedras. *South Carolina*—Eleanor Bull, Pub. Schs., Dentsville; P. M. Kirkpatrick, Anderson Co. Schs., Honea Park. *South Dakota*—Alice Gilbert, Pub. Schs., Huron; Ardath Van Tassell, Pub. Schs., Mitchell. *Tennessee*—Sam H. Ingram, St. Dept. of Educ., Nashville; Arthur Rauscher, Shelby Co. Schs., Memphis. *Texas*—Jessie F. Cardwell, Pub. Schs., Dallas; Lorena Haynes, Edgewood Pub. Schs., San Antonio; Gladys Henninger, Pub. Schs., Austin; V. J. Kennedy, Tex. Educ. Agency, Austin; Gladys Polk, Brazosport Pub. Schs., Freeport. *Utah*—Norma Jensen, Box Elder Sch. Dist., Brigham City; Areletta Williams, Davis Co. Sch. Dist., Farmington. *Virginia*—Sue F. Ayres, Charles City & New Kent Co. Schs., Providence Forge; Luther C. McRae, Pub. Schs., Portsmouth; S. G. Stewart, Augusta Co. Schs., Staunton; Hortense R. Wells, Pub. Schs., Norfolk. *Washington*—John Amend, Pacific Lutheran Coll., Parkland; Clifford M. Johnson, Highline Pub. Schs., Seattle; Ruth Wilcox, Pub. Schs., Edmonds. *West Virginia*—Martha Cottrell, Kanawha Co. Schs., Charleston; George M. Wood, Jr., Wetzel Co. Schs., New Martinsville. *Wisconsin*—Elsie Chell, Pub. Schs., Waukesha; Irene Kronenwetter, Co. Pub. Schs., Wausau; Fred Overman, Dept. of Pub. Instr., Madison. *New England (Connecticut, Maine, Massachusetts, New Hampshire, Rhode Island, Vermont)*—Cathryn R. Hoctor, Pub. Schs., Middletown, Conn.; Raymond W. Houghton, Pub. Schs., Warwick, R. I.; Roberta M. Kellogg, Brown Univ., Providence, R. I.; Karlene Russell, St. Dept. of Educ., Montpelier, Vt.; Mark Shedd, St. Dept. of Educ., Middletown, Conn. *Rocky Mountain Tri-State (Colorado, New Mexico, Wyoming)*—Clifford Bebell, Dept. of Educ., Denver, Colo.; Fred Nelson, Pub. Schs., Albuquerque, N. Mex.; Philip Perdew, Univ. of Denver, Colo.

ASCD HEADQUARTERS STAFF

(1201 16th Street, N.W., Washington 6, D.C.)

Executive Secretary, Margaret Gill

Associate Secretary; Editor, ASCD Publications, Robert R. Leeper

Associate Secretary, M. Karl Openshaw

Administrative Assistant, Virginia Berthy

Staff Assistants, Sarah Arlington, Betty Lou Atkins, Nancy C. Childs, Ruth P. Ely, Ruby J. Funkhouser, Carole Mang, Frances Mindel, Dolores J. Minor, Constance R. Reinhardt, Nancy J. Suitt, Betty Lou Wilson.